Jack Samson

The Bear Book

Foreword by
JIM RIKHOFF

Illustrated by
AL BARKER

The Amwell Press
Clinton, New Jersey

CONTENTS

FOREWORD

Men have always been fascinated by bears. Man's ancient religions revered the bear. Our North American Indians often regarded the bear as a sacred animal. Some of our oldest folklore—songs, art and story—center on the bear and the almost mystic quality that animal inspires in men's souls. There are probably more bear "legends" and "tall tales" than any other category of animal stories. I think man is intrigued by the bears about him for the simple reason that, in many cases, he identifies with the animal that often "walks like a man." The bear has become one of our favorite anthropomorphic creatures because the bear seems somehow closer to man than most creatures; even more so than the giant apes.

Perhaps the first book I can recall from my steadily retreating childhood was "The Bears of Blue River" by, I believe, Charles Major. I had been brought up in Indianapolis, so I was terribly excited by this book which was devoted to all sorts of adventures with a variety of ferocious bears rampaging over the the Indiana countryside back in the pioneer days of the early nineteenth century. Although I lived literally on the edge of White River, I never quite understood where the Blue River was. I was astounded that there had actually been real live bears in Indiana, a state that didn't have even a huntable deer population during the whole period I lived there, some twenty-five years off and on.

As I grew older and developed into an enthusiastic hunter, my interest in bears expanded accordingly. I now thought of them as a desirable quarry as well as the basis of interesting reading. As the years passed and I found myself in bear country at various times in my life, I hunted bears with a variety of methods. I first hunted them in North Carolina in 1955. I was younger then and made a gallant effort to follow a couple of Smoky Mountain ridge-runners and their hounds through the Joyce Kilmer National Forest. It was a terrific hunt, but somebody else shot the bear our hounds had treed. I would find that this was not an unusual occurence in future years. Later, I hunted them in Montana, Wyoming, Arizona and Idaho in the West. Usually, my bear hunting was sort of an extra added attraction to the more important elk and deer hunting at hand, but I actually spent two nights and mornings watching a dead horse bait in Wyoming. It was interesting, but hardly the way I'd like to spend much more of my life.

Finally, after years of fruitless bear hunting, I finally took a black bear with Chris Klineburger and Dee De Moss on Washington's Olympic peninsula. We followed Dee's Plott hounds up, down and through enough of that rain forest to dampen my enthusiasm for bear hunting for a number of years. Some years later, in the mid-sixties, I shot a 900-pound Alaskan Brown bear on the Alaskan Peninsula and I sort of hung up my guns on bears. After you've shot one that big, there doesn't seem much point in shooting another one just for the fun of it. Also, I've never forgotten that, after we had skinned the animal out on a high glacier, I couldn't help thinking how much he looked like a man.

Somehow I guess I'd rather watch and read about bears than shoot them now, but I certainly don't object to bear hunting as long as there is a good bear population to be harvested and the bears are taken by fair chase. In the meantime, most of my bear hunting is done vicariously while I search for new bear stories in the outdoor magazines and books. Being a confirmed bear nut, I asked Jack Samson to put together the "bear book to end all bear books" and I think he has done just that.

Any book that has bear stories by top writers like Ernest Thompson Seton, William Faulkner, Ben East, Frank Dufresne, Elmer Keith, Warren Page, Pete Barrett, Grancel Fitz, Fred Bear, Bob Brister and Jack O'Connor, plus a good many other talented gentlemen, has got to be a cherished addition to any outdoor library. When that book is edited by Jack Samson, who also happens to be the editor of *Field and Stream*, then you can be sure you have garnered yourself a most unusual anthology indeed.

I have known Jack for about fifteen years and he is one of those rare fellows that we all sort of half-admire and half-envy. He's an accomplished fresh water flyfisherman while also recognized as one of the country's leading salt water authorities. He's an avid shotgunner on one hand while enjoying a reputation as a skilled rifleman on the other. He writes as well as he edits and *that* is saying something! Meanwhile, as if his life weren't full to the proverbial brim already, he has turned out several of the most thoughtful and, I think, lasting contributions to the world of outdoor literature that we have been privileged to witness this century. Without going into a complete listing of his credits, it seems more than appropriate that mention be made of his excellent editing of "The Worlds of Ernest Thompson Seton," since one of Seton's pieces graces this volume.

Jack had been a newspaperman, war correspondent, magazine editor and general all-around writer for more years than he likes to admit. He has excelled in all of these vocations just as he has achieved high marks in his outdoor avocations. We at Amwell Press like to think that, in this bear book, he has brought all of it together in one fine volume that will add even more to his growing stature in contemporary outdoor publishing.

JIM RIKHOFF
President, Amwell Press

February 20, 1979
Speakeasy Hill
High Bridge, New Jersey

SOME THOUGHTS ON BEARS

Of all the writers I have chosen to present in this collection of bear stories, probably no one put the relationship between bears and people into better perspective than Frank Dufresne. Frank was far more of a naturalist than a bear hunter, but he spent a lifetime studying bears and had this to say on his subject:

"Ever since the appearance of their ancestors on earth, man and bears have been at odds. Beginning in the Pleistocene when giant cave bears towered over every other predator—of which man must be reckoned as one—our low-browed grandfathers were forced to cope with shaggy-haired beasts who stood twice as tall and outweighed them ten to one. For half a million years it was the bear, not man, who dominated the wilds, and it continued to hold the upper edge until the development of high-powered rifles within the past two hundred years. "In this short period—the blink of an eye in time—some of the bears have not adjusted their thinking to man's sudden supremacy. Some of them still believe they can whip any man in a fair fight, and that they have every right to run him out of the dwindling wilderness."

And that is where the trouble lies today. No one—conservationist, hunter, fisherman, "environmentalist" or preservationist—wants to see these great bears disappear from the wilderness of the North American continent. But the trouble is we are running out of habitat for bears. True, there are wilderness areas and national parks, but each year there are more and more tourists, hikers, fishermen, campers and backpackers flooding into these once-virgin regions where the bears held sway.

Unfortunately most of the younger generation today have been fed a great deal of nonsense about bears from a well-meaning Walt Disney, protectionists groups, motion pictures and television. For example, the TV show "The Life of Grizzly Adams" leads children to believe that James Capen Adams (his real name) was a protectionist who fought to keep people from killing his dearly-beloved bears. The truth is—and has been proven historically—that not only was James C. Adams a professional bear hunter who killed bears for meat and hides and bounty money but who also captured bears for zoos. One need only read *The Adventures of James Capen Adams, Moun-*

taineer and Grizzly Bear Hunter of California, by Theodore H. Hittell, published in 1860 (and republished in 1911 by Charles Scribner's Sons, New York) to find out that, while he liked and admired the grizzly bear, he killed it regularly. His first tame bear was named Lady Washington, acquired by Adams after he killed her mother in eastern Washington State in 1853 and captured her two cubs. He raised Lady Washington but did not have as much luck in completely taming her as he did in 1854, when he discovered a female grizzly still in her den one spring day in the Yosemite Valley. Adams killed the sow in her den and took both cubs and raised the smaller of the two. It turned out to be a fine pet, and he named it Ben Franklin. It remained with him for many years and even saved his life once when he was attacked by another grizzly.

Now all this history made fine grist for television writers, who saw all sorts of profit from inventing a fictional character who walks the world espousing the rights of wild creatures with a giant grizzly at his side. The kids ate it up—and still do. But to have told the truth would have been kinder and just a whole lot safer for some youngsters.

In the past several years youngsters have been killed and partially eaten by grizzlies in our national parks. Another misguided city boy a few years ago climbed over the wire and attempted to lie down with his "brother," a polar bear, in the Central Park Zoo in New York. The trouble was the polar bear had never seen television and killed the boy instantly. Authorities shot the bear for that. Instead I would have suggested some stiff fines and jail sentences for TV and movie script writers who grew up in big cities and tragically mislead the viewing public.

The great bears are slowly being pushed from their natural habitat by civilization. Hunting is not the reason for their decline, since federal and state game and fish departments still issue licenses for areas where the animals are plentiful. But the grizzly, the brown bear and the polar bear are huge, wild and extremely individualistic carnivores. They do not always do what the wildlife managers want them to do. Even the relatively small black bear has been known to inflict awful damage to humans who are careless. People insist on feeding these animals in national parks despite signs all about telling them not to. Tourists still get between a mother bear and her cubs and even perch their infant children on the backs of feeding bears to have their photographs taken!

Introduction

Ernest Thompson Seton's wonderful story about "Wahb," the cattle-killing grizzly from Montana's Bitteroot Mountains living for two months each year in the garbage dump in Yellowstone Park, is a classic. It appears in this book. And although Seton was guilty at times of anthropomorphism—attributing too many human traits to his fictional animals—he knew a lot about grizzlies.

There are many of us today who worry about the fate of the big bears. There has to be a better solution than locking them all up in zoos.

On the other hand, blindly accepting the grizzly and the Alaskan brown bear as a soulmate while fishing or backpacking is going to result in a lot of dead and mutilated people unless the big bears are scientifically managed.

The stories in this book are about encounters with bears—all the way from the days of Lewis and Clark to the present. They are not meant to terrify the reader. They are simply stories of bears and bear hunters. It would be foolish to place false human value judgments upon bears based on their encounters with man. Bears are neither "good" nor "bad." They simply are. They are bears.

ACKNOWLEDGMENTS

"The White Bears of The Lewis and Clark Expedition 1804–1806" is from *First Across The Continent*, Noah Brooks, Charles Scribner's Sons, New York, 1901.

"Wahb—Seton's Grizzly" is from *The Biography of a Grizzly*, Ernest Thompson Seton, The Century Company, New York, 1900.

"Ben Lilly's Bears" is from *The Ben Lilly Legend*, J. Frank Dobie, Little, Brown and Company, Boston, 1951. Copyright 1950 by J. Frank Dobie.

"Faulkner's Bears" is from *Big Woods*, William Faulkner, Random House, New York. Copyright 1931 William Faulkner.

"Ben East's Bears" is from *Bears*, Ben East, Outdoor Life, Crown Publishers, Inc., New York. Copyright 1977 Ben East.

"Phil Moore's Grizzly" is from *With Gun and Rod in Canada*, Phil Moore, Houghton, Mifflin Company, Boston and New York, 1922.

"Frank Dufresne's Bears" is from *No Room for Bears*, Frank Dufresne, Holt, Rinehart and Winston, New York. Copyright 1965 Frank Dufresne.

"Elmer Keith's Bears" is from *Keith—An Autobiography*, Elmer Keith, Winchester Press, New York, 1974. Permission of publisher.

"The Glacier Bear" first appeared as "My Quest for a Rare Bear," William A. Fisher, in *True's Hunting Yearbook*, copyright, 1961, Fawcett Publications, reprinted by permission of Mrs. Marylyn E. Fisher.

"Grizzly Adams and His Bears" is from *The Grizzly Bear*, William H. Wright, Charles Scribner's Sons, New York, 1909.

"Warren Page's Grizzly" is from *One Man's Wilderness*, Warren Page, Holt, Rinehart and Winston, New York, 1973. Permission of Mrs. Martha Page.

"O'Connor's Bears" is from *Hunting Big Game in North America*, Jack O'Connor, Alfred A. Knopf, New York, 1977. Permission of the late author.

Acknowledgments

"Monarch" is from *Monarch of Deadman Bay*, Roger Caras, Little, Brown and Company, 1969. Copyright 1969 Roger Caras.

"Of Grizzlies and the River" is from *North American Head Hunting*, Grancel Fitz, Oxford University Press, New York, 1957. Permission of Mrs. Betty Fitz Dingwall.

"Bears that Make My Memory Sweat," Slim Moore, *True's Hunting Yearbook*, 1959. Permission of publisher.

"The Day the Bears Come Out," Peter Barrett, *True Fishing and Hunting Yearbook*, Fawcett Publications, 1961. Reprinted by permission of the author.

"Polar Bear—1966," is from *Fred Bear's Field Notes*, Fred Bear, Doubleday and Company, Inc., Garden City, New York, 1976. Permission of author.

"Brown Bear the Hard Way," Bob Brister, *Field and Stream*, December, 1971. Reprinted by permission of the author.

"Grizzly Bears" first appeared in *Big Game Hunting in the West*, Mike Crammond, Mitchell Press, Ltd., Vancouver, British Columbia, 1965. Permission of publisher.

"Plenty of Bear," Russell Annabel, *Field and Stream*, April 1937. Permission of publisher.

THE BEAR BOOK

THE "WHITE BEARS" OF THE LEWIS and CLARK EXPEDITION
1804–1806

*In 1901 Charles Scribner's Sons, New York, published a book en-*titled First Across The Continent, *by Noah Brooks. It was the story of the Lewis and Clark Expedition of 1804–1806, the first party of white men to cross the continent south of Canada. They were the first white men to explore the region of North America between lands occupied by English-speaking settlers in the East and the Spanish-speaking peoples of the West. They crossed the valleys of the Upper Missouri, the Yellowstone and the Columbia River Basin and finally looked upon the Pacific.*

In the summer of 1803 Napoleon Bonaparte, then first consul of France, sold to the United States a parcel of land called the Louisiana Purchase. The price for this chunk of domain was fifteen million dollars. What was not fully realized at the time was how big it was. Roughly described, the territory comprised all that part of the continent west of the Mississippi River, bounded on the north by British possessions and on the west and south by dominions of Spain. This included such settled regions as Louisiana and Missouri as well as the great open territory to the north and west. At the time the entire population of the region, exclusive of the many Indian tribes that roamed over the vast tract, was barely 90,000 people, of whom 40,000 were Negro slaves. The civilized inhabitants were principally French, with a few Spanish, Germans, English and Americans. The dominion of the United States was now extended across the entire continent of North America. Few white men had ever crossed these trackless plains or scaled the towering mountains separating the Great Plains from the Pacific. There were Indian tribes in that vastness who had never seen the face of white men.

And there were bears, bears and more bears. There were black bears galore—which did not impress the early explorers much, but they were certainly impressed by a giant known scientifically as URSUS HORRIBILIS—an apt name—the grizzly. In 1795 Sir Alexander MacKenzie, the famous Canadian explorer, wrote: "The In-

3

dians entertain great aprehension of this grizzly bear and never venture to attack it except in a party."

A contemporary writer of the times, Brackenridge, also wrote this of the big bears: "This animal is the monarch of the country. The African lion nor the Bengal tiger are not more terrible or fierce. He is the enemy of many and literally thirsts for human blood. He seldom fails to attack. The Indians make war upon these ferocious monsters with the same ceremonies as they do with tribes of their own species, and in the recital of their great victories, the death of the bear gives the warrior greater renown than the scalp of a human enemy. The grizzly possesses an amazing strength and attacks and tears to pieces the largest buffalo . . ." Brackenridge was indeed impressed with grizzlies.

Grizzlies come in all shades and colors, and early naturalists called it the "variegated" bear for the tonal range of its pelts. Silver hairs give rise to the "silvertip" description of many observers and may have led to the description by early explorers of "white" bears. However, many were yellow in color—such as the huge golden grizzlies of California—and it is more likely that color phase accounted for the "white" description. For certainly no true white bear—such as the polar bear—traveled that far south of the polar ice pack.

In 1803, availing himself of the pretext of sending out an exploring expedition before the Louisiana Purchase had been completed, President Thomas Jefferson asked Congress to appropriate a small sum for just such a force. Congress put up $2,000 and Meriwether Lewis, a captain in the Army, was chosen to lead the expedition. Lewis chose a comrade, Lieutenant William Clark, also a native of Virginia, as his partner. The expedition was made up tof these two officers and twenty-six men. Nine of them were from Kentucky and were used to life on the frontier among the Indians; fourteen were United States soldiers who volunteered for the trip, two were French boatmen, one an interpreter of Indian languages and the other a hunter; and the last the black man York, a servant of Clark.

It was nearly a year before the expedition reached the headwaters of the Missouri River and approached the land of the Yellowstone. By then they had seen a number of "white bears," and the following accounts vividly illustrate how both the explorers and bears reacted to each other. It was April 1805.

The "White" Bears of Lewis and Clark

Noah Brooks

Game, which had been somewhat scarce after leaving the Yellowstone, became more plentiful as they passed on to the westward, still following the winding course of the Missouri. Much of the time, baffling winds and the crookedness of the stream made sailing impossible, and the boats were towed by men walking along the banks.

Even this was sometimes difficult, on account of the rocky ledges that beset the shores, and sharp stones that lay in the path of the towing parties. On the twenty-eighth of April, however, having a favorable wind, the party made twenty-eight miles with their sails, which was reckoned a good day's journey. On that day the journal records that game had again become very abundant, deer of various kinds, elk, buffalo, antelope, bear, beaver, and geese being numerous. The beaver, it was found, had wrought much damage by gnawing down trees; some of these, not less than three feet in diameter, had been gnawed clean through by the beaver. On the following day the journal has this record:—

"We proceeded early, with a moderate wind. Captain Lewis, who was on shore with one hunter, met, about eight o'clock, two white [grizzly] bears. Of the strength and ferocity of this animal the Indians had given us dreadful accounts. They never attack him but in parties of six or eight persons, and even then are often defeated with a loss of one or more of their party. Having no weapons but bows and arrows, and the bad guns with which the traders supply them, they are obliged to approach very near to the bear; as no wound except through the head or heart is mortal, they frequently fall a sacrifice if they miss their aim. He rather attacks than avoids a man, and such is the terror which he has inspired, that the Indians who go in quest of him paint themselves and perform all the superstitious rites customary when they make war on a neighboring nation. Hitherto, those bears we had seen did not appear desirous of encountering us; but although to a skilful rifleman the danger is very much diminished, yet the white bear is still a terrible animal. On approaching

5

these two, both Captain Lewis and the hunter fired, and each wounded a bear. One of them made his escape; the other turned upon Captain Lewis and pursued him seventy or eighty yards, but being badly wounded the bear could not run so fast as to prevent him from reloading his piece, which he again aimed at him, and a third shot from the hunter brought him to the ground. He was a male, not quite full grown, and weighed about three hundred pounds. The legs are somewhat longer than those of the black bear, and the talons and tusks much larger and longer. Its color is a yellowish-brown; the eyes are small, black, and piercing; the front of the fore legs near the feet is usually black, and the fur is finer, thicker, and deeper than that of the black bear. Add to which, it is a more furious animal, and very remarkable for the wounds which it will bear without dying."

Next day, the hunter killed the largest elk which they had ever seen. It stood five feet three inches high from hoof to shoulder. Antelopes were also numerous, but lean, and not very good for food. Of the antelope the journal says:—

"These fleet and quick-sighted animals are generally the victims of their curiosity. When they first see the hunters, they run with great velocity; if he lies down on the ground, and lifts up his arm, his hat, or his foot, they return with a light trot to look at the object, and sometimes go and return two or three times, till they approach within reach of the rifle. So, too, they sometimes leave their flock to go and look at the wolves, which crouch down, and, if the antelope is frightened at first, repeat the same manoeuvre, and sometimes relieve each other, till they decoy it from the party, when they seize it. But, generally, the wolves take them as they are crossing the rivers; for, although swift on foot, they are not good swimmers."

Later wayfarers across the plains were wont to beguile the antelope by fastening a bright-colored handkerchief to a ramrod stuck in the ground. The patient hunter was certain to be rewarded by the antelope coming within range of his rifle; for, unless scared off by some interference, the herd, after galloping around and around and much zigzagging, would certainly seek to gratify their curiosity by gradually circling nearer and nearer the strange object until a deadly shot or two sent havoc into their ranks.

May came on cold and windy, and on the second of the month, the journal records that snow fell to the depth of an inch, contrasting strangely with the advanced vegetation.

"Our game to-day," proceeds the journal, "were deer, elk, and buffalo: we also procured three beaver. They were here quite gentle, as they have not been hunted; but when the hunters are in pursuit, they never leave their huts during the day. This animal we esteem a great delicacy, particularly the tail, which, when boiled, resembles in flavor the fresh tongues and sounds of the codfish, and is generally so large as to afford a plentiful meal for two men. One of the hunters, in passing near an old Indian camp, found several yards of scarlet cloth suspended on the bough of a tree, as a sacrifice to the deity, by the Assiniboins; the custom of making these offerings being common among that people, as, indeed, among all the Indians on the Missouri. The air was sharp this evening; the water froze on the oars as we rowed."

The Assiniboin custom of sacrificing to their deity, or "great medicine," the article which they most value themselves, is not by any means peculiar to that tribe, nor to the Indian race.

An unusual number of porcupines were seen along here, and these creatures were so free from wildness that they fed on, undisturbed, while the explorers walked around and among them. The captains named a bold and beautiful stream, which here entered the Missouri from the north,—Porcupine River; but modern geography calls the water-course Poplar River; at the mouth of the river, in Montana, is now the Poplar River Indian Agency and military post. The waters of this stream, the explorers found, were clear and transparent,—an exception to all the streams, which, discharging into the Missouri, give it its name of the Big Muddy. The journal adds:—

"A quarter of a mile beyond this river a creek falls in on the south, to which, on account of its distance from the mouth of the Missouri, we gave the name of Two-thousand-mile creek. It is a bold stream with a bed thirty yards wide. At three and one-half miles above Porcupine River, we reached some high timber on the north, and camped just above an old channel of the river, which is now dry. We saw vast quantities of buffalo, elk, deer,—principally of the long-tailed kind,—antelope, beaver, geese, ducks, brant, and some swan. The porcupines too are numerous, and so careless and clumsy that we can approach very near without disturbing them, as they are feeding on the young willows. Toward evening we also found for the first time the nest of a goose among some driftwood, all that we had hitherto seen being on the top of a broken tree on the forks, invariably from fifteen to twenty or more feet in height."

"Next day," May 4, says the journal, "we passed some old Indian hunting-camps, one of which consisted of two large lodges, fortified with a circular fence twenty or thirty feet in diameter, made of timber laid horizontally, the beams overlying each other to the height of five feet, and covered with the trunks and limbs of trees that have drifted down the river. The lodges themselves are formed by three or more strong sticks about the size of a man's leg or arm and twelve feet long, which are attached at the top by a withe of small willows, and spread out so as to form at the base a circle of ten to fourteen feet in diameter. Against these are placed pieces of driftwood and fallen timber, usually in three ranges, one on the other; the interstices are covered with leaves, bark and straw, so as to form a conical figure about ten feet high, with a small aperture in one side for the door. It is, however, at best a very imperfect shelter against the inclemencies of the seasons."

Wolves were very abundant along the route of the explorers, the most numerous species being the common kind, now known as the coyote (pronounced *kyote*), and named by science the *canis latrans*. These animals are cowardly and sly creatures, of an intermediate size between the fox and dog, very delicately formed, fleet and active.

"The ears are large, erect, and pointed; the head is long and pointed, like that of the fox; the tail long and bushy; the hair and fur are of a pale reddish-brown color, though much coarser than that of the fox; the eye is of a deep sea-green color, small and piercing; the talons are rather longer than those of the wolf of the Atlantic States, which animal, as far as we can perceive, is not to be found on this side of the Platte. These wolves usually associate in bands of ten or twelve, and are rarely, if ever, seen alone, not being able, singly, to attack a deer or antelope. The live and rear their young in burrows, which they fix near some pass or spot much frequented by game, and sally out in a body against any animal which they think they can overpower; but on the slightest alarm retreat to their burrows, making a noise exactly like that of a small dog.

"A second species is lower, shorter in the legs, and thicker than the Atlantic wolf; the color, which is not affected by the seasons, is of every variety of shade, from a gray or blackish-brown to a cream-colored white. They do not burrow, nor do they bark, but howl; they frequent the woods and plains, and skulk along the skirts of the buffalo herds, in order to attack the weary or wounded."

Under date of May 5, the journal has an interesting story of an encounter with a grizzly bear, which, by way of variety, is here called "brown," instead of "white." It is noticeable that the explorers dwelt with much minuteness upon the peculiar characteristics of the grizzly; this is natural enough when we consider that they were the first white men to form an intimate acquaintance with "Ursus horribilis." The account says:—

"Captain Clark and one of the hunters met, this evening, the largest brown bear we have seen. As they fired he did not attempt to attack, but fled with a most tremendous roar; and such was his extraordinary tenacity of life, that, although he had five balls passed through his lungs, and five other wounds, he swam more than half across the river to a sand-bar, and survived twenty minutes. He weighed between five and six hundred pounds at least, and measured eight feet seven inches and a half from the nose to the extremity of the hind feet, five feet ten inches and a half round the breast, three feet eleven inches round the neck, one foot eleven inches round the middle of the fore leg, and his claws, five on each foot, were four inches and three-eighths in length. This animal differs from the common black bear in having his claws much longer and more blunt; his tail shorter; his hair of a reddish or bay brown, longer, finer, and more abundant; his liver, lungs, and heart much larger even in proportion to his size, the heart, particularly, being equal to that of a large ox; and his maw ten times larger. Besides fish and flesh, he feeds on roots and every kind of wild fruit."

On May 8 the party discovered the largest and most important of the northern tributaries of the Upper Missouri. The journal thus describes the stream:—

"Its width at the entrance is one hundred and fifty yards; on going three miles up, Captain Lewis found it to be of the same breadth and sometimes more; it is deep, gentle, and has a large quantity of water; its bed is principally of mud; the banks are abrupt, about twelve feet in height, and formed of a dark, rich loam and blue clay; the low grounds near it are wide and fertile, and possess a considerable proportion of cottonwood and willow. It seems to be navigable for boats and canoes; by this circumstance, joined to its course and quantity of water, which indicates that it passes through a large extent of country, we are led to presume that it may approach the Saskaskawan [Saskatchewan] and afford a communication with that river. The water has a peculiar whiteness, such as might be produced by a table-spoonful of milk in a dish of tea, and this circumstance induced us to call it Milk River."

Modern geography shows that the surmise of Captain Lewis was correct. Some of the tributaries of Milk River (the Indian name of

which signifies "The River that Scolds at all Others") have their rise near St. Mary's River, which is one of the tributaries of the Saskatchewan, in British America.

The explorers were surprised to find the bed of a dry river, as deep and as wide as the Missouri itself, about fifteen miles above Milk River. Although it had every appearance of a water-course, it did not discharge a drop of water. Their journal says:—

"It passes through a wide valley without timber; the surrounding country consists of waving low hills, interspersed with some handsome level plains; the banks are abrupt, and consist of a black or yellow clay, or of a rich sandy loam; though they do not rise more than six or eight feet above the bed, they exhibit no appearance of being overflowed; the bed is entirely composed of a light brown sand, the particles of which, like those of the Missouri, are extremely fine. Like the dry rivers we passed before, this seemed to have discharged its waters recently, but the watermark indicated that its greatest depth had not been more than two feet. This stream, if it deserve the name, we called Bigdry [Big Dry] River."

And Big Dry it remains on the maps unto this day. In this region the party recorded this observation:—

"The game is now in great quantities, particularly the elk and buffalo, which last is so gentle that the men are obliged to drive them out of the way with sticks and stones. The ravages of the beaver are very apparent; in one place the timber was entirely prostrated for a space of three acres in front on the river and one in depth, and great part of it removed, though the trees were in large quantities, and some of them as thick as the body of a man."

Yet so great have been the ravages of man among these gentle creatures, that elk are now very rarely found in the region, and the buffalo have almost utterly disappeared from the face of the earth.

Just after the opening of the Northern Pacific Railway, in 1883, a band of sixty buffaloes were heard of, far to the southward of Bismarck, and a party was organized to hunt them. The *bold* hunters afterwards boasted that they killed every one of this little band of survivors of their race.

The men were now (in the middle of May) greatly troubled with boils, abscesses, and inflamed eyes, caused by the poison of the alkali that covered much of the ground and corrupted the water. Here is an entry in the journal of May 11:—

"About five in the afternoon one of our men [Bratton], who had been afflicted with boils and suffered to walk on shore, came running to the boats with loud cries, and every symptom of terror and distress. For some time after we had taken him on board he was so much out of breath as to be unable to describe the cause of his anxiety; but he at length told us that about a mile and a half below he had shot a brown bear, which immediately turned and was in close pursuit of him; but the bear being badly wounded could not overtake him. Captain Lewis, with seven men, immediately went in search of him; having found his track they followed him by the blood for a mile, found him concealed in some thick brushwood, and shot him with two balls through the skull. Though somewhat smaller than that killed a few days ago, he was a monstrous animal, and a most terrible enemy. Our man had shot him through the centre of the lungs; yet he had pursued him furiously for half a mile, then returned more than twice that distance, and with his talons prepared himself a bed in the earth two feet deep and five feet long; he was perfectly alive when they found him, which was at least two hours after he had received the wound. The wonderful power of life which these animals possess renders them dreadful; their very track in the mud or sand, which we have sometimes found eleven inches long and seven and one-fourth wide, exclusive of the talons, is alarming; and we had rather encounter two Indians than meet a single brown bear. There is no chance of killing them by a single shot unless the ball goes through the brain, and this is very difficult on account of two large muscles which cover the side of the forehead and the sharp projection of the centre of the frontal bone, which is also thick.

"Our camp was on the south, at the distance of sixteen miles from that of last night. The fleece and skin of the bear were a heavy burden for two men, and the oil amounted to eight gallons."

The name of the badly-scared Bratton was bestowed upon a creek which discharges into the Missouri near the scene of this encounter. Game continued to be very abundant. On the fourteenth, according to the journal, the hunters were hunted, to their great discomfiture. The account says:—

"Toward evening the men in the hindmost canoes discovered a large brown [grizzly] bear lying in the open grounds, about three hundred paces from the river. Six of them, all good hunters, immediately went to attack him, and concealing themselves by a small eminence came unperceived within forty paces of him. Four of the hunters now fired, and each lodged a ball in his body, two of them directly through the lungs. The furious animal sprang up and ran open-mouthed upon them.

"As he came near, the two hunters who had reserved their fire gave him two wounds, one of which, breaking his shoulder, retarded his motion for a moment; but before they could reload he was so near that they were obliged to run to the river, and before they had reached it he had almost overtaken them. Two jumped into the canoe; the other four separated, and, concealing themselves in the willows, fired as fast as they could reload. They struck him several times, but, instead of weakening the monster, each shot seemed only to direct him towards the hunters, till at last he pursued two of them so closely that they threw aside their guns and pouches, and jumped down a perpendicular bank of twenty feet into the river: the bear sprang after them, and was within a few feet of the hindmost, when one of the hunters on shore shot him in the head, and finally killed him. They dragged him to the shore, and found that eight balls had passed through him in different directions. The bear was old, and the meat tough, so that they took the skin only, and rejoined us at camp, where we had been as much terrified by an accident of a different kind.

"This was the narrow escape of one of our canoes, containing all our papers, instruments, medicine, and almost every article indispensable for the success of our enterprise. The canoe being under sail, a sudden squall of wind struck her obliquely and turned her considerably. The man at the helm, who was unluckily the worst steersman of the party, became alarmed, and, instead of putting her before the wind, luffed her up into it. The wind was so high that it forced the brace of the squaresail out of the hand of the man who was attending it, and instantly upset the canoe, which would have been turned bottom upward but for the resistance made by the awning. Such was the confusion on board, and the waves ran so high, that it was half a minute before she righted, and then nearly full of water, but by bailing her out she was kept from sinking until they rowed ashore. Besides the loss of the lives of three men, who, not being able to swim, would probably have perished, we should have been deprived of nearly everything necessary for our purposes, at a distance of between two and three thousand miles from any place where we could supply the deficiency."

Fortunately, there was no great loss from this accident, which was caused by the clumsiness and timidity of the steersman, Chaboneau. Captain Lewis's account of the incident records that the conduct of Chaboneau's wife, Sacajawea, was better than that of her cowardly husband. He says:—

"The Indian woman, to whom I ascribe equal fortitude and resolution with any person on board at the time of the accident, caught and preserved most of the light articles which were washed overboard."

WAHB—SETON'S GRIZZLY

*It would be difficult to do a book on bears without including Wahb,
the hero of Ernest Thompson Seton's* The Biography of a Grizzly,
published in 1900 by The Century Company, New York.

*Seton, who lived from 1860 to 1946, was primarily a naturalist and
writer of children's books on nature. In addition he was a marvelous
sketch artist and a professionally-trained painter, having studied in
both London and Paris. Born in Scotland, he moved to Canada as a
youngster and grew up on the plains of Manitoba. There he grew
to know the creatures of the wilds as have few naturalists before him.
His* Life Histories of North American Animals *and later his* Lives
of Game Animals *were to gain him much fame as a naturalist and
many awards.*

*But his greatest fame was in his writing of some forty books on
wild creatures. His Lobo the wolf, silverspot the crow and Wahb
the grizzly were household words in America, Canada and Europe
around the turn of the century. He was once scolded by John Bur-
roughs for being a "nature faker," but the great naturalist later apolo-
gized at the urging of President Theodore Roosevelt, a mutual friend
of both men. Burrough's remark was probably touched off by Seton's
habit of attributing human traits to creatures of the wild—a practice
picked up by Walt Disney in later years and perpetuated by a number of writers and cartoonists in books, movies and on television.*

*In his children's books Seton usually pictured the hunter as the
"bad guy," red-eyed, unshaven and usually accompanied by a slath-
ering hound. He made a fortune writing for the children's market
and knew a good thing when he saw it.*

*But in the real world Seton himself was a sport hunter as well as
a fine naturalist. He was an excellent wing shot and loved to shoot
birds. In the company of many of his friends, such as the famous
zoologist and founder of the New York Zoological Society, William Hornaday, and Frank Chapman, curator of Birds at the American Museum of Natural History, he hunted many species of big
game. Most of these men were not only members of the venerable
Campfire Club of America but were founding members. In the records of the club today may be found awards made to these men for*

15

"successfully stalking and killing" such trophies as antelope, elk, deer, moose and many other species of big game in the East and West.

Seton was very fond of wolves and always placed a wolf's paw print after his signature. But he was also fascinated by big bears and spent a great many years studying them—particularly in the Yellowstone area. The story of Wahb takes the reader from the birth of the cub in the Bitterroot mountains of Montana to its death as an old bear in a gas-filled cave in Yellowstone. But in between Wahb had not only become a cattle and horse killer—as did many of the grizzlies of the early West—but a man-killer as well. I chose the chapter of Wahb being discovered spending his summers in the garbage dump next to the hotel in Yellowstone Park because it shows the conflicting nature of bears and illustrates some of Seton's best writing.

Wahb

Ernest Thompson Seton

Many years ago a wise government set aside the head waters of the Yellowstone to be a sanctuary of wild life forever. In the limits of this great Wonderland the ideal of the Royal Singer was to be realized, and none were to harm or make afraid. No violence was to be offered to any bird or beast, no ax was to be carried into its primitive forests, and the streams were to flow on forever unpolluted by mill or mine. All things were to bear witness that such as this was the West before the white man came.

The wild animals quickly found out all this. They soon learned the boundaries of this unfenced Park, and, as every one knows, they show a different nature within its sacred limits. They no longer shun the face of man, they neither fear nor attack him, and they are even more tolerant of one another in this land of refuge.

Peace and plenty are the sum of earthy good; so, finding them here, the wild creatures crowd into the Park from the surrounding country in numbers not elsewhere to be seen.

The Bears are especially numerous about the Fountain Hotel. In the woods, a quarter of a mile away, is a smooth open place where the steward of the hotel has all the broken and waste food put out daily for the Bears, and the man whose work it is has become the Steward of the Bears' Banquet. Each day it is spread, and each year there are more Bears to partake of it. It is a common thing now to see a dozen Bears feasting there at one time. They are of all kinds— Black, Brown, Cinnamon, Grizzly, Silvertip, Roachbacks, big and small, families and rangers, from all parts of the vast surrounding country. All seem to realize that in the Park no violence is allowed, and the most ferocious of them have here put on a new behavior. Although scores of Bears roam about this choice resort, and some-times quarrel among themselves, not one of them has ever yet harmed a man.

Year after year they have come and gone. The passing travellers see them. The men of the hotel know many of them well. They

know that they show up each summer during the short season when the hotel is in use, and that they disappear again, no man knowing whence they come or whither they go.

One day the owner of the Palette Ranch came through the Park. During his stay at the Fountain Hotel, he went to the Bear banquet-hall at high meal-tide. There were several Blackbears feasting, but they made way for a huge Silvertip Grizzly that came about sundown.

"That," said the man who was acting as guide, "is the biggest Grizzly in the Park; but he is a peaceable sort, or Lud knows what'd happen."

"That!" said the ranchman, in astonishment, as the Grizzly came hulking nearer, and loomed up like a load of hay among the piney pillars of the Banquet Hall. "That! If that is not Meteetsee Wahb, I never saw a Bear in my life! Why, that is the worst Grizzly that ever rolled a log in the Big Horn Basin."

"It ain't possible," said the other, "for he's here every summer, July and August, an' I reckon he don't live so far away."

"Well, that settles it," said the ranchman; "July and August is just the time we miss him on the range; and you can see for yourself that he is a little lame behind and has lost a claw on his left front foot. Now I know where he puts in his summers; but I did not suppose that the old reprobate would know enough to behave himself away from home."

The big Grizzly became very well known during the successive hotel seasons. Once only did he really behave ill, and that was the first season he appeared, before he fully knew the ways of the Park.

He wandered over to the hotel, one day, and in at the front door. In the hall he reared up his eight feet of stature as the guests fled in terror; then he went into the clerk's office. The man said: "All right; if you need this office more than I do, you can have it," and leaping over the counter, locked himself in the telegraph-office, to wire the superintendent of the Park: "Old Grizzly in the office now, seems to want to run hotel; may we shoot?"

The reply came: "No shooting allowed in Park; use the hose." Which they did, and, wholly taken by surprise, the Bear leaped over the counter too, and ambled out the back way, with a heavy *thud-thudding* of his feet, and a rattling of his claws on the floor. He passed through the kitchen as he went, and picking up a quarter of beef, took it along.

This was the only time he was known to do ill, though on one occasion he was led into a breach of the peace by another Bear. This was a large she-Blackbear and a noted mischief-maker. She had a wretched, sickly cub that she was very proud of—so proud that she went out of her way to seek trouble on his behalf. And he, like all spoiled children, was the cause of much bad feeling. She was so big and fierce that she could bully all the other Blackbears, but when she tried to drive off old Wahb she received a pat from his paw that sent her tumbling like a football. He followed her up, and would have killed her, for she had broken the peace of the Park, but she escaped by climbing a tree, from the top of which her miserable little cub was apprehensively squealing at the pitch of his voice. So the affair was ended; in future the Blackbear kept out of Wahb's way, and he won the reputation of being a peaceable, well-behaved Bear. Most persons believed that he came from some remote mountains where were neither guns nor traps to make him sullen and revengeful.

BEN LILLY'S BEARS

In 1951 J. Frank Dobie, the great Texas writer, wrote a book about a man who was probably the greatest lion and bear hunter that ever lived in America. His book, The Ben Lilly Legend *was published by Little, Brown and Company, Boston and should be a must in the library of any collector of outdoor writing. It is out of print now, but copies keep showing up now and then.*

Nobody, except perhaps Lilly and it is doubtful if he did, ever kept an exact count of the number of bears and mountain lions Lilly killed. He hunted them from his early boyhood in Louisiana until shortly before his death in 1936 at almost eighty near Silver City, New Mexico. He was the ultimate hunter—leaving his home or a camp or ranch on the spur of the 'moment and spending days or weeks on the trail of one of the big predators. He traveled on foot, either with or without dogs, depending upon his mood. He was incredibly strong and in his mid-fifties and early sixties could and did climb mountains and trail bears like a twenty-year-old. He slept out under the sky in clear weather and foul, seldom wearing more than denim trousers, a cotton shirt and old sweater—his battered sombrero the only covering for his head. He ate what he killed and could fast for days if need be.

During most of his life he hunted for the sheer need to do so, or for the love of it. Later—at age fifty-five—he took a job with the U.S. Forest Service in The Apache National Forest of Arizona as a guard-trapper at $75 per month. For six or eight years he hunted up and down the borders of Arizona and New Mexico, cleaning out the lions and bears. During those years he averaged about fifty lions and bear a year, collecting as much as fifty dollars each as a bounty. Then in 1916 he worked as a trapper for the U.S. Biological Survey, which paid him a salary of $100 per month. He worked on and off for the Survey for about four years until he quit to hunt on his own.

Cattle ranchers in those days paid well for professional hunters, and Lilly made enough ridding the big ranches of cattle-killing bears and lions to keep himself satisfied. He regarded his years as a professional hunter as the most exhilarating period of his life. He never "came down" from the mountains to stay in towns during the winter.

The old hermit hunted for lions when bears were in hibernation and for both lions and bears the rest of the year. After he had located a hunting range he would set up a series of hunting "camps." These were caches in natural shelters, and here he would store dried jerky made from the meat of bears and lions he had killed. Occasionally he would hire a man to carry supplies into the mountains, but more often he would carry the supplies himself or pack them in on a burro.

Although relatively unschooled, Lilly could both read and write and throughout his life claimed to be writing a book on his hunting. Frank Dobie found enough hand-written pages of this book to write his own after Lilly's death. In addition he was an accomplished naturalist and interested in everything that moved in the outdoors. Influenced in 1904 by Ned Hollister, a biologist with the Biological Survey, Lilly later in life learned to prepare study skins of birds and mammals, which he regularly sent to the Smithsonian in Washington.

His notes on wildlife have appeared in the scientific writings of Harry C. Oberholser's The Bird of Louisiana; *in Vernon Baily's* Birds of New Mexico; *C. Hart Merriam's* Review of The Grizzly and Big Brown Bears of North America; *and in Prentiss N. Gray's* Records Of North American Big Game.

The story in this volume, "That Taos Bear," perhaps best pictures the great Ben Lilly for the true legend he was.

That Taos Bear

J. Frank Dobie

In 1921, fourteen years after he had been "Chief Huntsman" to
Roosevelt, Ben Lilly again withdrew from solitude to guide the most
elaborately planned hunt the West has known since the Earl of Dun-
raven, led by Buffalo Bill and Texas Jack, bombarded the wapiti of
the Yellowstone. It was enterprised by W. H. McFadden, Oklahoma
oilman. For months before it started, promoter and sportsman Monroe H. Goode was spending his time and McFadden's money getting
men, dogs and equipment together. The plan was to start on the
Mexican border and hunt through the Rocky Mountains to Alaska.

Early in the spring four big wagons, each drawn by four big
mules, set out north from Lordsburg, New Mexico. With the wagons
was a train of pack mules, manned by professional packers, and
enough horses and horsemen to drive a trial herd to Montana. The
combined packs of dogs numbered forty-five, one dog alone having
cost one thousand dollars. There were enough guns and ammunition
to start a revolution in Nicaragua. A commercial photographer had
been hired out of his studio to take pictures. The chief cook had a
corps of helpers. The wagons held cases of maps, cases of Scotch,
and provisions both delicate and substantial in proportion. Tents and
servants assured comfort to ladies and gentlemen. The outfit had no
time schedule, no limit on cost. Fresh supplies could be obtained at
various points. Freehanded McFadden proposed to give his friends, in
groups and in relays, an outing to remember. He would have to be
absent from the expedition many times, but it was to go on just the
same. Side hunts would be made east and west, wherever the signs
pointed. For the first stretch of the hunt, through New Mexico, Ben
Lilly, was to be the main sign reader. His chief mission in life became to get McFadden a chance at a grizzly bear. Black bears and
mountain lions were also on the program.

Coming down the Mimbres River in a light spring wagon one day,
McFadden overtook his guide.

"I've been following a blue lion," Ben Lilly said.

23

"Blue, you say?"

"Yes, don't you want a blue lion? Here's the evidence." He took out of his pocket some blue hairs gathered from the under side of a crooked log on which the lion had rubbed his back. It was early June and lions were shedding.

"Well, get in the wagon and let's ride to camp," McFadden said.

"No, I'll get cold if I ride. I'll run ahead and open the gates." He had come nineteen miles that day and waded the Mimbres River eighteen times. He was going to camp to get his dogs, having been scouting without them.

The night turned out cold. McFadden insisted that the aging hunter sleep in a sleeping bag, near him. At two o'clock in the morning, Ben Lilly crawled out of it. "I'm choking to death," he said. "I'm going after the blue lion. Don't you want to go?"

"No."

"Then I'll see you in Silver City, and have the skull and hide."

This was Thursday morning. On Sunday morning Ben Lilly walked up to McFadden in Silver City, picking the flesh out of a skull with a knife, a fresh hide slung over his shoulder. "Here is the blue lion," he said.*

At night he would lie down in his blanket off to one side of the lighted, luxurious, tented camp. Often he boiled corn meal to eat instead of gorging on the profuse dishes provided by McFadden's cooks. If he did not leave before daylight to scout, he would be standing in blue denim awaiting emergence of shivering sheepskin-coated guests. Their ways were all right with him; his way of austere simplicity was the way he wanted for himself.

On June 29 he struck the trail of a grizzly in mountains above Taos. He followed it for thirty hours without letup, and when he quit it to notify his patron, be knew where the bear would be during the next thirty hours. Just at this point McFadden had to leave for the East on business. He left instructions for Lilly to keep the bear located until he could return. The hunting party moved on. All the rest of the summer and into the fall Ben Lilly shadowed the bear. He followed the wandering trail over northern New Mexico and into Colorado. He came to ground still warm from the grizzly's body, got left far behind. He sent in reports:

"*Saturday, August 6th, 1921.* Going north for Wheeler Peak in Colorado. I trailed him until dark. It rained that night and next day. It

*Not robin's-egg blue.

24

rains from one to three times every day. On Friday at 11 o'clock I found his track again, headed for Wheeler Peak mountains. I camped on his track. It come a big rain and hail that evening. I took it up at daylight and followed it until 11 o'clock. A heavy rain put the track out. He was going south on the head of Pueblo River. I saw several small bear tracks while trailing him. He was feeding on berries and yellow jackets. He robbed about ten yellow jacket nests and followed after cattle tracks. . . .

"This big bear will have a range of 65 miles when disturbed and will change at any time. I am fully determined to work out his habits. It hurts me to let a bear rest that is wanted. . . .

"I found 22 old beds in one space of about 300 yards. That spot had been used by four different grizzlies—an old she, two two-year olds, and this male. The other three bears have not used it for two years, but the big male used it this spring. . . .

"Spent 12 hours on 3 miles travel, picking my own route. If a bear had picked the route, I might have made only one mile a day. Whenever you want to see the roughest country, trail a grizzly. . . .

"I can tell a grizzly claw mark a year after it has been made on a tree. I can tell the tooth marks. A Monster bear will not come back to a carcass to eat after he finds a man has been around. Other bear will come and eat. An old male will strike out for another range as soon as he gets filled up. Even if it is twelve months later, show me where one of these big fellows has left his sign, and in a few minutes I can tell you what happened. . . .

"A black bear that is fat and is living on good mast in his home range is easier killed than one that has just emigrated to a section where the feed is poor. When frightened, the fat bear will tree; the migratory bear is ready to keep on rambling from one bad place to another."

Clouds might prevent the "old male" from seeing his own shadow, but he could not run away from his shadower. Now he was in high rough places he had "been using for years," the shadower reported, "and no one knows of these places except me." That the big bear might not learn he was being shadowed, Lilly would not allow his dogs to run other bear in the country, and the only dog he used to follow this one was tied to his belt.

In late fall, Ahab suspended for a little while his wrath for the monster grizzly and came down to hear some word from his patron. No word. With "a hundred pounds on my back," he went up again. He was sixty-five years old now. This was in the Sangre de Cristo

25

Mountains, in the Taos country. "We will never give that bear up. He has got to come—if I live. He can't get away. I know him too well to let him out, and he knows other people who are after him too well for them to get him. We will get him sooner or later—just as it suits you."

Now it was hibernation time. "My gun froze on the route. I didn't have a mouthful of meat for ten days." Mr. McFadden was on a luxury liner in the Atlantic Ocean, bound for Europe.

While the grizzly slept, Ben Lilly went to Taos to sit for the full-length portrait that his patron had commissioned Herbert Dunton to paint—"Buck" Dunton as his friends called him, "Dunton of Taos" as he magnificently signed his name. Grizzled hunters and grizzly bears were favorite subjects with Dunton. Lilly lived with him for twelve days, considered the portrait "true to life"—an opinion not shared by some—and reported that Dunton called it "the best piece he had ever done." In after times Dunton spoke of Ben Lilly's legs as his outstanding feature, along with his ability to read sign. In the spring the finished portrait, which is now in the New Orleans home of W. H. McFadden, was exhibited by the National Academy of Design in New York.

Ben Lilly was in Ponca City to get a string of McFadden dogs to take to Idaho, where the grand hunt had wintered. According to McFadden, he started from Ponca City on a train, but got out and walked and, upon arriving in Parma, Idaho, snow still on the ground, slept in the stockyards instead of going to the hotel where a room had been engaged for him. Idaho was the farthest north he ever hunted, though for years he yearned towards Alaskan bears.

He spent the summer of 1922 high up in the Rockies, attached to a camp that was frequently moved and that McFadden men but not McFadden himself dominated. His main object seems to have been to train his employer's dogs. According to his regularly kept diary, the dogs were lost a good part of the time. One of his own most cherished dogs got quilled by a porcupine and when finally found was blind and dying. One of his associates reported seeing a lion. "I am afraid he saw a coyote instead of a lion," Lilly mildly entered in the diary. He was mild also in entering the fact that target practice with pistols by a packer and a game warden confused the dogs and threw them off a hot bear trail. Once he rode a horse in order to keep company with a guest; then, just when he had a bear within reach, the guest insisted on fishing. The bountiful camp seemed to interest the campers more than hunting. He took "the grip." A dose

of Epsom salts gave him a chill; two pills made him worse. They moved into a sheep country; a sheep got into a bear trap he had set. He dressed the sheep's wound and felt hopeful that it would recover, but "looked up the sheep herder and left a check for $5" to pay the owner for damages.

Frequent rains blotted out tracks, but between the last of May and the first of August Lilly observed the tracks of thirty-nine bears. He knew the age, sex and character of each trackmaker: "One four-year-old male," "one three-year-old male," a "two-year-old female," "one track grown-size but not plain enough to tell sex," "one small female yearling," "a barren she," and so on. On Big Pistol Creek he saw "hair rubbed on trees by a light cinnamon and a dark brown bear traveling eastward five days ago." From "bites in trees," he decided that a grizzly male had made two trips into that section the spring and summer of the preceding year, but had not been back. Without explanation, he entered in the diary for Sunday, October 15, 1922: "Lay over in camp. Helped skin the bear." On another Sunday he hunted by mistake, having lost account of the days, but rested from all labor on Monday. Altogether, it was not a satisfactory season. "Things" were in the saddle.

That fall he came back south, stopping in Denver, and, as arranged by McFadden's office, going to the Brown Palace Hotel. Wearing his blowing horn and followed by three hounds, his bearded figure was the cynosure of all eyes. He told a reporter for the *Denver Post*, so the reporter said, that he wore the beard to keep mosquitoes off his face and the horn to call "the pups" in case they got lost in a train wreck or something like that. He did not think much of the backwoods language—manufactured in town—that the reporter made him speak. Trite, nonapprehending people often credited him with the vernacular that third-rate fictionists habitually put into the mouths of their rural characters. His mild protest recalls one made by Bigfoot Wallace to his biographer. "I know," Bigfoot said, "that my education is limited, but do give me credit for the little I have. People are not such fools as to think a man cannot be a good hunter or ranger, merely because he speaks his own language passably well."

He was glad to get back to the G O S range, where there were no camps to report to, no kennel dogs to interfere with his own, no voices to interrupt the silences. For years he continued to write McFadden letters about his dogs, the trails he had struck, the lions he had killed, the knives and pictures he was sending, the appropriateness of electing Mr. McFadden President of the United States—and "that Taos bear." "I will never feel right until we get him," he wrote, in April, 1925. That fall he was still "wild to get that bear." The final hunt was never made. Another rich man paid him $300 a month to tree lions for himself and his wife to shoot.

In these years of the 'twenties he virtually cleared the G O S and adjoining ranches of lions and bears. He was at the climax of enjoying his own prestige. He was a voluminous letter-writer and diary-keeper, but his diaries were scattered and lost. It seems to have been in 1924 that he began writing "my book." A California promoter encouraged him to imagine that a fortune-making film based on the proposed book would picture his hunting activities in the mountains. Like many people ignorant of the craftsmanship necessary for good writing, of the publishing business, and of the limitations of the book-buying public, he thought that a chronicle of his experiences and knowledge, once in book form, would bring a comfortable income "for the later years of life."

A mass-producer of Western fiction who came into the Silver City country sent him a note by a cowboy saying that he would be pleased to accompany him on a lion chase. After a good deal of trailing, the cowboy was able to deliver the note. Mr. Lilly read it slowly and then slowly penciled a courteous reply on a sheet of his pulp-paper tablet. He was after some stock-killers, he explained, and could not allow pleasure-hunters to interfere with business.

Royalties had made this Western writer acutely conscious of his own importance. Upon reading Ben Lilly's note, he turned to the cowboy bearer of it and blazed, "Apparently this old codger does not know who I am."

The cowboy shifted in his boots and grinned. "No, Mister," he remarked, "it ain't exactly that. You jest don't know who Ben Lilly is."

Everybody else knew. Over against Jerky Mountain, between the West Fork and the Middle Fork of the Gila River, a big "park" went—and still goes—by the name of Lilly Park. It is one of Mister Ben Lilly's tracks. He had already become a legend. People in town talked about the "big deposits" he had in banks, as well as about his checks written on aspen bark. In 1924 he had small amounts of money "laid up" in eleven or thirteen banks—he seemed unsure of the number—in El Paso, two Oklahoma banks, a bank or two in Arizona, and various New Mexico banks. Most of them closed when all the Western country went broke in the early 'twenties.

If a rancher or hunter anywhere in New Mexico or Arizona got to telling about some unusual experience he had had with a wild animal, he would likely add, "The first chance I get I want to ask Ben Lilly about that." Blunt Sloan ran a lion with dogs from nine o'clock one morning until five that afternoon before the lion treed. For a lion to stay ahead of running dogs that long is very unusual. When Blunt Sloan finally met Ben Lilly up in the aspens Lilly strengthened reliance upon his knowledge by saying that he did not know what possessed the lion but maybe he was mad.

After Charlie Saucier, while freighting in the Black Range, saw a grizzly standing on his hind legs slapping a steer, both its jaws having been broken, and then driving it off an open draw into timber, he consulted Ben Lilly on bear tactics. "I never saw a bear hug," Ben Lilly told him. "All I've ever seen fighting slapped."

Forest men concerned with the increase of porcupines, destructive to trees, consulted him. Yes, he thought that the destruction of lions would result in further increase of porcupines unless they were otherwise checked. He had often observed the fondness of lions for porcupine meat. He always cut open every animal he killed to learn about its diet. Though he had never seen the act, he was convinced that many lions knew how to roll a porcupine over and claw the body open without getting seriously quilled. Once he found a dead coyote with so many quills in its head that he judged they had prevented the coyote from eating and resulted in starvation.

Now and then he still sent specimens to the National Museum in Washington. How careful he was with the specimens is illustrated by an incident in which a young man named Edd Midgett took part. Late in 1923 Midgett was hunting on the Gila River, out from the famous Lyons Lodge, when he encountered Ben Lilly and "took up" with him. Stored carefully in a dry cave, the old hunter showed him the hides and skeletons of a female lion and two kittens, every bone minutely cleaned, to be shipped for mounting. One day the Lilly dogs struck the trail of a very old male lion. It leaped downward from a bluff into a piñon tree growing out obliquely into space 300 feet above the canyon floor. When a bullet from the Lilly .30–30 rifle took its life, the body lodged in a fork of the tree. Mr. Lilly had his ax, but to bring the lion carcass down by cutting the tree would mean crushed bones. This large, well-matured male was the very specimen to group with the female and the kittens already secured.

Mr. Lilly went to camp for two ropes and Old Smoky, his burro. He left Smoky on the canyon floor; then he scrambled ahead of the young man to the top of the bluff. Edd Midgett had climbed oil derricks. Now he swung down by rope from bluff to the base of the piñon, climbed its iced-over trunk, and fastened two ropes around the lion. He and Lilly managed to raise it to the bluff. The ground was covered with frozen snow. Ben Lilly sat down on it, tied one end of a rope around his waist, adjusted the lion's body carefully in his lap, and instructed Midgett to pull him down to Old Smokey. He turned himself into a sled to be dragged and braked over boulders rather than risk scraping a single hair from the lion's hide. In camp the two men, as well as the dogs, had a feast on panther steaks.

How many panthers and how many bears Ben Lilly killed is not very important. To judge him on that basis is like judging the intellectual level of a newspaper by how much it weighs. The claim that Lilly killed "thousands" is foolish. One admiring—that is, gaping with uncritical wonder—fool* asserts that he averaged a lion a day while hunting. Actually, if he averaged one every two weeks he figured he was doing well. He had good runs, of course. "In 1914," he recorded,

---

*"For fools admire, but men of sense approve."—Pope.

"I killed 9 mountain lions and 3 bears in one week." But this was a pocket, not a vein, as other statements from his diaries show: "I never struck a lion track from June 28th to the last of August, 1916. In another year I hunted all July and until the 25th of August and struck only 3 lion trails and lost them on account of rains. In 1912, I killed 47 bears and lions, about an equal number of each; in 1913, I killed 48 bears and lions."

During one month of the spring of 1832, Davy Crockett of Tennessee, who went into some places ahead of the bees, killed, according to his autobiography, 47 bears, making a total of 105 for less than a year. In 1904, Ben Lilly told Ned Hollister that he had killed 105 bears in Louisiana and Mississippi during the preceding quarter of a century. Too many Crocketts had gone before for him to make a Crockett record. Yet he was far superior to Crockett in hunting skills, and as an observer of wild life Crockett had absolutely nothing to report. In the West, Ben Lilly became more of a lion man than a bear man. What he saw in the animals he hunted is of more consequence than the numbers he slew. It is to be doubted if during his whole lifetime of hunting he killed more than a thousand bears and lions put together. Considering his time, this was an enormous toll.

The records of the Biological Survey show, according to Dorr H. Green, Chief of the Division of Predator and Rodent Control, that B. V. Lilly "took" predatory animals as follows during his intermittent terms of employment with the Biological Survey: October-December, 1916, 9 mountain lions; October-December, 1917, 8 mountain lions; February-December, 1918, 25 mountain lions, 8 bears, 2 bobcats; January-May 1919, 7 mountain lions; October-November, 1919, 2 mountain lions, 1 bear, 1 coyote; June 1-August 14, 1920, 4 mountain lions, 3 bears. He was killing too many bears; "services were terminated." At times during his employment with the Biological Survey, B. V. Lilly would be sent to some very difficult region to get some particularly elusive and destructive predator. During twenty-six and a half months of the years 1916–1920 that he worked for the Biological Survey, he reported the destruction of only 55 lions and 12 bears. It is doubtful if, during the remaining time of this period, he more than equaled that number.

In his "Mountain Lion Record for 1922," he tells of killing 10 lions between June 14 and September 26 and adds that his total over a period of years for the Alma (New Mexico) section, which included the Blue River country of Arizona, was 109 lions. His biggest kills, as deduced from the articles he published in the *Producer,* were 47 lions and bears (about equally divided) in 1912, in the Alma district; 48 lions and bears in 1913, in the same Arizona-New Mexico range; 1914 and 1915, also "good killing"; 42 lions on the G O S and Diamond Bar ranches during 4 months of 1919, after which the animals were much scarcer everywhere that he hunted.

In March, 1919, an article in the *American Magazine* reported that "during the past four years, in the Apache Forest Reserve alone, Lilly has tracked to death 154 lions, with 46 bears picked up on the side." Four years later, Fred Winn of the Forest Service, who knew Lilly very well indeed, reported that he had "disposed of over 400 mountain lions in Arizona, New Mexico and Texas." In 1943, Dr. A. K. Fisher of the Biological Survey wrote to Monroe Goode: "As I understand it, Lilly gave me his 500th lion, a fine male killed 30 miles north of the G O S Ranch, March 14, 1921. He very likely killed 50 to 75 after that, but of course this is a guess only." About the same time, E. E. Lee, noted Arizona hunter, wrote to Monroe Goode: "In the spring of 1925, Lilly told me he had just killed his 547th lion since 1912—'after they had begun to get scarce.'" On December 9, 1934, an article in the *Sunday Star* of Washington, D.C., evidently based on an interview with Ben Lilly, was entitled "Old Chap Has Killed 600 Lions." By this date the "old chap" had virtually ceased to hunt.

The Boones and the Crocketts skimmed the cream; Ben Lilly scooped up every drop of splattered milk from the cracks. In the letter of self-appraisal that he wrote Dr. J. B. Drake, in 1928, he said: "No other man will work as close as I have worked. I have worked in localities where not enough food could be carried to keep three men alive. I have worked where no water was to be had for 76 hours. In order to get to the animals I wanted, I went without food and water for days. I have stayed in snow from 3 to 12 feet deep for three weeks at a time and not even a blanket and I succeeded. I have followed a big grizzly for three days at a time, snow from 3 to 12 feet deep, never had a coat on, I killed him, and then I eat his meat. No other man will take such risks alone—not even a dozen other men together. I have killed the largest and best tribes of animals. I have hunted them so close that it would take longer for 100 of them to accumulate again than it took me to kill 1000."

No, numbers are not the index to Ben Lilly's career as a hunter.

FAULKNER'S BEAR

William Faulkner was one of America's best-known novelists and short story writers.

His novels and stories—for the most part—were about the anguish and social changes that took place in his beloved Deep South following the Civil War. Best known for his writings on family decay, he was nevertheless a writer of nature and hunting. Faulkner was a quail hunter and an excellent shot.

In 1949 he was awarded the Nobel Prize for Literature. His best known works are The Sound And The Fury, As I Lay Dying, Sanctuary, Light In August, Absalom, Absolom, The Unvanquished, The Hamlet, Go Down Moses, Intruder In The Dust, Requiem For A Nun, A Fable, The Town, *and* The Mansion.

But among his least-known works appeared some of his greatest writing. In 1931 he published a book about his beloved Mississippi called Big Woods. *It was a collection of essays and short stories, and one of the stories was called "The Bear." It was the story of an old bear which had been hunted for a long time by many hunters with dogs. I have excerpted the section that deals with the last hunt, when the bear was killed. It could stand alone as a classic in writing about bears.*

The Bear

William Faulkner

There were five guests in camp that night, from Jefferson: Mr. Bayard Sartoris and his son and General Compson's son and two others. And the next morning he looked out the window, into the gray thin drizzle of daybreak which Ash had predicted, and there they were, standing and squatting beneath the thin rain, almost two dozen of them who had fed Old Ben corn and shoats and even calves for ten years, in their worn hats and hunting coats and overalls which any town Negro would have thrown away or burned and only the rubber boots strong and sound, and the worn and blueless guns and some even without guns. While they ate breakfast a dozen more arrived, mounted and on foot: loggers from the camp thirteen miles below and sawmill men from Hoke's and the only gun among them that one which the log-train conductor carried: so that when they went into the woods this morning Major de Spain led a party almost as strong, excepting that some of them were not armed, as some he had led in the last darkening days of '64 and '65. The little yard would not hold them. They overflowed it, into the lane where Major de Spain sat his mare while Ash in his dirty apron thrust the greasy cartridges into his carbine and passed it up to him and the great grave blue dog stood at his stirrup not as a dog stands but as a horse stands, blinking his sleepy topaz eyes at nothing, deaf even to the yelling of the hounds which Boon and Tennie's Jim held on leash.

"We'll put General Compson on Katie this morning," Major de Spain said. "He drew blood last year; if he'd had a mule then that would have stood, he would have——"

"No," General Compson said. "I'm too old to go helling through the woods on a mule or a horse or anything else any more. Besides, I had my chance last year and missed it. I'm going on a stand this morning. I'm going to let that boy ride Katie."

"No, wait," McCaslin said. "Ike's got the rest of his life to hunt bears in. Let somebody else——"

"No," General Compson said. "I want Ike to ride Katie. He's already a better woodsman than you or me either and in another ten years he'll be as good as Walter."

At first he couldn't believe it, not until Major de Spain spoke to him. Then he was up, on the one-eyed mule which would not spook at wild blood, looking down at the dog motionless at Major de Spain's stirrup, looking in the gray streaming light bigger than a calf, bigger than he knew it actually was—the big head, the chest almost as big as his own, the blue hide beneath which the muscles flinched or quivered to no touch since the heart which drove blood to them loved no man and no thing, standing as a horse stands yet different from a horse which infers only weight and speed while Lion inferred not only courage and all else that went to make up the will and desire to pursue and kill, but endurance, the will and desire to endure beyond all imaginable limits of flesh in order to overtake and slay. Then the dog looked at him. It moved its head and looked at him across the trivial uproar of the hounds, out of the yellow eyes as depthless as Boon's, as free as Boon's of meanness or generosity or gentleness or viciousness. They were just cold and sleepy. Then it blinked, and he knew it was not looking at him and never had been, without even bothering to turn its head away.

That morning he heard the first cry. Lion had already vanished while Sam and Tennie's Jim were putting saddles on the mule and horse which had drawn the wagon and he watched the hounds as they crossed and cast, snuffing and whimpering, until they too disappeared. Then he and Major de Spain and Sam and Tennie's Jim rode after them and heard the first cry out of the wet and thawing woods not two hundred yards ahead, high, with that abject, almost human quality he had come to know, and the other hounds joining in until the gloomed woods rang and clamored. They rode then. It seemed to him that he could actually see the big blue dog boring on, silent, and the bear too: the thick, locomotive-like shape which he had seen that day four years ago crossing the blow-down, crashing on ahead of the dogs faster than he had believed it could have moved, drawing away even from the running mules. He heard a shotgun, once. The woods had opened, they were going fast, the clamor faint and fading on ahead; they passed the man who had fired—a swamper, a pointing arm, a gaunt face, the small black orifice of his yelling studded with rotten teeth.

35

He heard the changed note in the hounds' uproar and two hundred yards ahead he saw them. The bear had turned. He saw Lion drive in without pausing and saw the bear strike him aside and lunge into the yelling hounds and kill one of them almost in its tracks and whirl and run again. Then they were in a streaming tide of dogs. He heard Major de Spain and Tennie's Jim shouting and the pistol sound of Tennie's Jim's leather thong as he tried to turn them. Then he and Sam Fathers were riding alone. One of the hounds had kept on with Lion though. He recognized its voice. It was the young hound which even a year ago had had no judgment and which, by the lights of the other hounds anyway, still had none. *Maybe that's what courage is*, he thought. "Right," Sam said behind him. "Right. We got to turn him from the river if we can."

Now they were in cane: a brake. He knew the path through it as well as Sam did. They came out of the undergrowth and struck the entrance almost exactly. It would traverse the brake and come out onto a high open ridge above the river. He heard the flat clap of Walter Ewell's rifle, then two more. "No," Sam said. "I can hear the hound. Go on."

They emerged from the narrow roofless tunnel of snapping and hissing cane, still galloping, onto the open ridge below which the thick yellow river, reflectionless in the gray and streaming light, seemed not to move. Now he could hear the hound too. It was not running. The cry was a high frantic yapping and Boon was running along the edge of the bluff, his old gun leaping and jouncing against his back on its sling made of a piece of cotton plowline. He whirled and ran up to them, wild-faced, and flung himself onto the mule behind the boy. "That damn boat!" he cried. "It's on the other side! He went straight across! Lion was too close to him! That little hound too! Lion was so close I couldn't shoot! Go on!" he cried, beating his heels into the mule's flanks. "Go on!"

They plunged down the bank, slipping and sliding in the thawed earth, crashing through the willows and into the water. He felt no shock, no cold, he on one side of the swimming mule, grasping the pommel with one hand and holding his gun above the water with the other, Boon opposite him. Sam was behind them somewhere, and then the river, the water about them, was full of dogs. They swam faster than the mules; they were scrabbling up the bank before the mules touched bottom. Major de Spain was whooping from the bank they had just left and, looking back, he saw Tennie's Jim and the horse as they went into the water.

Now the woods ahead of them and the rain-heavy air were one uproar. It rang and clamored; it echoed and broke against the bank behind them and reformed and clamored and rang until it seemed to the boy that all the hounds which had ever bayed game in this land were yelling down at him. He got his leg over the mule as it came up out of the water. Boon didn't try to mount again. He grasped one stirrup as they went up the bank and crashed through the undergrowth which fringed the bluff and saw the bear, on its hind feet, its back against a tree while the bellowing hounds swirled around it and once more Lion drove in, leaping clear of the ground.

This time the bear didn't strike him down. It caught the dog in both arms, almost loverlike, and they both went down. He was off the mule now. He drew back both hammers of the gun but he could see nothing but moiling spotted houndbodies until the bear surged up again. Boon was yelling something, he could not tell what; he could see Lion still clinging to the bear's throat and he saw the bear, half erect, strike one of the hounds with one paw and hurl it five or six feet and then, rising and rising as though it would never stop, stand erect again and begin to rake at Lion's belly with its forepaws. Then Boon was running. The boy saw the gleam of the blade in his hand and watched him leap among the hounds, hurdling them, kicking them aside as he ran, and fling himself astride the bear as he had hurled himself onto the mule, his legs locked around the bear's belly, his left arm under the bear's throat where Lion clung, and the glint of the knife as it rose and fell.

It fell just once. For an instant they almost resembled a piece of statuary: the clinging dog, the bear, the man astride its back, working and probing the buried blade. Then they went down, pulled over backward by Boon's weight, Boon underneath. It was the bear's back which reappeared first but at once Boon was astride it again. He had never released the knife and again the boy saw the almost infinitesimal movement of his arm and shoulder as he probed and sought; then the bear surged erect, raising with it the man and the dog too, and turned and still carrying the man and the dog it took two or three steps toward the woods on its hind feet as a man would have walked and crashed down. It didn't collapse, crumble. It fell all of a piece, as a tree falls, so that all three of them, man, dog and bear, seemed to bounce once.

He and Tennie's Jim ran forward. Boon was kneeling at the bear's head. His left ear was shredded, his left coat sleeve was completely gone, his right boot had been ripped from knee to instep; the bright blood thinned in the thin rain down his leg and hand and arm and down the side of his face which was no longer wild but was quite calm. Together they prized Lion's jaws from the bear's throat. "Easy, goddamn it," Boon said. "Can't you see his guts are all out of him?" He began to remove his coat. He spoke to Tennie's Jim in that calm voice: "Bring the boat up. It's about a hundred yards down the bank there. I saw it." Tennie's Jim rose and went away. Then, and he could not remember if it had been a call or an exclamation from Tennie's Jim or if he had glanced up by chance, he saw Tennie's Jim stooping and saw Sam Fathers lying motionless on his face in the trampled mud.

The mule had not thrown him. He remembered that Sam was down too even before Boon began to run. There was no mark on him whatever and when he and Boon turned him over, his eyes were open and he said something in that tongue which he and Joe Baker had used to speak together. But he couldn't move. Tennie's Jim brought the skiff up; they could hear him shouting to Major de Spain across the river. Boon wrapped Lion in his hunting coat and carried him down to the skiff and they carried Sam down and re-turned and hitched the bear to the one-eyed mule's saddle-bow with Tennie's Jim's leash-thong and dragged him down to the skiff and got him into it and left Tennie's Jim to swim the horse and the two mules back across. Major de Spain caught the bow of the skiff as Boon jumped out and past him before it touched the bank. He looked at Old Ben and said quietly: "Well." Then he walked into the water and leaned down and touched Sam and Sam looked up at him and said something in that old tongue he and Joe Baker spoke. "You don't know what happened?" Major de Spain said.

"No sir," the boy said. "It wasn't the mule. It wasn't anything. He was off the mule when Boon ran in on the bear. Then we looked up and he was lying on the ground." Boon was shouting at Tennie's Jim, still in the middle of the river.

"Come on, goddamn it!" he said. "Bring me that mule!"

"What do you want with a mule?" Major de Spain said.

Boon didn't even look at him. "I'm going to Hoke's to get the doctor," he said in that calm voice, his face quite calm beneath the steady thinning of the bright blood.

"You need a doctor yourself," Major de Spain said. "Tennie's Jim——"

"Damn that," Boon said. He turned on Major de Spain. His face was still calm, only his voice was a pitch higher. "Can't you see his goddamn guts are all out of him?"

"Boon!" Major de Spain said. They looked at one another. Boon was a good head taller than Major de Spain; even the boy was taller now than Major de Spain.

"I've got to get the doctor," Boon said. "His goddamn guts——"

"All right," Major de Spain said. Tennie's Jim came up out of the water. The horse and the sound mule had already scented Old Ben; they surged and plunged all the way up to the top of the bluff, dragging Tennie's Jim with them, before he could stop them and tie them and come back. Major de Spain unlooped the leather thong of his compass from his buttonhole and gave it to Tennie's Jim. "Go strait to Hoke's," he said. "Bring Doctor Crawford back with you. Tell him there are two men to be looked at. Take my mare. Can you find the road from here?"

"Yes sir," Tennie's Jim said.

"All right," Major de Spain said. "Go on." He turned to the boy. "Take the mules and the horse and go back and get the wagon. We'll go on down the river in the boat to Coon bridge. Meet us there. Can you find it again?"

"Yes, sir," the boy said.

"All right. Get started."

He went back to the wagon. He realised then how far they had run. It was already afternoon when he put the mules into the traces and tied the horse's lead-rope to the tail-gate. He reached Coon bridge at dusk. The skiff was already there. Before he could see it and almost before he could see the water he had to leap from the tilting wagon, still holding the reins, and work around to where he could grasp the bit and then the ear of the plunging sound mule and dig his heels and hold it until Boon came up the bank. The rope of the lead horse had already snapped and it had already disappeared up the road toward camp. They turned the wagon around and took the mules out and he led the sound mule a hundred yards up the road and tied it. Boon had already brought Lion up to the wagon and Sam was sitting up in the skiff now and when they raised him he tried to walk, up the bank and to the wagon and he tried to climb into the wagon but Boon did not wait; he picked Sam up bodily and set him on the seat. Then they hitched Old Ben to the one-eyed mule's saddle again and dragged him up the bank and set two skid-poles into the open tailgate and got him into the wagon and he went and got the sound mule and Boon fought it into the traces, striking it across its hard hollow-sounding face until it came into position and stood trembling. Then the rain came down, as though it had held off all day waiting on them.

They returned to camp through it, through the streaming and sightless dark, hearing long before they saw any light the horn and the spaced shots to guide them. When they came to Sam's dark little hut he tried to stand up. He spoke again in the tongue of the old fathers; then he said clearly: "Let me out. Let me out."

"He hasn't got any fire," Major said. "Go on!" he said sharply.

But Sam was struggling now, trying to stand up. "Let me out, master," he said. "Let me go home."

So he stopped the wagon and Boon got down and lifted Sam out. He did not wait to let Sam try to walk this time. He carried him into the hut and Major de Spain got light on a paper spill from the buried embers on the hearth and lit the lamp and Boon put Sam on his bunk and drew off his boots and Major de Spain covered him and the boy was not there, he was holding the mules, the sound one which was trying again to bolt since when the wagon stopped Old Ben's scent drifted forward again along the streaming blackness of air, but Sam's eyes were probably open again on that profound look which saw further than them or the hut, further than the death of a bear and the dying of a dog. Then they went on, toward the long wailing of the horn and the shots which seemed each to linger intact somewhere in the thick streaming air until the next spaced report joined and blended with it, to the lighted house, the bright streaming windows, the quiet faces as Boon entered, bloody and quite calm, carrying the bundled coat. He laid Lion, bloody coat and all, on his stale sheetless pallet bed which not even Ash, as deft in the house as a woman, could ever make smooth.

The sawmill doctor from Hoke's was already there. Boon would not let the doctor touch him until he had seen to Lion. He wouldn't risk giving Lion chloroform. He put the entrails back and sewed him up without it while Major de Spain held his head and Boon his feet. But he never tried to move. He lay there, the yellow eyes open upon nothing while the quiet men in the new hunting clothes and in the old ones crowded into the little airless room rank with the smell of Boon's body and garments, and watched. Then the doctor cleaned and disinfected Boon's face and arm and leg and bandaged them and, the boy in front with a lantern and the doctor and McCaslin and Major de Spain and General Compson following, they went to Sam

Fathers' hut. Tennie's Jim had built up the fire; he squatted before it, dozing. Sam had not moved since Boon had put him in the bunk and Major de Spain had covered him with the blankets, yet he opened his eyes and looked from one to another of the faces and when McCaslin touched his shoulder and said, "Sam. The doctor wants to look at you," he even drew his hands out of the blanket and began to fumble at his shirt buttons until McCaslin said, "Wait. We'll do it." They undressed him. He lay there—the copper-brown, almost hairless body, the old man's body, the old man, the wild man not even one generation from the woods, childless, kinless, peopleless —motionless, his eyes open but no longer looking at any of them, while the doctor examined him and drew the blankets up and put the stethoscope back into his bag and snapped the bag and only the boy knew that Sam too was going to die.

"Exhaustion," the doctor said. "Shock maybe. A man his age swimming rivers in December. He'll be all right. Just make him stay in bed for a day or two. Will there be somebody here with him?"

"There will be somebody here," Major de Spain said.

They went back to the house, to the rank little room where Boon still sat on the pallet bed with Lion's head under his hand while the men, the ones who had hunted behind Lion and the ones who had never seen him before today, came quietly in to look at him and went away. Then it was dawn and they all went out into the yard to look at Old Ben, with his eyes open too and his lips snarled back from his worn teeth and his mutilated foot and the little hard lumps under his skin which were the old bullets (there were fifty-two of them, buckshot, rifle and ball) and the single almost invisible slit under his left shoulder where Boon's blade had finally found his life. Then Ash began to beat on the bottom of the dishpan with a heavy spoon to call them to breakfast and it was the first time he could remember hearing no sound from the dogs under the kitchen while they were eating. It was as if the old bear, even dead there in the yard, was a more potent terror still than they could face without Lion between them.

The rain had stopped during the night. By midmorning the thin sun appeared, rapidly burning away mist and cloud, warming the air and the earth; it would be one of those windless Mississippi December days which are a sort of Indian summer's Indian summer. They moved Lion out to the front gallery, into the sun. It was Boon's idea. "Goddamn it," he said, "he never did want to stay in the house until I made him. You know that." He took a crowbar and loosened the floor boards under his pallet bed so it could be raised, mattress and all, without disturbing Lion's position, and they carried him out to the gallery and put him down facing the woods.

Then he and the doctor and McCaslin and Major de Spain went to Sam's hut. This time Sam didn't open his eyes and his breathing was so quiet, so peaceful that they could hardly see that he breathed. The doctor didn't even take out his stethoscope nor even touch him. "He's all right," the doctor said. "He didn't even catch cold. He just quit."

"Quit?" McCaslin said.

"Yes. Old people do that sometimes. Then they get a good night's sleep or maybe it's just a drink of whisky, and they change their minds."

They returned to the house. And then they began to arrive—the swamp-dwellers, the gaunt men who ran traplines and lived on quinine and coons and river water, the farmers of little corn- and cotton-patches along the bottom's edge whose fields and cribs and pig-pens the old bear had rifled, the loggers from the camp and the sawmill men from Hoke's and the town men from further away than that, whose hounds the old bear had slain and traps and dead-falls he had wrecked and whose lead he carried. They came up mounted and on foot and in wagons, to enter the yard and look at him and then go on to the front where Lion lay, filling the little yard and overflowing it until there were almost a hundred of them squatting and standing in the warm and drowsing sunlight, talking quietly of hunting, of the game and the dogs which ran it, of hounds and bear and deer and men of yesterday vanished from the earth, while from time to time the great blue dog would open his eyes, not as if he were listening to them but as though to look at the woods for a moment before closing his eyes again, to remember the woods or to see that they were still there. He died at sundown.

Major de Spain broke camp that night. They carried Lion into the woods, or Boon carried him that is, wrapped in a quilt from his bed, just as he had refused to let anyone else touch Lion yesterday until the doctor got there; Boon carrying Lion, and the boy and General Compson and Walter and still almost fifty of them following with lanterns and lighted pine-knots—men from Hoke's and even further, who would have to ride out of the bottom in the dark, and swampers and trappers who would have to walk even, scattering toward the little hidden huts where they lived. And Boon would let nobody else dig the grave either and lay Lion in it and cover him and then General Compson stood at the head of it while the blaze and smoke of the pine-knots streamed away among the winter branches and spoke as he would have spoken over a man. Then they returned to camp.

BEN EAST'S BEARS

Ben East was born in 1898 in the farming country of Michigan. During his career as an outdoor writer Ben East wrote more than 800 stories of adventure in the wilds. But it is in the area of bears that Ben is considered an expert. He spent years interviewing hunters, trappers, homesteaders, game wardens, wildlife biologists and anyone who would talk to him about bears.

All kinds of bears fascinated East—from the eastern black bear to the huge polar bears of the Arctic ice floes. He hunted bears himself and had many a close brush with death as a result.

Of all his bear stories I like the one about his first—and almost fatal —encounter with a giant polar bear in 1937 along the eastern shore of James Bay.

I have chosen this story as one of his best:

Last Shell in the Rifle

Ben East

I have never heard it said better than by Captain Peter Freuchen, the renowned Danish adventurer and explorer who married an Eskimo girl and lived many years in Arctic Greenland.

"No more beautiful animal walks on four feet," he told me once when we were talking about the polar bear.

No matter how long I live, I'm sure I shall never forget the first one I saw outside a zoo. He was standing on a rocky headland, at the top of a cliff that rose vertically from a boulder-littered beach, staring out over a gray and empty reach of sea. A gale was sweeping down from the northwest, savage surf was smoking along the beach, and the sky was black with the clouds of a violent rain squall. Save for the handful of us aboard the schooner, the bear could well have been the only living thing in that wild, storm-swept world.

He was as magnificent an animal as I shall ever lay eyes on. His white pelt was faintly tinged with yellow, and standing motionless at the top of the cliff, he could have been a bear carved out of old ivory. Yet there was about him something wonderfully alive, too, something that proclaimed his rightful place in that desolate, lonely seascape.

It was the summer of 1937. An Ontario man who had hopes of setting himself up in the guiding and outfitting business, taking clients into remote and rarely visited places in the far north, had organized a trip that summer along the east shore of James Bay and into the lower end of Hudson Bay.

He chartered the Venture, a weather-beaten forty-three-foot schooner, auxiliary powered with an old Diesel engine, owned and skippered by Jack Palmquist, then the only free trader competing with the Hudson's Bay Company on James Bay.

Palmquist's crew consisted of a Cree deckhand and a good-humored Eskimo who tended the ancient Diesel as a mother tends a child. Neither spoke English, but the skipper, married to a pretty mission-educated Cree girl, was fluent in her language. The Eskimo also spoke Cree, so there was always a way around the language barrier.

At the trading post and summer camp of the Crees at Eastmain, Palmquist also took aboard a leather-faced Indian pilot to see us through the bleak island-sheltered channels along the coast we would travel. No charts of those waters existed then, and only a Cree who knew them from a lifetime of canoe travel and remembered each island, each headland, each clump of stunted spruce trees could follow the maze of channels and avoid the reefs.

The outfitter had hired three guides and a cook and there were nine clients in the party. I was one of them. We were the first sportsmen to penetrate that wild and roadless country. It was a region that only an occasional roving prospector, the Mounties, missionaries, and the men of the HBC had ever seen. Apart from them it belonged to the Crees and a handful of coastal Eskimos.

Incidentally, the outfitter's plans fell through after one summer, so for many years we were the last as well as the first party of guided sportsmen to travel that coast.

I have roamed the back country of this continent for fifty years, from the Great Smokies and the diamondback-infested flatwoods of Florida to Maine, from the Texas desert to the Aleutian Islands of Alaska, but that treeless and lonely country that I call the land of midnight twilight was the most fascinating place I have ever seen.

The land was untouched, the people primitive, living by the trapline, the fishnet and the gun. We saw steel traps set on low driftwood posts to catch owls for the cooking pots of the Crees; we heard loons called to the gun and shot for the same purpose. At the trading posts we saw summer camps of as many as five hundred nomad Cree trappers, living in roomy wigwams as they had before the whites came.

We fished the virgin pools of whitewater streams where three-pound speckled trout rose to flies, spinners—or even small strips torn from a red bandanna. It was an easy matter for two or three rods to take in a couple of hours all the trout the party could eat at three meals. We had no way to keep fresh meat aboard the Venture, so we lived for many days on a diet of trout and learned to our surprise that it palled rather quickly.

For ten days we camped beyond the sight of trees, carrying our tent poles along and relying on driftwood for our cooking fires. We tramped mossy barrens where ptarmigan were far more plentiful than ruffed grouse back home. When autumn came those treeless barrens would also be alive with geese, beginning their fall flight from summer homes still farther in the north.

Seals followed our schooner, and at night white whales blew close enough to awaken us. The half-wild sled dogs of a dozen Indian and Eskimo camps howled us to sleep time and again. Every minute of the trip was pure adventure.

There was no hunting. The Quebec government was keeping the wildlife, from waterfowl to seals and polar bears, in trust for the Crees and Eskimos, who needed it. But Howard Cooper, a hunting partner of mine from Kalamazoo, Michigan, and I carried collecting permits obtained by two museums back home, authorizing us to take for scientific purposes any birds or animals we chose.

Toward the end of July, the Venture dropped anchor off Long Island. Not the Long Island you have heard about all your life. This one is a rocky sliver of land three or four miles offshore near the southern end of Hudson Bay. We had come now to polar bear country. We left most of the party camped on the island, and Palmquist and his crew took Cooper and myself on a bear hunt.

It was a strange place to look for polar bears. We headed for a small group of treeless islands, not shown on any map we had, lying thirty or forty miles off the coast. We were farther south than the latitude of Juneau, Alaska. Yet the HBC post managers, the Crees and our skipper had all assured us that we would find bears summering on those islands. At the Fort George post a Cree had even shown us the pelts of three, a female and two cubs, that he had killed only that spring on the adjoining mainland.

We found the island we were looking for but it had no shelter for a boat, and raging seas, driven by a gale screaming down from the ice fields five hundred miles to the north, kept us from going ashore. We found a sheltered harbor on a smaller island half a mile away and landed without difficulty. It was from there that I saw my first polar bear, looking out to sea from his rocky headland.

We watched him for hours through binoculars and spotting scope. In late afternoon the storm subsided and we got a freight canoe ashore on the beach below the cliffs.

Cooper and I and Tommy Lameboy, our old Cree pilot, landed in the canoe. Lameboy had no rifle. Cooper and I were each carrying Model 99 Savages in .300 caliber. At the time I thought them adequate. I would not think so today.

The island was about two miles long and half as wide, rising in vertical cliffs at one end, sloping down to submerged reefs at the

other. The top was a rolling expanse of low hills and ravines, all rock and moss, with no vegetation taller than clumps of arctic willow that did not reach to a man's knee. But there were plenty of places for a bear to hide, and ours had disappeared. He had watched our boat as it neared the island, and taken to his heels.

We separated; Cooper and Lameboy headed for the far side of the island, I set out to search the broken sea cliffs. The job was on the hairy side, for there were places where I could round a big rock and meet the bear only three or four steps away. I was moving slowly and carefully when I heard a shot rap out from the direction Cooper had taken, followed almost at once by another. I scrambled to the top of the cliff for a look.

I made out the small figure of my hunting partner, three-quarters of a mile away, but I could see nothing of the bear. While I watched, Howard fired a third shot, and to my astonishment I heard the 180-grain softpoint go whining angrily over my head as a ricochet.

If Cooper was firing toward me the bear must be somewhere between us. And then I saw him, half a mile away, out of rifle range for Howard, running toward me like a big white dog that I had called. I learned later that Cooper had not really had him in range at any time, but had shot in the hope of sending him back my way. He succeeded better than he expected.

I learned something else later. The bear did not know I was there. The face of the cliff behind me was broken by a ravine that ran all the way down to the beach, and there was a well-used bear trail in the bottom of it. That was, in all likelihood, his customary path to the sea and he was coming to use it.

I was aware of mixed feelings. I wanted him to keep coming, for from the time I planned the trip I had wanted more than anything else to take a polar bear. But at the same time, although I had used a rifle for years, starting with a .22 as a boy, I was no crack shot and this bear was the first game I had ever confronted bigger than a whitetail deer. Could I deal with him? Well, I'd soon find out.

I went down on one knee to escape his attention, and watched him come. He dropped out of sight in a shallow dip but when he came up on my side of it he was still on course, traveling at a lumbering, ground-eating run.

I tried my first two shots while he was still too far away for accurate shooting with iron sights. They were clean misses and he paid them no attention.

The next one scored. He braked to a stop, swinging his head from side to side like a big white snake caught by the tail, biting savagely at the top of both shoulders. When it was all over I learned that my 180-grain softpoint had hit him in the back just behind the neck, too high to do any real damage, and had gone through under the heavy layer of fat that padded him, just deep enough to cut muscle and draw blood. I suppose it must have burned like a branding iron.

From his actions I was sure he would go down in a second or two, and in my lack of experience with dangerous game I made a bad blunder. I scrambled to my feet, ready to move closer and put in a finishing shot.

I never got the chance. The instant I stood up he saw me for the first time. He swerved and came for me in a deadly, businesslike charge, head down, running as a cross dog runs to bark at a passing car.

I shot too fast and threw away one more chance to stop him, and as he closed the distance between us to less than thirty yards I felt cold fear of a kind I have never known before or since.

I had started with one shell in the chamber of the Savage and four in the magazine. I had used four. That meant only one was left. There would be no time for reloading and all my confidence that I could kill the bear had evaporated.

Afterward I could not remember firing the fifth shot but my subconscious, if it took over, did a far better job than I had been doing. I heard the whiplash report of the .300 and the bear collapsed as if lightning had struck him. His head dropped between his front legs, he fell and skidded to a stop, rolled almost in a ball. Not so much as a shudder of movement stirred him anywhere.

I sidled away then while I fed five fresh hulls frantically into the rifle. When that was done I began to feel ready for more trouble if it came. I stood and watched for three or four minutes, waiting for some sign of life in the bear. Then I saw Tommy Lameboy coming across the island at a run, only a hundred yards away. Although un-armed, the old Cree was not running to me. He was running to the bear.

I could not let let him arrive until I was sure it was dead. I walked in with the safety off and prodded the big ball of white fur in the neck and ribs. There was no answering quiver, and I stepped back and waited for Tommy.

Together we rolled the bear over enough to pull his head out from beneath his body. The round hole of my last bullet was trick-ling blood just above the nose, dead center between the eyes. It had mushroomed in the brain and there was hardly a piece of bone bigger than a silver dollar left intact in the skull from the jaws back.

Before we moved the bear I went back and found the five empty cases I had ejected from the rifle. I wanted to know just how close he had been when I killed him. I stepped it off, seventeen paces. Fifty-one feet. I hardly wonder that I had been frightened or that for many nights afterward I dreamed of his final rush, dreamed he was standing over me ready to finish me off. It was a dream that brought me awake in a cold sweat each time.

We hoisted the bear aboard the schooner and took him back to the camp on Long Island unskinned. There Alagkok, our pleasant little Eskimo engineer, offered to take the pelt off.

Alagkok knew no English and of course could not write. But I have never seen hands more deft with a knife.

Three days later, on a somewhat bigger island thirty or forty miles to the south, Cooper made his bear hunt.

The party found anchorage for the Venture in a small harbor and Howard went ashore with Palmquist, Lameboy, and Roy Maguire, one of our guides. Almost at once they found a line of big bear tracks leading up across the sand of the beach, the footprints still wet with water that had dripped from the bear's legs. He had come in from the sea less than an hour before.

Half a mile farther on Cooper spotted a patch of white behind a tangle of driftwood just above the beach. At first he took it for snow, but when Palmquist put a question to Tommy Lameboy the old Cree replied with a firm "Wahb'esco!" the name for polar bear in his language.

The hunters were within a hundred yards of the bear when it heard or winded them and sat up on its haunches. Cooper told me afterward that it was so big it reminded him of a short-legged, burly white horse. He broke its back with his first shot, ran in close and finished it cleanly with a second softpoint in the neck.

Unfortunately, at that time neither Howard nor I was aware of the Boone and Crockett system of measuring and scoring trophies. As a result, the skull of that bear was never measured. But his body measurements, taken with a steel tape before he was skinned, revealed a polar bear of extraordinary size.

He measured 18 inches between the ears, 52 around the neck just behind the head, and 10½ feet from tip of nose to tip of tail. I still believe he would have stood very high on the Boone and Crockett record list.

He was skinned the next morning and the hunters came back to our camp at the mouth of a small river fifty miles south of Cape Jones. Two families of Crees sailed their canoes in behind the Venture, and in return for a sweater, a few pounds of flour, tea, sugar and some canned fruit, the women agreed to flesh the pelt of the big bear.

The scene that evening, lighted by a big driftwood fire behind our camp, is printed indelibly in my memory. Cooper had killed a second bear, to which his collecting permit entitled him, an immature animal that weighed around three hundred pounds, and brought it back to the mainland unskinned. The Cree women took the pelt off before they went to work on the big one, and we gave them a big kettle of the meat.

While they worked by firelight on the bear pelts, their men got two wigwams up and baked bannock for supper. In the dim twilight of that subarctic midnight a grease-rimmed kettle of bear stew was bubbling on the fire and the whole party of Crees was hunched in an eager, grinning circle around it.

The last sound we heard in our sleeping bags that night was the wild and doleful howling of a gaunt, ill-fed Indian sled dog, staked on a babiche leash beside one of the wigwams. His nose was full of the scent of bear short ribs but such feasts, alas, were not for him, and he sang his hunger song long after silence had settled over the camp.

The rest of the smaller bear Cooper gave to Tommy Lameboy, and when we reached the Fort George trading post, where the old Cree was camped for the summer, we witnessed a strange and ancient Indian ritual. The bear carcass was ferried ashore in one of our freight canoes, and a group of Crees picked the big canoe up bodily with the bear in it, six or eight men on either side. They lifted it to their shoulders and carried it ceremoniously through the camp of some five hundred Indians to Tommy's wigwam. There it was cut up and divided among many families, in keeping with Cree custom when a big animal is killed.

One of the most surprising things about that long-ago bear hunt was the fact that it happened only about a hundred miles farther, as a crow flies, from Sault Ste. Marie in my home state of Michigan than the distance from that same city south to Detroit. The white bear of the North is not always an animal of the arctic ice.

PHIL MOORE'S GRIZZLY

I have no idea who Phil Moore was except that he sure liked to hunt and fish, wrote fairly well about both subjects, had a sense of humor and published a book back in 1922 called With Gun And Rod In Canada. *It was published by Houghton Mifflin Company of Boston and New York.*

Moore was not the world's greatest sportsman by today's standards —having allowed his guide to shoot a couple of bear cubs for bounty—but one must remember that this was more than fifty years ago in Canada and the black bear was considered a pest.

But for the most part Moore had a wonderful time on his many hunting and fishing trips and, of all his stories, I found the one that follows to be the most interesting. He ran into a grizzly that almost did him in and it was quite a tale!

Shooting a Grizzly
with a Coffee Pot

Phil Moore

In August, 1901, I started from the little town of Vernal, Uintah County, Utah, situated in Ashley Valley, accompanied by a young guide of the faith by the name of David. We were going hunting, and incidentally to visit the old Dead Man Mine way up on the north side of Baldy Mountain, some one hundred miles from town. The abandoned mine was located just below snow-line, and had an elevation of ten thousand feet.

David was a very quiet boy with a pleasant disposition; a first-class prospector, guide, and hunter. He had a crippled hand. From his mild and retiring personality one would conjecture that he might have crippled that hand in his mother's sewing-machine, or perhaps jammed it in the cellar-door. I learned later that he carried this deformity as a result of performing some of his duties as deputy-sheriff, particularly while persuading a couple of outlaws to accompany him to jail. I also learned that one went to jail and the other to the cemetery. Uintah County in the old days was a nice isolated place to live in, and an unostentatious place in which to die. As intimated above, however, you would never guess from appearances that David had any notches on his gun.

With the white cap of Baldy Mountain gleaming in the noon sunshine, we left the old Government trail, and turning sharply to the north-west rode up a long draw, or canyon, to the edge of a mesa, made a lunch camp beside a mountain torrent, hobbled the horses and turned them out to feed. Packing up after lunch, we crossed a most beautiful grassy park on top of this tableland. It was a vast undulating sea of grass with clumps of cedars here and there, like ships riding at anchor.

Toward night David said we were in a fine deer country, and should soon begin to see elk, and bear tracks as well. We camped that night on the northern edge of the mesa, and next morning travelled down a short canyon partially wooded with quaking-asp and cottonwoods. There was a good footing for the horses, but no fresh tracks were in sight. By noon we were making elevation again at every mile. We were in the foothills of Baldy Mountain. Hardly half a mile from our camp-fire the hoof-prints of a bunch of ponies came into our trail, going also toward our objective. David said they belonged to a bunch of Uintah Utes going on a deer-hunt. He explained to me that the Ute Indians made a sort of general holiday of their hunting. All went on horseback spread out in a great half-moon, sometimes stretching for a couple of miles, with the object of driving deer or other game before them into the mouth of some blind canyon, or draw. In that way they could be more certain of getting them than by individual hunting. Our chance of getting any game short of the snow-line on Baldy Mountain seemed pretty slim. As the tracks we were following were hardly two days old, we would likely run into this bunch of Indians sometime within twenty-four hours.

About the middle of the next afternoon we came up to their camp. I first saw it from the top of a little knoll in the foothills, and it was in the distance a most picturesque sight. There were perhaps a dozen wigwams pitched on the side of a "creek" (even a mountain torrent is known as a "creek" among the Mormons). There were ponies and dogs, and papooses and squaws, scattered indiscriminately over the landscape. The wigwams, covered with different shades of deer and elk hides, old pieces of canvas and tattered blankets, and a few burlap bags thrown in for good measure, gave a crazy quilt effect in the blue, late afternoon atmosphere. It really would have made a colourful and interesting painting for a Remington to extend himself upon.

Personally I never yet saw a picture of an Indian camp that seemed real. One misses the smell so. When we were a quarter of a mile away a gentle, evening northwest breeze drifted indolently and carelessly among the tepees, and thence wafted the perfume toward our ungrateful and misunderstanding nostrils.

"Gosh, David! what's that awful smell? There must be something dead around here!"

"Them's Indians, pardner. They don't stink half as bad when they're dead as when they're alive."

Dave said this with a perfectly serious face, and I wondered if he referred to the old adage that the only good Indian is a dead Indian, and if it applied to the Indian smell as well as to his life.

With my olfactory nerves tremendously disciplined, I accompanied Dave into the camp. He dismounted, but I did not. At his suggestion I had caught up the pack-mare and led it with a turn of the larigo attached to the hackamore around the horn of my saddle. Indian kids sometimes, slyly assisted by their elders, would jokingly stampede a well-packed animal, and before you could find your pack-horse, the diamond- or loop-hitch would become strangely unfastened, the contents of the pack or panniers might be scattered among the rocks and underbrush, and although the papooses, squaws, and even bucks would help scour the country for your goods and chattels, they would be curiously inefficient when it came to finding things and bringing them to you. The inevitable blanket, so nonchalantly worn by all classes of Ute Indians when not actually fighting, dancing, or hunting, always struck me as a convenient place for concealing other people's possessions.

Dave held council with the Chief in the Ute language, and after proffering a chew of tobacco, which was readily accepted, mounted his horse and joined me.

The Utes had huge smoke fires going, and hundreds of pounds of venison strung upon baling wire in the dense fumes. The Chief told David they had had good hunting, and had killed some forty blacktail in a steep blind canyon, the mouth of which showed to the south about half a mile beyond the camp.

We rode straight on to the north-west, following an old creek bed up Baldy Mountain. Toward night the going began to get steep. There was no marked trail. Our path was interspersed with rocky stretches covered with quaking-asp and beautiful little open grassy meadows, or parks, as the Mormons call them. We camped that night beside a crystal mountain pool, my aneroid barometer showing an elevation of five thousand five hundred feet. The feed was excellent for the horses. There were fresh elk tracks, and although the night was cool, it was clear and not windy. We did not hobble the horses, as Dave said they would not leave the good level feeding-ground of the park for the rough country we had quit. I have noted that when packing through the mountains of the West, as you make altitude and get into a country strange to your horses, they are more dependent upon their masters, and are not so apt to stray far from the camp-fire. It may be they feel the need of the protection of human beings, as it is in these mountains that both the grizzly bear and cougar have their homes. There is no doubt that a grizzly will attack a horse if he can get the opportunity. Burros and colts are often victims of the cougar. Whether the latter would have the temerity to attack a full-grown horse, I am not prepared to say.

Dave caught seven or eight little speckled trout, which we had for supper.

Speaking of the supper we ate that night reminds me of all the other meals upon that trip, and makes me appreciate the wonderful luxury of the grub we eat in Nova Scotia compared to what we packed in the old days. Our complete menu consisted of flour, salt pork, baking-powder, coffee, sugar, salt, a few onions and half a dozen cans of tomatoes. The tomatoes were only to be used if we got short of water while crossing the Bad Lands, which border the Rocky Mountains upon this particular part of the American continent. The juice in a can of tomatoes is better to drink when suffering from thirst than the best water you can pack in a canteen. Owing to the can having no opening except what you make with your knife, it is never used except as a last resort, and consequently the juice is not idly sipped at as the water is apt to be when in a screwtop canteen. The old-timers told me that many a man's life had been saved through this habit of carrying canned tomatoes for an emergency. My personal experience bears this out. You will gather from the limited store of provisions we carried that every meal consisted of baking-powder bread made in the fryingpan, salt pork, black coffee, and such meat or fish as we happened to kill along the way. At times we picked and ate various kinds of berries. As strange as it may seem to the pampered guide and "sport" of the East, fryingpan bread, fried pork and coffee tasted good three times a day and every day in the week. Mountain air might have had something to do with it. If our friend, the sauce-maker of "57 varieties" of fame, could bottle some Rocky Mountain air and sell it for the sharpening of the jaded Eastern appetite, he could discard the original "57," and, calling the new mixture "Oxynitrogen Piquant à la Rocky Mountain," double the sales.

The next day we climbed slowly toward snow-line, hunting as we went, leading our horses much of the time, and using our field-glasses where the country was open enough. After lunch we espied one small band of sheep on a shoulder of Baldy Mountain itself, but they were too far off to shoot at or go after. This night we camped under one of the ridges, making the fire on the edge of a snow-water lake. This lake gave rise to one of the many streamlets or creeks fed by the eternal snows of the mountain peak.

As we are but slowly progressing to the incident of the coffee-pot and the grizzly, I am going to continue loitering and tell a fish story.

The tiny lake before our camp was ice-cold and perfectly clear, having a pebbly bottom. It did not seem to be over two feet deep and was full of speckled trout. They were so thick that I thought at first they were suckers. I fired my six-gun at a big one near the surface and killed it. After wading in and taking up the dead fish in my hands, and incidentally freezing my feet, I discovered I had a most remarkable specimen. It was about eighteen inches long and had all the markings of the Eastern brook-trout. But it was the leanest fish I had ever seen, being about the same proportions as a skinny pickerel. In Dave's presence I cleaned it and took from its stomach another lean-looking trout, seven or eight inches long. For curiosity's sake I cut this fish open, and found within it the skin and bones of another small trout. I imagine that if I had had a microscope I could have gone on discovering fish of a descending scale in size, *ad infinitum.*

As there were no bushes or grass around the edge of that pond and no mud on the bottom, there was no feed, and these trout must have lived and propagated and cannibalized since Adam threw away the core. The only outlets to the lake were little rivulets passing through the loose formation forming the bed of the watercourse leading down the mountain. To add to the mystery of the phenomenon, the water in this pond must have been solid ice six months out of the twelve. Dave said that he knew for a fact that the trout in these high altitudes stayed in the ponds all winter frozen in the ice, and came to life again in the spring. We didn't cook the trout because it did not have flesh enough upon it to warrant wasting the fat required for frying.

Looking for signs of spawn around the edge of the pond revealed nothing, nor was there a characteristic place for a spawning-ground. If one could judge by a trout's teeth, the way you judge the age of a horse, the trout I shot was a thousand years old.

Crossing the ridge and dropping down the other side, a vast natural amphitheatre or bowl stretched before our eyes, like the crater of an extinct volcano. Upon the farther side of the crater we could distinctly see a white quartz vein cutting vertically down through the formation, its lower end being lost in the accumulation of overburden in the bottom of the crater. A turquoise lake a few hundred yards across, surrounded by deserted cabins, completed the picture. The sides of the bowl were dotted with location monuments of stone. Dave took me quite a détour to pass one of these close at hand. Obeying his suggestion to dismount and examine this old "stake," I was interested to see him kick out from among the rocks a few ancient bleached bones and a much rusted rifle-barrel.

Dave said that an old prospector who was the original owner in fee simple of these bones had been obsessed with the idea that all the other inmates of the camp were going to try to jump his claim. Consequently he stayed on guard day and night. When the mines turned out to be a non-paying proposition and the inhabitants had stampeded out of the country, this old prospector was convinced that it was simply a ruse to lure him away from his claim. So he had sat there untiringly with his rifle across his knees to guard his property, ever since. The Indians found him, but being superstitious left him alone. They named the place "Dead Man Mine."

Upon closer examination we found the cabins still partly furnished; old rusted mining tools lying around, a couple of black-smiths' outfits, much moulded and rusted cases of canned goods, mice-riddled blankets, cooking utensils, etc. After a casual inspection one would have thought that the miners had left the day before and were expected back any moment.

I carefully sampled such of the quartz as I could get at, both on the surface and in a short tunnel, quartered my samples down to the smallest possible bulk for convenient carrying on our pack-mare; and climbing the southern and lower side of the crater, we topped the low ridge, and waving farewell to the tenacious old miner, started our descent. For two miles we travelled down the most treacherous rock slides it was ever my bad fortune to encounter. Then we entered fallen timber. Forest fires and wind had made this canyon almost impassible for anything but snakes and birds.

We dismounted, and with an axe in one hand and reins in the other, we hewed, scrambled, crawled, and twisted through a maze of giant jack-straws. When it was nearly dark the timber began to take a more upright position. To my relief we came to what Dave called an "elk park." It was a series of small meadows with bunches of cottonwoods and quaking-asp between them, and fine grass for the horses. Elk tracks and elk beds were all around us.

We were too tired, scratched, and sore to hunt. Unsaddling and unpacking our lagging animals, we turned them loose. I unstrapped my heavy cartridge-belt and six-shooter and hung them on the branch of a tree, glad to be rid of the dangling weight. Hearing the gurgle of a mountain stream a little way off, I picked up the coffee-pot and went for water while Dave built a fire and opened the provisions. I walked perhaps fifty yards before coming to the bed of the creek. The spring torrent had washed away the gravel, leaving a little bank a couple of feet above the surface of the brook. Taking the coffee-pot by the nozzle and putting my left arm around a cottonwood to help me maintain my balance, I reached down and dipped a potful of water and slaked my thirst.

As I was drinking I heard the stones rattling on the other side of the brook behind some bushes. Glancing, somewhat startled, in the direction of the noise, I discerned a big black shapeless mass. It moved, then growled, and believing it to be a bear, and having heard that bears were timid when confronted by unexpected sights and sounds, I emitted a lusty yell and threw the coffee-pot full of water at the dark growling shape.

Its identity was immediately established. It stood up on its hind-legs, gave a most convincing snarl, and started toward me. I started up the tree. There were no branches on this old cottonwood within ten feet of the ground, but I went up that smooth trunk like an electric shock. The interim between the time I started to climb and the time I got my legs over the branches is a very short and hazy period in my life. I have a distinct recollection, however, as I pulled myself safely up into the branches, of seeing the bear in the brook at the foot of the tree just scrambling upright. The left half of my hunting-shirt was torn completely off, and my upper left arm was burning and bleeding badly. I do not know to this day whether the bear had jumped and made a slash at me with his paw, or whether my shirt and arm were torn as I climbed into the tree. Evidently the bear had jumped, and striking on the edge of the bank when he came down, had rolled over into the water.

Naturally wishing to get assistance from Dave, I yelled "Bear!" at the top of my lungs. He came running through the bushes with a can in his hand. It being a great country for bees and wild honey, he thought I had yelled "Bees!" and was coming to get the honey. Catching sight of me in the tree and the bear beneath it at almost the same instant, he made tracks for his gun, touching only the high spots. It is a well-known fact among hunters that the much-touted Eastern champion sprinters really do not hold the world's records. The only way that a man can be made to run fast is to have a grizzly chase him. The bear started after Dave, but by shaking the limbs and hollering I succeeded in attracting his attention to such an extent that he decided not to leave the sure thing up the tree for the chimerical and flighty Mormon. Besides, I was in good flesh, bleeding profusely, and David was quite scrawny.

In a couple of minutes the bear and I heard a slight crackling in the bushes, toward which we immediately turned our heads, only to be startled by the sharp crack of a 45-70 and a blinding flash. The bear grunted and started straight for the flash. Again I shouted and shook the branches while David did a semicircular sprint. The bear returned snarling and growling to the tree. He reached up almost to the lower branches, and with a few emphatic pats of his paws ripped bark and wood out of that old trunk as though it were made of cheese. Then he started to bite it. If it had not been for the timely crack of my friend's rifle from another quarter, I veritably believe he would have gnawed that tree down in six bites.

The bear started again for the flash of the gun. After jumping a few yards toward the bushes from which the bullet came, he fell down. I shook the branches of the tree again and repeated my hurrah. The bear jumped to his feet and came toward the tree. He was limping badly. I could hear Dave make another spurt through the mountain laurel to a new point of vantage. The way he was running around he must have been trying to make the bear think that there were five or six men firing at him. Again from a bush the rifle cracked. This time the bear squalled and rolled over and over, trying to strike at the small of his back with his fore-paws. He rolled into the water, then got up and gave himself a shake. Limping off over the stony bed of the brook, he finally disappeared in the bushes on the other side. I could hear him grumbling and whining as he scrambled up the steep side of the mountain.

Fearing that a yell to David would attract the bear's attention and call it back to the tree, I gave a low whistle. Dave answered in kind, and in a minute or two appeared sneaking along as if stepping on eggs, with his gun cocked and at the ready, darting his sharp little eyes at every corner in the growing dusk.

"Where is he?" whispered David.

"He's gone up the mountain on the other side," I replied, as I slid stiffly down the trunk of the faithful cottonwood.

"My Gawd!" he exclaimed, as he saw me bloody and half denuded. "Did he take a crack at yer?"

"Nothing serious," I explained, at the same time making speedy tracks for the proximity of my own firearms. I decided then and there never again to be without them a second when on the trail.

Reaching the camp-fire, which Dave had already started, we found the horses stampeded, but our grub and outfit where we had left them. Building up a good bright fire, David proceeded to dress my arm by the simple process of washing with cold water and sewing up a cut about two inches long by half an inch deep, square across the left biceps. White linen thread and a coarse needle which we carried for "housewife" emergencies did the trick. After this operation we packed in plenty of dry fuel, of which there was an abundance near our camp-fire, and after an unrelished supper we stayed awake all night—David, for the purpose of keeping the fire, and I, on account of the pain in my arm.

At daylight we started to track the horses, my arm in a handkerchief sling, both of us carrying rifles. We succeeded in rounding them up about half a mile down the canyon, at the lower end of a series of little parks, and drove them back. After hobbling them and having lunch, Dave suggested that we pull out at once for Vernal, where my arm could have the attention of the local surgeon. Although the wound was painful, its being on the left arm did not incapacitate me. But it annoyed me just enough to make me so irritated at that bear that I could have eaten him raw if I could have come up to him. I explained all this to Dave, and he finally consented to help me hunt him.

We found his tracks where he had crossed the brook. David stooped down and picked up something. It was the coffee-pot, flattened out as if a steam-roller had run over it. The bear had bled a great deal, so it was not difficult to keep on his trail. I fully expected to find him dead at any moment. We followed him up the mountain clear to snow-line. When he struck the snow he evidently kept right on going. As it was four in the afternoon, we had to give it up and return to camp. After another painful night we saddled up and started down the canyon for Vernal.

It was about one hundred miles away. We were on the trail two nights and three days.

The surgeon in Vernal pulled out the stitches and said it was a good job.

Nova Scotia bears can climb trees. I often think it's a wise provision of Providence that they do not combine with this talent the disposition of the Rocky Mountain grizzly.

FRANK DUFRESNE'S BEARS

Frank Dufresne was first a naturalist and secondly a writer, hunter and fisherman. He was a great lover of bears—all kinds—and probably knew as much about them as any man alive.

One of the most admired of America's nature writers, Dufresne was an associate editor of Field & Stream, *and his articles appeared frequently in such magazines as* Colliers, Readers Digest, The Saturday Evening Post *and* Pageant. *He also wrote books, and his best-known are* Animals and Fishes of Alaska, The Great Outdoors, The Lure of The Open *and the book from which this story was taken:* No Room For Bears, *published by Holt, Rhinehart & Winston, New York, in 1965.*

Most of the bears in his book were not man-killers. He had a great affection for bears, and his worst fear was that they would be forced into extinction from such habitat as his beloved Admiralty Island. Many of his forty years in and around bear country were spent in Alaska, where he was director of the Alaska Game Commission.

If the bear were to write its own autobiography it probably would come out reading just about the way Frank Dufresne did it in No Room For Bears.

But this chapter—about a bear which was unlike most of the bears Dufresne ran across—is a classic in fear and suspense.

The Twenty-fifth Bear

Frank Dufresne

Ever since the appearance of their ancestors on earth, man and bears have been at odds. Beginning in the Pleistocene when giant cave bears towered over every other predator—of which man must be reckoned as one—our low-browed grandfathers were forced to cope with shaggy-haired beasts who stood twice as tall and outweighed them ten to one. For half a million years it was the bear, not man, who dominated the wilds, and it continued to hold the upper edge until the development of high-powered rifles within the past two hundred years.

In this short period—the blink of an eye in time—some of the bears have not adjusted their thinking to man's sudden supremacy. Some of them still believe they can whip any man in a fair fight, and that they have every right to run him out of the dwindling wilderness. My friend, Hosea, the greatest bear student I ever knew, used to say that about one grizzly out of twenty-five is ready to do battle against a human for reasons best known to themselves. "Unfortunately," Hosea would add slyly, "they don't wear numbers on their backs like football players so you never can be sure when you've met the twenty-fifth bear."

I knew what he meant, because I had searched unsuccessfully for one of these "twenty-fifth" bears. It had all started when a forest ranger was mauled to death by a grizzly while cruising timber on Admiralty Island. His death was to start another public outcry to remove all protection on Alaskan bears, put a bounty on the killers, poison them, get rid of them all. Of the several fatal attacks and maimings of humans by grizzlies, the case of the forest ranger was to create the most attention.

But, of course, the ranger would never know about this furor. All he knew was that a bear lurked nearby in the rain forest and that he would take no chances with it. The minute he laid eyes on it he would drop it in its tracks. He couldn't afford to be careless. It was too dark; the bear would be too close. So the ranger had made up his mind to shoot quickly if the animal showed the first sign of a fight.

Evidence of its nearness was clear to a woodsman of the forest ranger's experience. There was the much used wallow hole filled with still roily water, and the huge padded prints in the soft mud alongside. A spruce tree near the game trail down which the ranger and his unarmed helper were traveling had been shredded of its bark as high as he could reach with the muzzle of his rifle. Matted brown hair clung to the oozing pitch. In the trail itself was the real payoff —a half-eaten salmon fresh out of the creek.

The ranger held up his hand in silent, tense warning to his young aid, who was following close with a bulky packload of camp supplies. The rifle came out of the crook of his left arm; his right index finger slid inside the trigger guard, and his thumb pressed hard against the safety lever. This might have to be quick.

He listened carefully. There was no sound except that of their own heavy breathing and the flop-flop of spawning coho salmon in the small stream that ran around the bottom of the knoll on which they stood. Both men were dead sure now that the bear was near; that it must have sensed them and had chosen to stand its ground. You get to feel things like this when your job is scouting timber on the primitive forest lands of Admiralty Island with its estimated population of 1,600 bears!

Later, when I talked with the young backpacker, he told me he saw the grizzly first, and hissed an excited warning to the ranger. Silent as a shadow, the bear had risen off its bed between three closely growing hemlocks and faced them with lowered head. The distance was twenty feet. For a half minute the small eyes stared at them. The helper said he would never forget; they were like two red marbles. He saw the black, rubbery lips separate to bare yellowed teeth.

At the crash of the rifle the young backpacker told me he jumped off the knoll and went rolling and clawing down through prickly devil's-club to the creek bottom. Wrestling out of his pack, he scrambled to a smallish tree and swarmed up until he reached a point level with the knoll-top. The ranger was not in sight. The bear was bouncing about insanely with movements so fast it was all a blur to the helper's eyes. When the beast backed away for a second he saw the ranger face down on the ground trying to push himself up with his arms. The helper got one horrified glimpse of clothing ripped to

rags, of bloody, gaping wounds. Then the bear rushed in again, roaring and mauling and shaking the man until he was limp.

The helper said he didn't recall too clearly what then happened. At the sight of his partner's stricken body, he dropped to the ground and climbed up the knoll hoping in some vague way to recover the rifle and get in a telling shot with it. But when he reached the ranger he knew it was too late. The bear had vented its rage and fled the scene. There was nothing to do except try to bandage the awful wounds, build a campfire, and keep a death watch through the ensuing night.

He had trouble locating the rifle. A blow of the bear's paw had spun it from the ranger's hands and sent it flying far into the brush. It had been fired once, the empty brass case ejected, and a fresh cartridge fed halfway into the firing chamber. Here was mute testimony of the terrific speed of the charge, because the ranger had been fairly adept in the handling of firearms. He must have had less than a second from the time he fired the first hurried shot until the beast struck him down.

When the young helper showed me the spot a few days later it was our hope to destroy the bear before it attacked another human. An Indian tracker picked up the footprints and we followed them into the high meadows above timber line before they faded out. There was no sign of blood. A year elapsed before Hosea came to see me with what he said was a hunch. He reasoned that if the bear had not been wounded too severely, with the passage of time it might return to its old fishing hole.

It was a rainy, gloomy day on the 16th of October—a year to the day since the attack—when Hosea left his gas boat at the mouth of the river. Before rowing ashore in a small skiff, he instructed his boating companion to wait aboard until noon of the next day before attempting to follow his trail up the river. "I was up against a wily, dangerous grizzly," said the guide later. "Having once been stung by a rifle bullet and having killed the man who fired the shot, that bear would have a savage reception ready for the next human to invade its domain." But Hosea had confidence in his own ability and told his shipmate to listen for shooting late in the afternoon. If there had been a successful encounter he would fire three fast shots.

In the lower stretches of the river Hosea saw almost no sign of bear that day. The early runs of humpback and dog salmon were over and the carcasses of spawned-out fish had been washed into the bay by heavy fall rains. But up in the narrow headwaters Hosea knew that the late spawning cohos would still be threshing out their redds in the gravel, and that each favorite site would have its quota of bears. He saw two yearlings searching the empty riffles ahead, and waited until they went into the timber before proceeding. He had no intention of letting them squall an alarm to the bears upstream.

At noon the guide reached the forks where the particular stream he was seeking joined the main river. There had been dozens of small tributaries, but Hosea was too good a woodsman to stray off the penciled directions I—as director of the Game Commission—had made for him. As he told me later, he found part of a rusted kerosene lantern abandoned by the litter-bearing party the year before, and noted places where the blueberry bushes had been axed away to let the carriers through with their lifeless burden. As he neared the scene of the killing, Hosea said, he became extremely cautious, stopping to test the wind and sometimes standing motionless for minutes at a time. It was a spooky sort of place under the canopy of giant trees, fog-shrouded and dim. Few men would care to venture alone here to match wits with one of the wiliest and most savage of all wild game.

The distance was now less than a quarter of a mile to the knoll. Hosea deliberately waited for the late afternoon hours in the hope of catching the bear out in the stream where he could spy it first. When he could see the pool, there were parts of salmon on the bank where a bear had eaten its fill. Was it the same bear? As Hosea eased lightly past the deep imprints of a grizzly, its fetid odor hung heavy in the dank air, and he knew he was very close. In spite of his long experience among these bears, Hosea admitted to a prickly feeling along his scalp. "I could feel death all around me," he confessed.

At the foot of a leaning windfall where a giant hemlock had been uprooted by a windstorm and crashed into the forks of another tree, Hosea stopped to recheck his rifle again. He was carrying his favorite .30-06 sporter, equipped now with receiver sight with open aperture for fast shooting. The cartridges were well-tested 220-grain open point, expanding—deadly if they struck a vital spot. Hosea had heard that the forest ranger had trusted his life to regular Army issue hardpoints, filed square for dumdum effect. The guide had no faith in such makeshift ammunition. Removing first one hand and then the other from the damp gunstock, he wiped them dry against the wool shirt under his light slicker-jacket. His eyes measured the trunk of the windfall, selecting steps among the exposed roots where he could mount in a hurry if need be.

"I'd come far enough," said Hosea. "I'd gambled on the grizzly being at this spot. But now all I heard were cohos in the creek and the drip-drip of rain."

Call it premonition, sixth sense, or what you will, Hosea, who was not in the habit of loading the chamber of his rifle until he was ready to fire, now drew back the bolt and eased a cartridge into firing position. The operation was barely audible—a light, oily *snick*. But it triggered an explosive roar, followed by a crescendo of trumpet-blasts that reverberated through the forest. The spine-chilling outbursts seemed to come from everywhere. The instant he heard them Hosea mounted quickly to the windfall and ran upward until he stood on the leaning trunk fifteen feet above a dense patch of devils-club. He knew now that the beast had been watching for him. With the hateful scent of man full in its nostrils it had been silently closing in for the attack at the very second Hosea's hunch had caused him to work the bolt of his rifle. Hosea thinks the grizzly still remembered the slight, metallic click that had preceded a rifle blast on another October day.

In its baffled fury the bear thrashed about in the heavy cover trying to flush out the man enemy. By climbing to a point overhead, Hosea had suddenly cut off his fresh scent. Air currents with their tendency to swirl upward were all at once lost to the bear. Looking down on the crazed beast now, there was no longer any doubt in

Hosea's mind that this was the grizzly that had taken a man's life. In all his years of working among the bears of Southeastern Alaska he had never witnessed such rage; had never seen a bear so determined to attack. Unable to see its foe, its roars and rapidly ejaculated *chuff-chuff-chuff* of clashing teeth changed to whining eagerness.

Midway in its crashing leaps the bear suddenly froze motionless. A vagrant down-scent had carried Hosea's location to its nose. It rose on hind feet and for ten long seconds looked upward to study the face of the enemy. Hosea's shot was cool, unhurried and accurate. There was no need for a second cartridge. Watching the slumped carcass to make certain it was all over, Hosea retraced his steps to the ground and moved forward to prod the bear in the back of its neck with the toe of his boot. Gripping one of the big furry ears he swung the bulky head around to look for wounds. Down near the shoulder was a long, healed scar that might have been the near miss of another bullet. The guide's shot had exploded a vertebra to cause instant death.

Telling us about it, Hosea wasn't proud of the achievement. "That grizzly knew I was gunning for him just like the forest ranger had tried to kill him the year before. He was fighting for his life and he knew it." Hosea turned to me with a question: "If you had been the grizzly what would you have done?"

Without waiting for a reply because he was sure what it would have to be, Hosea finished his account of the twenty-fifth bear. He said that night was coming on fast when it was all over. There would be barely time enough to get back to the beach before pitch darkness settled over the wet forest. His partner on the boat would be worried. Turning away from the downed bear, Hosea swung the muzzle of his rifle upward and sent three fast shots crashing through the tree tops.

73

ELMER KEITH'S BEARS

*No book on North American big game could be written without in-
cluding at least one account of a hunt by Elmer Keith—a legend in
both the hunting and gun fields.*

*Elmer Keith was born in 1899 and grew up in Montana on a cattle
ranch until moving to Idaho in 1929 to become a hunter and guide.*

*The rest of his life has been spent in hunting over most of the
world. A true "diamond in the rough," Keith has advocated so many
changes and developments in the gun and ammunition field that it
would take this chapter alone to cover them. A natural shot, he is
as adept with handguns as with a rifle and pistol. His books* Sixguns
and Shotguns *are considered classics in their field. If there is one
thing generations of shooters will remember Keith for—besides his
great ability as a storyteller—it is his fondness for large-bore guns.
Keith has always been a "magnum man" and one of the best-known
jokes about Elmer among gun enthusiasts and big game hunters is
that Elmer's idea of the perfect big game gun would be "the camp
stove moving at about 3,200 foot-pounds per second of muzzle
velocity!"*

*Keith is as American as Will Rogers and will remain a classic him-
self for years after he is gone.*

*He has done so much hunting that it is difficult to pick out any
one story that represents his best experience. It is simply a matter of
personal choice. I like this excerpted part of a chapter from his autobiography* Keith, *published by Winchester Press in 1974. The chapter was called "Canada And Alaska Again" and was about a trip
Elmer took in 1939.*

Canada and Alaska Again

Elmer Keith

In the spring of 1939 I went into partnership with Arthur Kinnan, a brother of Marjorie Kinnan Rawlings, who wrote *The Yearling*. He had a good 56-foot boat with a good sea hull and an old make-and-break 20-horse motor. We proposed to run parties up to Alaska and guide big-game hunters up there, especially for bear. We put in ten days on Lake Union (I believe they called it), repairing the boat, painting it and getting everything in shape before we went through the locks and out to sea. We decided to run the same inside passage I had gone up in 1937 with the Ellinger party. Nelson Busick, who ran the Lord Baltimore Hotel in Baltimore, was the first to book with us for a brown bear hunt. Art's crew consisted of an ex-sailor, his wife, Martin the cook, myself and Kinnan to do part of the work and all of the navigating. Jack and I had the wheel, four hours on and four hours off. I remember it took us ninety-three hours from Seattle to Ketchikan. About a hundred miles up the coast, that old make-and-break engine, which took up half of the bottom of the boat, quit on us. It also had a make-and-break ignition system. Jack and I put the dory over the side, let out a sea anchor, and rowed for all we were worth to keep the tide from piling us on some rocks. When we were still a quarter-mile off the rocks, the wind and tide carrying us in, Art finally got the motor going and we headed on for Alaska. When the old motor was going good it sounded just like this: "Let's quit and go fishing, let's quit and go fishing, let's quit and go fishing."

While crossing Queen Charlotte Sound, Jack and I put up a small sail he had on the aft deck and that spanked us along considerably faster. It upset Art's navigation, however, and where we should have turned to port and gone through a passage in the islands, we went on north. Finally two small mountains showed up over the horizon. Art took one look at them and said, "Make a 180, Elmer. You and Jack and that darn sail of yours has carried us past the entrance where we should have turned." The only bad trouble we had, however, on the trip was while we were up in British Columbia territory on the inside passage. We had two 500-gallon tanks of gasoline in the hold. and one of them sprung a leak. Art discovered it when he went down to check the motor while we were traveling.

We pulled into the nearest Canadian port, but as soon as he discovered this everything was shut off. He said, "Nobody strike a match or light of any kind." We opened all the portholes and doors to air the thing out. We got out the bilge pump and the whole bilge was full of gasoline. We pumped it all out into the sea. The trip did not cover going into a Canadian port so we had to go to the Customs Officer and the old chap took us up to his office. He was a big man with a big red beard. He said, "This is going to be painful and take a bit of time." So he got out a quart of Scotch and gave us a drink, and Art finally satisfied him as to why we pulled into this port, and what we were up against. He had quite a few papers to fill out and sign.

The next proposition was gasoline. Art said he hadn't brought any cash along. He had a bank account up in Alaska and we needed more gas to get to Alaska than we carried. I happened to look across the bay and I saw a Standard Oil dock so I said, "Let's get the boat and go over there. I've had a Chevron card since 1938." I'd gotten it the year before. So we rowed over. They agreed to sell us all the gas we needed. So we bought another 500 gallons in 50-gallon drums, loaded the gas on the afterdeck, roped the barrels on and headed on out for Alaska.

One night while I was on the wheel, I thought I saw a log ahead, and as the inside passage was full of floating logs from the big log booms that had been towed to port, I turned the wheel hard over to the right to miss it. I stuck my head out of the pilot house and we just barely bumped it. Then a flashlight appeared out of that so-called log. Instead of a log it was an Indian out there in his canoe asleep, fishing.

It was uncanny the way Art could navigate. I remember one evening he set a course, laid out the chart, had his watch hanging by the binnacle light, and he specified how many minutes, hours he would run on each course, exactly when to turn and take another course, and he went to sleep in the bunk. Jack and I were four hours on and four hours off all night. At daylight the next morning we passed between two head lands, not much over 100 or 150 yards off either side of the boat, and a bell buoy there which he told us we'd pass between. How he ever figured that navigation so fine and that we didn't run into land was more than I could understand. At any rate, we were exactly on course and the bell buoy was on our left, just as he specified it would be after running all night and changing course several times.

Another night, about two o'clock in the morning, I ran into a heavy fog bank. It was so thick you could cut it with a knife, couldn't see anything. But I was on course exactly as he had written it out. Soon I heard people talking all around me, and then I heard some ships' bells. At that I kicked the bunk and woke Art up. He said, "Where are we?" I said, "I'm right on course, but stick your head out the window and listen." One second of that and he said, "Turn her 180, Elmer, quick." So I spun the wheel, put her on 180 degrees and around we came. We went out of the fog bank in just a few minutes, but just as we got out of the fog bank Art hollered, "Hard over to the right again, Elmer." And I did. As I looked back, up there was the bow of a big freighter hanging right out over us. The wash from it almost upset our 56-foot boat, but it missed us. Then from behind it came three more ships, one behind the other. How they ever got through without somebody getting run down in that fog bank I'll never know. I told Art, "I've had enough of this." So we pulled over into a little bay, got Jack up and he threw the lead until we got into a little cove where there was good anchorage and we proceeded to put in six hours' sleep.

We spent some time in Ketchikan, then went on up to Petersburg where Art had hired Jim Allen as a guide. We also took on Nelson Busick there for his bear hunt. He had flown up to Alaska. At high tide we took off and went over to Admiralty Island. There we hunted for a time and then Art wanted to go across to Baranof, but a huge storm kicked up. Allen, the guide, informed us that if the

weather wasn't too rough for Art and Jack and me he'd like to go on across and start hunting over there. So we took off. The waves were plenty high and it was awfully rough. Jack and I both had to stay on the wheel and then it almost made a whip-cracker out of us. However, the ones to get sick were Nick Busick and Jim Allen, the guide. The rest of us weathered it fine. We hunted all three islands, Admiralty, Baranof and Chichagof, and also some smaller islands for black bear.

First on the ticket was to get some black bear. Art knew of an island that was simply loaded with black bear. I never saw so many in one day in my life. We took the sea dory and went up a stream running in for a short distance, then got out and walked up the stream. There was quite a good trail that the bears had made along there while they were fishing for salmon. The river was loaded with humpies and dog salmon. In fact, the salmon were so thick the river was roped up. I believe if they had held still, one could have walked across the pools on the backs of salmon. Nelson was shooting a .30-06 rifle with Peters 225-grain belted bullets. Formerly, Gus Perret and I had designed that bullet for Remington, but we wanted a soft point and instead of a soft point they made it full-jacket with a big hollow point and a belt of supporting metal just back of the point. We found it would not expand enough for black bear, and hardly enough even on grizzly, before the trip was over.

Nelson shot the first black through behind the shoulders at about 50 yards. He simply whirled his head around, snapped at the entrance hole and went off into the brush. We never did find him. The next one he shot did the same thing, only this one was up a tree and Nelson knocked him out. He regained his feet and took off. We still didn't have a hide, and in that almost tropical vegetation, we couldn't trail them—there were bear tracks everywhere. The third black Nelson shot he knocked over, and when the bear got up, he knocked him over again. So I whipped the old .333 OKH I had with me off my back, and just as the bear was hitting the brush across the river, I hit him in the tail-end. We later found that the 300-grain bullet lodged in his left jaw. That finished him and we had one bear hide.

After skinning him out and putting the hide and skull on the packboard, we worked farther up the creek and cut in again. We saw a bear fishing down below us about 150 yards. There were quite a lot of big rocks in the stream. Nelson shot at him but he shot low and hit a rock right at the stern of the bear. I believe a fragment of the jacket hit the bear. Anyway he sat up from his fishing, slapped himself on the rump as hard as he could several times. It was a comical sight, that bear pounding himself. I believe he thought a bee had stung him. Anyway, Busick clobbered him in the shoulders the next time, and he had his two black bear. Those 225-grain bullets just drilled, didn't seem to expand hardly at all.

As we were going back to where we'd left the dory, another black bear came out from us across the creek. The creek at this place wasn't over forty feet wide, and this black bear was spoiling for a fight. He'd walk along, ruffle up his hair, look at us, then walk back, just acting like a dog running along by another dog trying to pick a fight. I didn't want a black bear hide and had no way of getting across without bringing the dory clear up the creek, so we didn't bother him. But that was the most belligerent black bear I ever saw.

Martin was a good cook and we had plenty of food aboard, so we lived quite well and had good bunks in the boat. It's really the only way to hunt bear in Alaska, to my notion—on a good boat of this sort. Shore camps are just out. It rains all the time. Everything is wet and soggy farther north on the peninsula where the ice is only about four to six inches underneath the top soil.

We next hunted Baranof Island. We anchored out in the bay, took the sea dory and went ashore and went up a beautiful salmon stream.

After killing one big old sow, we encountered a much better bear while hunting on a little cove on a bay. This was a beautifully furred grizzly, typical grizzly, not brownie. He was frosted clear down the shoulders, to the elbows. The first shot was about 80 yards. The bear was just tipping over to go fishing in the creek. Nelson—or Nick, as we called him—caught him forward of the right flank, and the bullet came out low in front of his left shoulder. The bear swapped ends and came back by us. Nelson shot him again through the lungs right behind the shoulder. The bear swung his head and snapped at the bullet entrance and went into the devils club and brush, heavy timber up a very steep mountain.

There was a bear trail about thirty yards to the right of where the bear entered the jungle. Jim Allen said, "I don't like to take Nick in there for that bear," so I told him I'd trail the bear if he'd work up the trail from the right and try to get Nick a shot if I located the bear. I had a .400 Westley Richards double-rifle and I knew I could stop any bear with that if I had any chance for a shot. The bear was bleeding quite heavily and I managed to trail him up the hill about

300 or 400 yards. It was quite steep. I finally came to a big log. I could hear Nick and Allen, the guide to my right as they climbed up a well-worn bear trail.

When I came to this big log—it was chest high—I reached my hand up to climb up on it, but just on the other side, there sat the grizzly. He opened his mouth and hissed at me, so I swung the double rifle around, covered him and I whistled for Jim and Nick, to find if they could hear me. They answered me. I said, "Can you see the bear? He's just over this log from me." Jim said, "I can see him all right." I asked Nick, "Are you in the clear so that you can find a hole with no brush to deflect your bullet? If you can, shoot him through the head." Nick said, "You're all in the clear," so he shot.

Down went the grizzly in a pile. Jim Allen came running over, vaulted the log. He straddled the bear and got him by the ears and lifted his head up. He said, "My ain't he a beauty." Just then the grizzly came to life, came up on all fours. Jim Allen let out one wild yell, and went over the log, over the top of my hat and I think he went about thirty feet down the steep slope. The bear started hissing again, but I don't think he knew what he was doing. He was pretty badly hit from the shot in the head, but Nick had missed the brain. So I told him, "Shoot again, and this time, hit him at the base of the ear." Nelson shot again and that did the trick. He was a beautiful furred grizzly. I don't like wounded grizzlies on the end of my gun barrel, but this was another time when it happened.

Nelson still wanted a bigger bear. Jack wanted a bear and offered to take one of these on his license and to let Nelson kill another one. We moved to another island. This time there was quite a salmon stream that came in by a cannery. It was so full of salmon that it didn't look as if there was water enough to float another one. At the mouth there was an Indian and his squaw. They had a sea dory and she had a rope about thirty feet long with several hooks tied on it about four feet from the bottom, with a boulder on the end of it. She'd heave the boulder into a pool there, wrap the rope around herself and head for shore. Each time she'd bring out from one to three flopping salmon. The Indian would knock them in the head with a club and throw them in the boat. When the boat was loaded to within about six inches from the top, they'd get in and paddle over to an island. There they'd dress all the fish, put sticks in them to hold them open flat. They'd split them and hang them up in the trees to dry. How they ever dried though was beyond me, because on that whole month's trip I saw the sun just once. The rest of the time it was either drizzling or pouring rain.

Allen, Nelson and I worked up this stream for about two miles, finding fresh killed salmon and some big bear tracks. One track crossed a gravel bar, and sunk into the gravel a good two inches. I jumped up and down and I couldn't dent that gravel that that bear had sunk into for two inches. This track looked very similar to one we had seen on the other island. So we worked cautiously on up the stream. Nelson was following Allen, and I was bringing up the rear of the procession, when I saw a big bear come out in the middle of the stream. This portion of the stream was swifter and much shallower than it had been down near the tidewater where the pools were deep. The big bear walked out in the middle. He was a jet-black grizzly or brownie. At any rate there was not a white hair on him, and he was a big bear.

I whistled low. The bear turned his head and looked at me. Nelson turned around and saw me and I just pointed. His eyes were two question marks and I made the motion to shoot. He'd quit the .30-06 with the 225-grain Peters belted and had my .333 OKH with 300-grain bullets, 60 grains of 4350 powder behind them with Winchester 120 primers. I had my big .400 double and I watched. Nick shot the bear in the shoulders, square broadside, the range probably 30 yards. It just looked as if his front feet flew out each way and he came down on his big belly and his nose in the river. His ears wiggled but that was all.

Nelson shot again in his neck but it wasn't necessary. He was so big and heavy, he just lay there and the stream backed up and flowed around him on each side. He was far too heavy for the strength of the three of us to move at all so we waded out and skinned him right there in the river. It was quite a job. Then we got his big hide on my packboard, including the feet and skull. I didn't take time to skin out the paws. It made a terrific load.

When we'd headed down the trail a couple of miles, we met Art Kinnan. He'd been part way up and he heard the shots, so he came on up. The first bullet had evidently expanded when it hit the wet hide. They were Kynoch 300-grain with thin jackets. Anyway it tore an inch entrance hole in that bear and where he lay down in that river a rope of blood squirted out for four feet as big as my thumb for several seconds after he went down from his heart beat. The slug had taken off the top of the heart and lodged, fully expanded, in the far side of the right lung. It entered from the left side. The one he placed in the neck broke the neck and stayed there in the heavy muscles on the other side of the vertebrae.

Jim and I were both tired from the heavy load, we'd been trading off, so Art Kinnan took on my packboard. After we'd gone down the trail a quarter-mile, he found a good big log and sat down on it, but he didn't figure the weight of the bear hide and he got a little too far back. Over Art went, his long legs sticking up in the air on top of the bear hide and pack board! Jim and I pulled him back and we headed on back down to the sea dory, thence on out to the boat.

This bear hide, spread out on the deck of Art's boat with no one touching it, squared nine feet. It was a nice bear. One toe and claw of one front paw was missing. I don't know whether from a trap or whether another bear had bitten it off. He was jet black, with a big hump on his shoulders, and I'd estimate his weight at around 800 pounds, possibly 900. Anyway it was all we could do to turn him over in the river while we skinned him. After that we took Busick back to Petersburg where he boarded a plane for his trip back home. He had his four bears.

On the way back to Petersburg we passed several glaciers. They hung out from the cliffs and were continually breaking off into the sea. There were also icebergs sticking up all around us, and Jack was kept pretty busy dodging them. We arrived at Petersburg in good shape and tied up near the end of a floating dock. These docks were made to rise as the tide came in and lower as it went out. The harbor was full of shipping and all around in the harbor, every now and then, I could see the black fin of a killer whale cruising around. Seaplanes would come in and land. By this time it was raining again and those seaplanes would break through the fog, it looked to me like, only 200 yards above the bay. They'd find an opening between the ships and splash down.

One night Art and I were sitting in the cabin, pilot house, waiting for the tide to come in so we could go down country towards the States. There was a bunch of halibut fishermen came in, three boats of them as I remember, and they were celebrating. They had a big catch of halibut and had made a lot of money. One of them, a Norwegian, had been up town. There the radio station played all night all kinds of Norwegian music, dance music. This Norsky came back down to the end of the dock with a little miniature radio in one hand, playing tunes, and a quart of whiskey in the other hand. He got out on the end of the dock right near the tip of it and was dancing to this tune. The rain was pouring down but he had on a slicker, rain hat, hip boots. Finally he danced too far to the end, and off he went.

I jumped up, opened the door and grabbed the boat hook to pull him out. Art grabbed me by the shoulder and pulled me back. He said, "You can't drown them fellows. Sit down and watch the show." So I did, feeling sure that he'd sink. Up he came, however, with his thumb over the top of the whiskey bottle which he carefully placed on the dock. Then he went down again and he came back with the radio. This time he heaved himself out on the dock, picked up the whiskey and had a drink, picked up the radio and it wasn't working. He shook it and threw it in the sea, finished the bottle, threw it in too, and went back up town. Within an hour he was back with a new radio and another bottle of whiskey.

THE GLACIER BEAR

Bill Fisher was a well-known big game hunter and photographer. But probably he was never more frustrated in his wildlife photography, or on a hunt, than he was on an Alaskan hunt for the rare glacier bear.

The story was first printed by Fawcett Publications, Inc. in their True Magazine *hunting annual in 1961 and later in a fine book called* Great True Hunts, *published in 1967 and edited by now-senior editor of* Field & Stream, *Peter Barrett.*

The very fact that Fisher got his rare trophy was testimony to his great ability as a hunter and rifle shot. He also got his photograph of the unusual bear—a color variation of the black bear found only in a remote section of Alaska.

It is a facinating account.

My Quest for a Rare Bear

William A. Fisher

It was the most disturbing decision I'd faced in two decades of big-game hunting. There, not 400 yards above me, stood the rarest animal I'd ever hunted. He blended so elusively into his surroundings that I thought for a moment I'd imagined him. A little shiver went through me as I remembered that the Alaskan Indians fear this animal, believing that it is possessed by the spirit of a medicine man.

Even in the heart of the animal's limited territory, to get so much as a look at a glacier bear was great good fortune. Many hunters had tried before me and come away half-convinced that this bear of silky blue pelt is capable of completely disappearing into the ice when pursued.

It was an easy shot for a rifle, but impossible in that failing light for the camera. I let him go, finally, on the chance that he'd still be feeding in the area when light returned. If I'm destined for hell, I know what mine will be like—I'll forever be trying to decide whether to shoot or not.

That was the dilemma. I had to have light enough and get close enough to catch the phantom bear on film as well as in my rifle sights if I were to realize the full objective of this hunt. While it's quite a trick to collect a glacier bear with a rifle, far more difficult is his capture on film. So far as I know, no one had taken a good picture of a living glacier bear, though men have spent months and years trying to photograph him.

Over a long period of planning this hunt, I had come to realize that the danger in an ordinary bear hunt—the pitting of self against the strength and ferocity of the animal—would be lacking in the search for a glacier bear. If I found him, the hunt would be over. To impart a special challenge to this quest, I determined to bring back both a trophy bear and photographs of it alive.

I first heard of the glacier bear 20 years ago on my first hunt in Alaska. Chugging up the Stikine River in a small powerboat with a veteran hunter and his Indian guides, I listened fascinated to an argument that ran on from Petersburg to Dease Lake. The hunter, after a trophy moose on this trip, wanted all the dope he could get on the glacier bear. The Indians kept maintaining that no white man ever would get one, that the bear was a spirit that could disappear at will into the glaciers of its habitat. Kid-style, I was fired with determination to take this phantom bear.

My chance didn't come until I'd gathered trophies of all other North American bears. During the intervening years, I picked up every scrap of information extant on the glacier bear. It proved remarkably thin.

The glacier is a variety of the black bear known to scientists as the mutation *Euarctos emmonsii;* but so rare that news of a single prize trophy spreads like wildfire all through Alaska. His total count is no more than 500, concentrated where tidewater glaciers of the St. Elias Range spill down the wild west faces of the mountains into the Gulf of Alaska.

Not more than a dozen, all told, can be seen in the trophy rooms of American hunters and in our museums. Though several capable expeditions have sought to bring back the living animal for display in zoos—and what an attraction that would be!—it has never been accomplished. The inaccessibility of its homeland forever stands guard over the blue glacier bear.

Habitat is limited to two coastal areas, Glacier Bay National Monument and the mountains inland from the narrows at the head of Yakutat Bay. Glacier Bay is *the* place, I learned, but it's a closed area. Alaska Fish and Wildlife answered my request for permission to take a single specimen in Glacier Bay with the information that the President himself actually couldn't get into the bay with a rifle.

I turned to my good friends the Welsh Brothers of Bellingham, Washington, who own and operate a salmon cannery at Yakutat, the little town at the entrance to Disenchantment Bay. They offered to keep an ear bent to the native grapevine for me, and there the matter rested until their telegram came one day last May. A native had spotted a fine boar bear on a beach littered with stranded icebergs. The animal was just out of hibernation and likely to stay put at sea level, where food supplies were most abundant early in his season.

I grabbed my hunting kit and flew to Alaska at once from Seattle, arriving at Yakutat by charter plane on a mild spring evening to discover that Barney, Bill and Bob Welsh had done everything in their power to insure the success of the hunt. They had ready for me a

28-foot boat captained by the owner, Landon Gilbert, a retired Coast Guard C.P.O., and a veteran native guide named Harvey Milton. I was delighted with them both. Harvey was a tall, dignified Indian in his late 40's with the broad features and bright black eyes of the coastal people. In past summers he had helped guide Dr. Oshin Agathon of the Explorers Club on his quest for a habitat group for the Carnegie Museum's Hall of Mammals, the most recent specimens taken. Even better, he'd talk about the glacier bear. To some extent, Harvey had conquered his superstitious fear of the animal. But he disconcerted me a little by heaving and choking with suppressed laughter when I told him I had just one week in which to photograph and collect one.

We wasted no time. Piling my gear on board, we swung out from the cannery dock into a confusing maze of waters rarely visited, and then only by native seal hunters. In five minutes we were away from civilization, threading through a chain of islands still as untouched as they were when seen first by Russian explorers 250 years ago.

Inland, all eyes scanned the bleak beaches isolated in coves between long stretches of mountains plunging abruptly into the sea and glaciers chopped off by the melting warmth of salt water. Bears wander along at low tide in the early hours and at dusk, seeking out

new shoots of vegetation, carrion left behind by the dropping tide, and sea foods.

Suddenly I spotted movement in misty, early morning light. An eagle flapped on a rocky point, alternately tearing chunks from a fox it had killed and fighting off gulls and terns.

We all had our fingers crossed as the boat approached the head of Disenchantment Bay filled with floating icebergs crumbled from the termini of two huge glaciers. Ours was the first craft to enter this dangerous, glittering, blue-white world that spring. The bay constricts at its deepest point inland to no more than a mile as it makes a hairpin turn south and west under ice-hung mountains rising to 18,000 feet. The south fork, a narrower body of water, is called Russell Fiord.

This eerie locale, a meeting place of ice, rock and sea, was our headquarters for the hunt. This inlet into the most heavily glaciated area of North America is the home of the glacier bear.

I began to question Harvey closely, for the Indian guide has probably seen more glacier bears in his lifetime than any other man.

"Just how big are they?" I asked.

"They're not large at all—a little smaller than the average black. Two hundred pounds would be a big boar. Their food is scarcer than the black's."

"What do the cubs look like?" I was anxious to know. "Does their color change as they mature?"

Harvey does not think so. He last saw a glacial bear a year ago. It was a silver-gray sow with darker markings, accompanied by two cubs. The sow was true glacier, but both cubs were black. He also has seen a black sow with one silver-blue glacier cub and one black cub. He believes that they interbreed with blacks, but points out that they are seen so seldom that no one knows too much about them. In addition, many natives who do see them consider it a bad omen, and keep it secret. The Indians explain that the hair down the back of a glacier bear is very thick and matted like that of an Indian medicine man, proof that the bear is possessed of a shaman's spirit.

I climbed out on the bow with a long pike pole and we forgot bears for hours as we groped our way through the ice pack, pushing hard away from 'bergs and saying a silent prayer that none would prove "turners" until we got by. We were nearly into Russell Fiord when my ears were bombarded by a thunderous roar. A half-mile away the face of Hubbard Glacier began to sag outward, a chunk half a block long breaking off and sending a mushroom of water a hundred feet into the air. I watched the great wave of the disturbance rush toward us across the water, tossing icebergs into a wild dance. In moments it struck us like a small tidal wave. Gilbert quartered the oncoming water and we were safe enough in a clear space among the floes, but to me it seemed a major crisis. Five days later the roaring of collapsing ice walls and rushing of wake had become commonplace.

Now began the long grind. Slowly we cruised the fabulous shoreline of Russell Fiord, taking turns at the wheel, always with two binoculars turned to the mountain slopes rising dizzily above us.

I had a tendency to look too high, following brown bear tracks winding around the crests of the snow-clad peaks in a maze of trails. Harvey pointed out to me that the smaller black bears seldom go this high. I questioned this, but it proved true. Not long after, I was following tracks in the snow with the glass when I came upon the first bears of the trip. High on a steep snowfield were a big Alaska brown and her two cubs. Later we saw two more brownies, but no blacks. By 11 P.M. it was too dark to see, so we called it a long Alaskan day.

By the small hours of the morning Gilbert was up and had coffee perking. He was becoming as obsessed with the glacier bear as I, but Harvey remained stolidly skeptical of the whole idea. The last hunter in the area was Dr. Agathon, who devoted two entire summers to collecting his museum group. One great point in our favor was the fact that we were hunting 18 to 20 hours a day, which would pile up the equivalent of a month's hunting in a week. My worst handicap was the fact that I'd never seen one of these animals.

Two days later we had circled Russell Fiord completely, checking innumerable brown bear tracks—almost twice as big as the small blue bear's—on the lonely beaches.

Once Gil spotted a tiny bay and headed slowly in to anchor. The fiord here was about eight miles across and can kick up pretty rough in a sudden Alaska storm. I was standing in the bow with my head and shoulders out through the hatch when Gil's hoarse whisper broke the peaceful chug-chug of the motor echoing back from the mountains.

"Look at the size of that bear!"

"Where?"

"On the beach! Where do you think?"

We were only a hundred feet off the beach in the uncertain half-dark of near midnight. I poked my head out again but couldn't see a thing. I ducked my head back down, hitting it one hell of a crack on the hatch cover. Now I could see lots of things—all red. I rushed back to Gil and Harvey in the cabin, who were both exclaiming over the size of the bear, now no more than 30 feet away. Gil cut the power and threw the gear and we drifted silently toward the dark beach. They kept pointing and shaking me in exasperation. Finally I saw the bear as it reared up on its hind legs.

It was a tremendous animal, large even for a Kodiak. He'd heard the noise of the boat but the wind was from the shore, so he hadn't scented us, and in that poor light the boat must have looked to his dull, near-sighted eyes like another iceberg. He stood for several seconds and then as the wind eddied, caught the first hint of man. He reached out with both forepaws, thrusting his massive head forward, and scooped air in toward his nostrils again and again. At last he got our scent, wheeled, still standing, and made a terrific lunge into the heavy mass of brush rising behind him.

We dropped anchor in our tiny bay and prepared for a brief rest. On a hunch, I dug into the ice chest and brought up a large slab of bacon which had acquired a patina of green mold. It wasn't fit to eat but it might attract bears In spite of Harvey's protests, I gouged a hole through one corner of the slab and went ashore in the dinghy with my prize. I found a likely alder in full view of the boat, climbed it until it bent under my weight, and tied the bacon as far up as I could reach.

At 3 in the morning I was awakened by a shot fired from the .22 Hornet by that dirty stinker, Gilbert. A wolverine had nosed down the beach, looking for the source of the strong bacon odor. When Gil appeared on deck the wolverine took off down the beach in a shambling, bearlike run. As I came on deck Gilbert still was cussing. He'd nicked the wolverine—he'd seen it roll head over heels midway in its passage up the beach.

At his insistence, we retrieved the pungent bacon and soon were back to work with the glasses.

By the next day we had completed the second circumference of Russell Fiord and again were in the ice pack. We turned our attention to the headwaters of Disenchantment Bay. Studying the terrain here, I was convinced that this was the logical area for a small bear to survive. Its main hazard to life, besides man, is the big brown. I never have seen a black bear brave enough to approach the salmon streams staked out by browns. I believe the lesser bears keep out of brown territory, literally taking what is left. Disenchantment Bay, well named, would make a poor supermarket for browns. In two hours our boat had worked its way through the ice and we were in fairly open water near the strange hump of Egg Island with only occasional 'bergs to worry us.

The sun was warm on my back as I stretched out on the forward deck of the cruiser, coffee fresh and hot at my elbow. My eyes burned from nights on end of little sleep and from the steady day-long glassing. I closed them and started an argument with my better judgment which was telling me to get ashore and climb to a vantage point. I was more than half asleep when Harvey, the impassive Indian, exploded as suddenly as a man seated on a digger wasps' nest. Jumping up and down, pointing wildly, he attempted to control a yell into a choked whisper.

"Look, look, look! Glacier bear! What I tell you? I find him, I tell you I find him. Shoot! Shoot!"

Harvey lost all skepticism in that electrifying moment.

I swung my glass into line with his wildly waving arm and all I could get was a glimpse, for the adrenalin was pumping so fast that I couldn't hold steady. Binocular, Harvey's brown arm—the whole works was going up and down. I didn't get a chance anyway, for Gil grabbed the glass out of my hands with an "I'll be damned!"

The animal was a beauty. He was the pale blue, or true glacier bear color—a very light blue-gray fur tipped with dark blue-black, the color lending an ephemeral quality to his presence. He was as hard to believe as a red-and-gold zebra. He was feeding low on the face of the mountain, just below a heavy outcropping of granite rock. I judged the distance as about 500 yards from the boat. All I had to do was row ashore, climb 100 yards, and take my cinch shot.

Instead of reaching for my rifle, I picked up a photographic light meter while Harvey jittered tensely at my side. I was out of luck—the afternoon sun suddenly had lost all power. The sensitive little needle in the meter refused to respond to the faint light.

Harvey hissed at me that the trophy was so rare I'd better get moving with the Weatherby and forget the camera. Gil promptly agreed with him.

"You'll never get another chance," they argued. "He won't wait for you—all bears are great travelers."

But I'm like the boy who wanted to look at his ice cream cone instead of eat it. I wanted to collect this bear as much as I've ever wanted anything, but I was going to gamble on the fact that he'd be obscured from sight for no more than five hours in the short northern light.

I wanted to move the boat farther down the beach and watch from there but Harvey cautioned against it. The boat must look to the bear like any ice floe, but movement would give us away. We stayed put and watched the blue bear until full dark. He seemed tranquil and at peace with his world as he browsed on new green buds of alder and cottonwood. He was as large as they come in this unfriendly habitat, somewhere around 200 pounds. Through the glass his face, paws and median line down the length of his back appeared darker than the rest of his body. He fed slowly, searchingly, working his way along the rock as far as he could go; then he'd back out of the cul-de-sac in order to turn around.

Over and over again he stripped growth buds delicately from the brush with his teeth. His feeding manners were those of a gentleman among bears, completely different from the grizzly, who bangs along with the insolence of the almighty. He displayed the unconcern of one secure in his own home, like a suburbanite mowing his own lawn.

Part of this impression of gentleness came from the ethereal aspect of the bear—it is hard to believe that any animal of such delicate color can be tough. By dark he appeared to be working his way toward the snowy summits of the mountains.

We were back on watch by 2:30 in the morning but were unable to locate him. I tried to convince myself that he was lying down. In that position his color would have blended so well with the rock that he would be impossible to spot. The sun rose and climbed high to light up this eerie world in which we trespassed, and still no bear. Harvey's "I told you so's" had me thinking that I'd figured it wrong as I combed the mountainside, foot by foot, with my binocular. The roll of the boat distracted me and threw my scanning off, so I went ashore and continued the vigil from the top of a prominence used by seals as a basking rock.

By 6 o'clock I'd given it up and come back on board for coffee, rubbing my aching eyes for some relief from the throbbing pain, when Harvey began to tremble with excitement again. He found the maltese bear in almost the same place as he'd been feeding before—just 100 yards higher on the mountain. How the devil did he get clear down here without being spotted? Harvey shrugged his shoulders and muttered,

"Bear magic."

To all natives, bears have superhuman qualities. Harvey is sure that this one will appear only when the light is too far gone for the camera. Harvey handed over my rifle with a look that spoke as eloquently as a billboard.

"Damn fool! Here's your second chance. Don't miss it."

Gil seconded him.

"Don't push your luck too far," he begged.

I was tempted cruelly.

"We'll wait until morning," I decided at long last. The men stalked off in disgust and I settled down to watch the bear until dark. He didn't move around much, just followed the same careful pattern upward toward the peaks.

I woke at 3 in the morning to find Harvey already in position on the seal rock. In an hour I motioned him in for some food.

He grunted sourly, "No bear—he's probably gone."

I bolted my eggs and coffee and took my turn on the rock. In 15 minutes I had him spotted! The bear had moved clear around to a series of brush-covered rock ledges near the top of the mountain and appeared to be heading for snowfields at the crest. He couldn't have chosen a tougher spot for us.

I rushed back to the boat to plan an attack. The only way to get at him was from above, as there was far too much heavy alder and buck brush below. The one way up was an awesome hogback that jutted out between this mountain and the next peak, knifing out half-way up a precipitous canyon. We talked it over. Harvey stated flatly that it couldn't be done—that no one could climb the hogback, or even reach it. Any effort to make our way up would be so noisy we'd spook the bear for sure. We'd pass within 200 yards of him. He could hear us, but we couldn't see him.

An hour's watch made it clear that the bear had no intention of moving down. Our patience was wearing thin—not with the bear, but with this indecisiveness.

There was just one choice open. Since the bear wasn't coming down, I'd have to go up. Harvey was convinced that the climb was impossible and bowed out of a venture that appeared useless to him. Gil offered to tag along. Once we began the climb, the bear would be wholly out of our sight. We worked out a set of signals with Harvey. He was to wave his arms up, or to the side, to indicate the bear's position; and should the bear disappear over the mountain his red hat on the end of a broom handle would signal failure.

We started up the stream bed centering the canyon, the logical approach to the ridge, in good order, Gil carrying the 400mm. camera on a gun-stock mount. Four feet of soft snow on the banks of the swift creek had lost all but the thinnest crust in the warm spring sun. It wouldn't take our weight. We fell through again and again, soaking to the waist in minutes. Despite an agonizing struggle upward over hidden boulders and downed trees, we reached the base of the hogback in an hour.

Then it got really rugged.

The big camera, lashed to Gil's packboard, kept getting caught in grasping alder branches until Gil, repeatedly thrown off his feet, was in a seething rage. Each time it was more difficult to rise. The slope now was at about 40°. We were scratched and bloody in every exposed spot, our clothes in tatters. Gil, recklessly shoving upward, slipped off a snowy foothold and fell 15 feet into a mass of alders.

His patience snapped as he found he couldn't get to his feet. Clutched in the tangle, he yelled.

"What the hell am I doing in the middle of this damned mountain? I'm no mountain climber. We'll never find the bear anyway—he could hear us coming a mile away. I'm going back down!"

I didn't say much, but I wasn't surprised to hear Gil thrashing his way upward behind me a few minutes later. We came at last to an enormous slash of upended rock rising out of the tangle. I inched my way out on it and signaled the boat and Harvey. His motions indicated that the bear was still in sight above us. We continued to fight our way up, foot by foot, damned if we'd give up now. In an hour we gained 600 feet to another pinnacle from which I could see the boat. Harvey swung the red hat in the awful signal that the bear had gone over the top. He was right all along—we'd spooked the bear with our racket.

Bushed, bleeding, utterly let down after all that work, we decided to go on up to the top. Fifty feet farther along we found the bear's tracks in snow and brush. Though we knew now that we were too late, still the tracks gave us something to follow, some faint glimmer of hope. We were too tired to use our heads at this point anyway. There seemed nothing to do but slog along the tracks, water squishing out of our boots at each step, faces stinging with the lash of the brush and our spirits at an abysmal low.

We came out on high sloping snowfields of the summit and saw that our bear had gone over the top and down into heavy brush on the far side.

The mountain here dropped into a high, narrow valley, headwaters of a creek. Across the valley rose endless barren peaks, line after line against the horizon as far as the eye could see. We circumvented the rocky summit jutting skywards from the snowfields and looked for another way back down to the beach. An avalanche path descended clear to the base of the mountain on the south side. This was risky, we knew, but the snow seemed stable on this face. We were tired enough to pick any route in preference to the way we had come up. I checked it over with my binocular, hunting for the best way down and looking for telltale outwashes of recent avalanches.

Suddenly the glass was filled with the blue bear, still proceeding at his leisurely pace. He was at the bottom of the avalanche path, just crossing a creek to the steep slopes of the neighboring mountain. I handed the glass to Gil and watched him change in an instant from an exhausted man, sagging under his pack, to a hunter again. The bear was 2,000 yards away and hundreds of feet below us.

I knew he couldn't see us at this distance, so we took off straight down the avalanche path at a running glissade. Halfway down we dug in our heels and came to a stop. The bear was poking around indifferently in the creek bed. We started stalking, silent in the snow, using every hump to stay out of sight in the hope that we could get to within a hundred yards and use the big camera. For once the light was splendid, the sun riding the three-quarter mark in the heavens.

At the next rise we peeked over and saw with dismay that something had spooked the critter. While we were still 800 yards away he started up the opposite slope like a gunned Bugatti.

"There go your pictures!" yelled Gil. "Look at that bugger go!"

He was right. But I still had my Weatherby. The grade was too steep for a good shot. I dropped another couple of hundred yards in great sliding leaps to reach a gentler slope. I had to choose a hellish spot, throwing myself down in the snow with my body slanted downward at a 45° angle. I threw the rifle upward and found the galloping bear, now 500 or 600 yards away, in my sights. At the last possible moment I touched one off. I couldn't see a thing.

"He's down! He's down! He's staying down!" Gill yelled from above me.

I looked through the binocular but saw only a field of blood-red. Blood was pouring down my face and into my eyes from a gash in the forehead. The angle of the shot was so great and my position so poor that the edge of the scope was almost touching my forehead when I shot. A handful of snow stopped the bleeding in a few minutes. When the dizziness subsided we slid down to the stream bed and climbed the opposite slope to our trophy.

He was as beautiful as he'd appeared in the glass for the past three days. The soft, silky underfur, deep as a tycoon's office rug, tipped in shadowy dusk that changed pattern as the hand was drawn over it, made the handsomest bear hide I'll ever see. We looked at it a long time, marveling at the texture, which is not coarse and oily like that of black bears. Gil told me that sea otter hunters first brought a few pelts back to Russia for the nobility, who valued them almost as highly as they did the otter skins. Few ever have seen the pelts since then.

Timid as he appeared, this bear surely made a monkey out of me. Two days before I could have shot him easily while my coffee cooled on the deck of the boat. Now I'd climbed all over hell's half acre and literally had to knock myself out to get a shot. But in the end, the shaman-bear won. The big camera never left its packboard. To get the picture shown on the opening page of this article, I had to have my bear mounted and then photograph it against an appropriate background.

I suffered mixed emotions as we sat in the wet snow, smoking, musing over the hunt and contemplating the trophy. Always when I'd taken a trophy Kodiak or polar bear, the immediate reaction was a sense of triumph and accomplishment. With this fellow it was different. I had a sense of elation, surely, but tinging the pleasure was the knowledge of defeat. I had come to this jumble of unknown mountains to photograph a blue glacier bear alive, in action, as well as to collect the specimen. I got him, but the phantom bear took me, too.

Somehow I respect him even more for this.

GRIZZLY ADAMS AND HIS BEARS

No account of bears would be complete without mentioning both Ben Lilly and James Capen "Grizzly" Adams. Both were superb bear hunters.

The modern TV version of Adams's experiences with grizzly bears would be laughable if it were not so tragically wrong. The "show-biz" types who produced the series for television may have been responsible for a number of injuries and possibly several deaths at the hands of bears the past few years.

They picture Adams as a man who loved grizzlies and hated hunters or anyone who would take the life of an animal. Their characterization of the grizzly "Gentle Ben" is true in that it was a tame bear. But that does not mean all grizzlies are tame nor is it safe to consider one as a "brother" with whom one may lie down and sleep with in the wild. Such anthropomporphism is not only stupid but dangerous.

James Adams was a bear hunter who killed bears for skins, food and bounties and who captured bears for zoos. He tamed several bears, as you will find out by reading about him in this excellent book on bears called The Grizzly Bear *by a fine hunter-naturalist named William E. Wright, published first by Charles Scribner's Sons in 1909.*

James Capen Adams

William H. Wright

And so we come to James Capen Adams. Adams was born in Medway, Mass., in October, 1807. He was trained as a shoemaker, but as soon as he attained his majority he joined a company of showmen as a collector of wild animals and hunted for them in the woods of Maine, New Hampshire, and Vermont. Later a tiger, belonging to the show, having disabled him while he was training it, he invested all his means in boots and shoes and started for St. Louis in search of health and a fortune. Finding neither in this outpost of civilization he joined the rush to California, where he arrived in the fall of 1849, having come overland *via* Mexico. Here for three years he engaged, with varying success, in mining, trading, and stock-raising, and finally becoming disgusted with the world and his fellows, in the fall of 1852 he took to the mountains and became a hermit, a hunter, and a purveyor of wild animals to shows and menageries.

At first he took no especial interest in grizzlies and, indeed, avoided them. He says: "I frequently saw him [the grizzly]; he was to be found, I knew, in the bushy gorges in all directions, and sometimes, in my hunts, I would send a distant shot after him; but, as a general rule, during this first winter, I paid him the respect to keep out of his way; and he seemed somewhat ceremonious in return. Not by any means that he feared me; but he did not invite the combat, and I did not venture it." Later on he "considered it a point of honor to give battle in every case."

But had he been merely a hunter, merely even an uncouth knight-errant of the mountains, sworn to perpetual pursuit of the grizzly dragon, his story would not concern us. It was because he dealt in living grizzlies as well as dead ones; because for all his sworn enmity he admired, understood, and even loved them, and was the first white man to domesticate them; because, although he was neither a student nor even an educated man, he was yet, within the limits of his interest, an accurate observer, that I rank him so high as a light-giver on the subject of these animals. The story of Adams's career is told in a book called "The Adventures of James Capen Adams, Mountaineer and Grizzly Bear Hunter of California," written by Theodore H. Hittell, published in 1860, and long since out of print.[1] I have already told how the discovery of this book excited my interest in hunting, and in the grizzly; but some years ago, wishing to refresh my memory in regard to it, I obtained a copy only after much searching.

Adams, in this book, describes several of his expeditions; one undertaken in May, 1853, in company with a young Texan named Sykesey and two Indians, in the course of which he visited Washington and Oregon Territories, and after collecting many animals, including both black and grizzly bears, took them to Portland and shipped them to the East; one undertaken in the early spring of 1854 to the Yosemite Valley; and one later in the same year across the Sierra Nevada and to Salt Lake City. These expeditions brought him into contact with the grizzly throughout the greater part of its range in what is now the United States, and he recognizes and comments upon the distinction between the grizzlies of California and those of the North. The grizzly, he says, is "the monarch of American beasts, and, in many respects, the most formidable animal in the world to be encountered. In comparison with the lion of Africa and the tiger of Asia, though these may exhibit more activity and bloodthirstiness, the grizzly is not second in courage, and excels them in power. Like the regions which he inhabits, there is a vastness in his strength which makes him a fit companion for the monster trees and rocks of the Sierras, and places him, if not the first, at least in the first rank of all quadrupeds."

Again he says: "There are several varieties of the grizzly bear; or, to speak more properly, perhaps, the species has a wide range, extending to the British possessions on the north, to New Mexico on the south, and from the eastern spurs of the Rocky Mountains to the Pacific Ocean. His size, general appearance, and character vary with the part of this great region in which he is found; for, although courageous and ferocious in the Rocky Mountains, he is there neither so large nor so terrible as in the Sierra Nevadas, where he attains his greatest size and strength. The grizzly of the Rocky Mountains seldom, if ever, reaches the weight of a thousand pounds; the color of his hair is almost white; he is more disposed to attack men than the same species in other regions, and has often been known to follow

[1]Republished, 1911, by Charles Scribner's Sons, New York.

upon a human track for several hours at a time. Among hunters he is known as the Rocky Mountain white bear, to distinguish him from other varieties. The Californian grizzly sometimes weighs as much as two thousand pounds. He is of a brown color, sprinkled with grayish hairs. When aroused he is, as has been said before, the most terrible of all animals in the world to encounter, but ordinarily will not attack man except under peculiar circumstances. The grizzly of Washington and Oregon Territories resembles the bear of California, with the exception that he rarely attains so large a size and has a browner coat. His hair is more disposed to curl and is thicker, owing to the greater coldness of the climate. He is not so savage, and can be hunted with greater safety than either the Californian or Rocky Mountain bear. In New Mexico the grizzly loses much of his strength and power, and upon the whole, is rather a timid and spiritless animal."

It was on his first expedition, somewhere in eastern Washington, that, having shot an old grizzly that was followed by two yearling cubs, and having, after many difficulties and repeated failures, captured the youngsters, Adams came into possession of Lady Washington, destined thenceforth to be his companion and servant. She was already old enough to resent the restriction of her liberty, and it was not until he had supplemented kindness with discipline that she accepted her new position in the scheme of life. "From that time to this," Adams says, "she has always been with me; and often has she shared my dangers and privations, borne my burdens, and partaken of my meals. The reader may be surprised to hear of a grizzly companion and friend, but Lady Washington has been both to me.

He may hardly credit the accounts of my nestling up between her and the fire to keep both sides warm under the frosty skies of the mountains, but all this is true." The details of her training, the gradual augmentation of her liberty, the way in which she came to follow him to the hunt, and finally to consent (at first under protest) to bear the trophies of these joint expeditions back to camp on her back, makes fascinating reading, and Adams seems, naturally enough, to have valued her affection. But the following year her nose was put out of joint. During one of his hunts in the Yosemite Valley, in the spring of 1854, he located the winter quarters of a grizzly bear, from which the occupant had not yet emerged, and deciding, from the sounds that reached him in his careful reconnoitering, that the occupant was a female with young, he determined to watch for her appearance, kill her, and secure the cubs. The adventure proved a thrilling one, and at its conclusion he found himself in possession of a grizzly bear so small and helpless that he only succeeded in raising it by inducing a greyhound, that accompanied the party and had a young family of her own at the time, to adopt it in lieu of two out of her three offspring. She objected strenuously at first, but soon gave in gracefully, and Ben Franklin and his foster-brother grew up in amity, and continued to be sworn allies through life. Ben, having never known the world under any other guise, accepted it frankly as he found it. He not only did not have to unlearn the habits of the savage, but seems never to have developed them, at least not toward his master. He was never chained, slept for the most part in Adams's company, and when at last the ultimate test of allegiance was unexpectedly presented to him, he took sides unhesitatingly with his adopted master against his own relations. Adams, while accompanied by Ben Franklin, was attacked by a wounded grizzly. Ben instantly joined in the fight, and, though himself badly bitten, saved his master's life. From that time on he was the apple of Adams's eye, his inseparable companion, and of all living things on earth the best beloved.

One is reminded of a quaint story, quoted by several of the early commentators, of a grizzly bear once domesticated by a tribe of northern Indians. On the occasion of a visit from members of another tribe, the bear's owner, for a joke, ordered the bear to get into one of the canoes belonging to the visitors. The bear obeyed, but the owner of the canoe, resenting the intrusion, struck him, and, "since the bear had come to be regarded as one of their family" by the hosts, the blow was the cause of an intertribal war.

Ben accompanied his master on several of his later trips, and more than once, suffering from blistered feet, limped after the outfit in improvised moccasins. On one occasion it was only by the most heroic devotion that Adams rescued him from the desert, where the bear had fallen exhausted, and lay, bending imploring eyes upon his master, as he left to search for water and help. We have no record of the manner of Ben's death, but one can well imagine, after reading Mr. Hittell's book, with what a heavy heart Adams must fiinally, in 1859, have sailed for home without him.

Adams also trained and, in a sense, domesticated, two other grizzlies. One of these, called "Funny Joe," he captured as a young cub on his expedition to Salt Lake; the other came to him in an entirely different way, as a result of the same trip. At one of their camps near the Emigrant Trail they thought it necessary to mount a guard at night. "The guard usually consisted of two persons, relieved at midnight by two others. The last guard on one particular night were Tuolumne and one of the Indians, who reported to me in the morning that a strange bear had entered camp, made the acquaintance of Lady Washington, and after a *tête-à-tête* of an hour or so had retired again in a very peaceful and orderly manner to the mountains from which he came. They had not called me because of my fatigue during the day, they said, and because the visitor had been so civil that they did not think it necessary to disturb me. I, however, directed that if such a case should occur again, they should not fail to let me know.

"The next night the visitor returned, and being informed of it, I got up. It was about midnight, but the moon was shining, so that we could easily see him approach the Lady, who was usually chained at night. I took my rifle with the intention of killing the beast, but, on second thought, concluded it would be more to our advantage to give him the freedom of the camp, and accordingly did not disturb him. He remained until dawn and then retired. On the occasion of his return the next night—for, like a royal lover, he was very attentive—Gray advised that he should be killed, but I opposed the proposition, and, for aught I know, he still roams in his native haunts."

Here is one of the times when one could wish that Adams's interest had had a more scientific bias. It is only roughly that we are able to set from seven to nine months as the approximate time before Lady Washington gave birth to a male cub. Adams named him Frémont, but he seems to have done little credit to his romantic begetting and his noble parentage, either in intelligence or looks.

In the *American Naturalist* for May, 1886, under the title of "Domestication of the Grizzly Bear," John Dean Caton, LL.D., discusses Adams's adventures, describes his taming of Lady Washington, Ben Franklin, and Frémont, and says that at first he looked upon this book as an entertaining romance or at least as much embellished. But that, "upon inquiring in San Francisco, I met reliable persons who had known him well and had seen him passing through the streets of that city followed by a troupe of these monstrous grizzly bears, which paid not the least attention to the yelping dogs and the crowds of children which closely followed them, giving the most conclusive proof of the docility of the animals." This is the only reference I have ever seen made to Adams's book, and Mr. Caton's glimpse of him in the streets of San Francisco is interesting, and, if that were needed, confirmatory.

In 1907, having been informed By Dr. C. Hart Merriam that the author, Mr. Hittell, was still living in San Francisco, I wrote to him asking for some information about the origin of the book and his recollection of Adams. In reply I received the following letter:

SAN FRANCISCO, *December* 15, 1907.
MR. W. H. WRIGHT.

Dear Sir: Your letter in relation to "The Adventures of James Capen Adams, etc.," has given me great pleasure. The book, unfortunately, was published in the exciting and excited days of 1860, just before the breaking out of the Civil War, and was never properly placed before the public; but it is gratifying to find that it did here and there reach readers who became interested in it. It is possible, and indeed, likely, that it will be republished, and, if so, it will contain a preface giving an account of how I became acquainted with Adams and came to write his story, and a postscript relating to his death and what became of his big bears, so far as known to me.

Your own work in hunting and studying the grizzly excites my lively interest, and particularly so as you say my book, to some extent at least, directed your attention to the subject. As to the questions you ask, or any other inquiries you may make, I will cheerfully give you all the information within my knowledge.

Ben Franklin, Adams's favorite bear, died in San Francisco; but as my papers are not at hand, I cannot be certain just now about the exact date. According to my recollection, it was in the summer of 1859. About the end of that year Adams went East, carrying his animals in a sailing vessel around Cape Horn, but without his finest specimen. I knew Ben Franklin well, often played with him, and on several occasions rode on his back. The picture of him and his master, given at the head of Part Second of my book, entitled "Adams and Ben Franklin," presents excellent portraits. Lady Washington and Samson were both, as I understand it, taken to New York and exhibited there by Adams under the auspices of Barnum. I do not know what became of them. Ben Franklin was caught, as a small cub, in the spring of '54; Lady Washington, as a larger cub in 1853, and Samson, as a large bear, in the winter of 1854–5; that is, if Adams was truthful in his statements to me, as I thought and still think he was. As to Samson's weight, my recollection is that Adams said he had had him weighed on a hay scales. His show bills in San Francisco gave fifteen hundred pounds as his weight and I never heard it disputed, but as he was doubtless the big bear exhibited in New York, it is possible that the exact weight could be ascertained there.

As to Adams's death, Barnum, in his autobiography, gives an account of it, and I know nothing more than he tells except a few items found in the newspaper at the time. My recollection is that he died in Massachusetts. There was a depression in his skull just above the forehead, which he said was caused by a blow from a bear in the early part of 1855, as related on pages 313 and 314 of my book. On his passage around Cape Horn, on his way to New York, he, according to report, had a fight with an ape or baboon, which tore the wound afresh, and, though it healed again sufficiently to enable him to go about and attend to business, he eventually died from the effects of it.

As to the comparative sizes of Ben Franklin and Lady Washington with Samson, I should say that the latter was nearly, if not quite, twice as large as either of the others; so far as I know he was the same bear that was exhibited in the Eastern States in 1860. He was untamed and had be kept in a very large and strong cage, though I never saw him very wild.

In reference to getting Adams's story, I was in the newspaper business at the time, and could get only an hour or two a day to spend with him; and, as he talked, I wrote down what he said, usually in his own language, but sometimes with some changes to make it more grammatical. He knew little or nothing about the geography of the country, and I therefore could not locate him except in very general terms. He did not, on any occasion, appear to exaggerate, and told nothing improbable, though I had to wonder how he could remember so distinctly the particulars of his various hunts. I still have my notes of his talk. My object in writing the book was to tell his story in his own way, and I added nothing to the substance of his narrative except a few supposed embellishments and a little sentiment, besides literary order, expression, and arrangement. I have to thank Dr. Merriam for directing you to me, and hope my answers to your inquiries will be satisfactory.

Hoping to hear from you again, believe me,

Very sincerely yours,
THEODORE H. HITTELL.

To my mind, when I was a boy, this old man Adams was the prince of all hunters. Boone and Crockett and Carson seemed one-candle-power lamps to this old arc light of an Adams, and in some ways I feel so still. Adams, of course, was not a naturalist. He was not, except in his capacity as a hunter, trader, and trainer of wild animals, interested in natural history, that is to say, he was only interested in those habits and in those traits of the animals he dealt with that had to do with his success. But he was of a quicker intelligence and of a more independent nature than most of his kind; he insisted upon using his own eyes, he had a widely varied experience, and his reminiscences abound in observations of interest, and of at least conditional value. I shall more than once refer to them as occasions arise.

WARREN PAGE'S GRIZZLY

Warren Page was one of the great gun writers of our times. He and Jack O'Connor, both of whom died only recently, vied with each other for decades in Field & Stream *and* Outdoor Life *for the major share of the gun audience in what, with* Sports Afield, *has been called the "Big Three" of the outdoor magazines. Their "feuds" were legendary, but one suspects they got along well enough personally. Since I knew both I am fairly certain they considered it good publicity to take opposing views on guns, ammunition and ballistics.*

Warren came to Field & Stream *in 1948 after serving as a gunnery instructor in the Navy during World War II. A graduate of Harvard and a former English teacher at Lawrenceville prep school, Page had no trouble with the written word.*

Former Field & Stream *Editor Hugh Grey told me when Page applied for a job with the magazine it was to fill the position as fishing editor. The magazine had just hired a young ex-G.I. named A. J. McClane for the job, but Grey said he was in need of a shooting editor. Warren told Grey he did not know a great deal about the field but that if he were allowed to try he would learn it. He literally fell asleep with books on handloading, cartridges, guns and ballistics on his chest for months after taking the job. He not only learned it well but became one of the finest big game hunters in America. He was to travel around the world for a quarter of a century, hunting with the great and near-great for* Field & Stream *until he resigned in 1972 to take over as head of the National Shooting Sports Foundation.*

Warren and I got to be friends when I became managing editor of Field & Stream *in 1970. We also served together, until his death, as fellow members of the board of governors of his beloved Campfire Club of America. Warren wrote a tight, hard grammatical story. He never wasted words and his copy needed little editing. This is a sample of his best writing.*

Snowshoe Grizzly

Warren Page

By the time Bob Kuhn, Bud Branham, and I had zipped up our sleeping bags we'd made a fair start on the subject of bears. We'd covered bloody-fanged charges real and imaginary, agreed that no North American animal stirs a hunter's adrenalin like a husky grizzly, and that bears are more fun than people.

But we still weren't much closer to a record-quality spring grizzly than when we first stepped off a plane at Anchorage on April ninth —into a foot of new snow. That had meant three to ten feet in the mountains. During the ski-plane flights in to Branham's Rainy Pass Lodge and then to one of Bud's trapping cabins, we'd seen little sign of bear. Sheep on the peaks, moose and caribou tracking up the valleys, but only at one spot the wallowing "road" a big bruin makes through the spring thaw. Binocular prospecting had located one bear trail across Portage Creek. We'd try him in the morning.

Before the bacon sizzled we were back in the ursine debate of the evening before. This time on the differences, if any, between brownies and grizzlies.

"Back at Rainy Pass," Bob said, "Ray Harris told me coastal bears chase salmon three hundred miles up the Kuskokwim. They brownies or grizzlies?"

"All the straight-snouted, big-headed, hump-shouldered bears along the Rockies and along into Siberia are of the grizzly family, Bob," I replied. "Thirty-odd types according to one naturalist, fortunately now discredited. A Cold Bay bear fat on salmon naturally grows a bigger skull than a timberline grizzly living on berries. The Boone and Crockett Club people had to draw a line somewhere."

"Well," put in Bud, "I've seen saltwater bears back pretty high, but it's reasonable to classify as brownies all the grizzly types within seventy-five miles of tidewater and those further back as grizzlies. These critters come in half the colors in your paintbox, Bob, but any grizzly you find up here, a hundred and fifty miles in, will be a mountain bear."*

And so we snowshoed around the mountain toward the old tracks. They crossed Portage Creek above where it flows into the upper Skwentna. Downstream five moose humped black against the snow. Moose were old stuff. But then my 7 X 35's picked out a new trail wallowing upcreek. The bear had started across the frozen stream, but the drag of wet-thawed snow or the icy bluff of the south bank had turned him back to our side. Where?

"I don't think he went over the range," said Bud. "Fresh out of hibernation, his pads will be tender. Let's go."

Noon sun had us shedding jackets before we reached the new tracks. They were fresh. No crusting around the edges, great dish-pan-sized wallows. In deep snow a thousand-pound bear—and the paw marks bottoming each hole showed this one was a buster—can't walk on top. He swims along, bulldozing his way with brute strength.

Nothing to it but point our snowshoes along the trail up a scramble-and-grab gully into the timber. The bear's broad-beamed road wound aimlessly to a low-branched spruce where he'd dug out a snoozing place. He'd left there only minutes before. Silver-tipped chocolate hairs were still unfrozen where body heat had thawed the snow. But he'd torn out at a swimming gallop, ramming his way straight up the steep mountainside.

A half hour of trailing through frost-squeaky snow only proved what we already knew. "He's taken out," decided Bud. "Bedded close to the creek, he scented us when we battled up that gully. No sense in a marathon."

Fagged out, we stopped on a bald ridge for another look over the country, but every sagging muscle snapped alive when Bob muttered under his binoculars, "What's that on the edge of the timber, in that fringe of alders?"

Bud and I followed his direction to a sentinel spruce just below the bare snow-sweep of the peak. We could pick out a dark blob.

"Winter-killed moose, Bud?" I queried. "Live one wouldn't feed that high in April."

---

*Since the writing of this story, and since the occurrences therein, Boone and Crockett has twice altered the brownie-grizzly line. The present line of distinction is generally the crest of the Alaska and Chugach ranges, little more realistic than the original seventy-five-mile line.

"Nope, that's your bear—see how light he shows? He's going to lie down. Think you can make it?"

No need to answer—we'd come too far to let aching ankles keep my scope cross hairs off that bear.

Stripped of all surplus gear, we followed the ridge toward that marker spruce. Wind in our faces was a help when the fast pace meant opened shirts.

The timber thinned, and we shuffled up through patches of cotton-woods and alder tangles. Fifteen minutes' climb and then a puff. Repeat, endlessly. No admiring the scenery, though we were not far west of Mount McKinley. Just snowshoe up.

Closer now and I was easing each web into Bud's tracks to make the least possible snow-squeak. A mess of alders and the single spruce. In this tangle, if I flubbed the shot, we'd be under an avalanche of mad grizzly.

Bud stopped. There was a lump in the brush snarl ahead a hundred yards. A brownish lump, silvery.

No time for binoculars—up with the .35 magnum and look through the scope. Thank heaven for 4X at such times. We were on the grizzly. But no killing shot from there. Through calf-thick alder stems only his head showed clear. I couldn't smash a bullet into that skull, not when I knew he was a record-sized bear.

Up the slope to get a clear angle. Now turn slow. And my left snowshoe trembled down across the right just as the bear came up! Broadside, clear. Tanglefoot or not, my two-hundred-and-seventy-five-grain slug cannoned into his shoulder.

With a bawling roar the grizzly flinched, sagged, struggled into the finisher. A last kick sent snow flying. We had a bear, half a ton of square-headed grizzly.

The fading afternoon left time for Bob to sketch only a few pictures if we were to make the cabin before black dark. Next day it was a long haul to skin out the perfect hide and an anxious wait until we could boil the skull and measure it on the square. 15 ⅛ x 10 meant 25 ⅛ points raw. 'Way up on the list. It could shrink only a hair before the official measurement, I knew.

So there was nothing shrinking about the chap who later boarded the Anchorage-Seattle flight and tenderly stowed a carton under his seat. With that bear-smelling package, he was no violet either. But he was happy.

O'CONNOR'S BEARS

Like Warren Page, Jack O'Connor came from a writing background to the shooting editor job on Outdoor Life *in 1941. He was born in the hunting country of Arizona and knew a lot more about hunting in the beginning than Page did, but one would be foolhardy to try and say who was the better at their respective jobs at the time of their deaths.*

Jack received a degree in journalism from the University of Missouri in 1927 and later was a professor of journalism at the University of Arizona. He became so wrapped up in the outdoor field that he eventually went with Outdoor Life *and remained as its shooting editor until 1972; he retired for a short time but returned to writing about guns and hunting for the "vertical" or specialized gun magazines until his death in 1978. He died about a year later than Page, his old rival.*

He wrote books in addition to his years of magazine writing. The best-known are Big Game Animals of North America, Complete Book Of Rifles and Shotguns, Jack O'Conner's Big Game Hunts, Complete Book Of Shooting *and* The Rifle Book, *republished in a third edition by Alfred Knopf at the time of his death.*

*Jack was a pro's pro. His writing was always exciting and his facts and figures accurate. It is tough to pick out a story as one of his best, but certainly this account of his grizzly bear hunt, from "*Hunting Big Game In North America, *published by Knopf in 1977 was typical of his marvelous ability to tell a hunting story.*

How to Handle a Grizzly

Jack O'Connor

In the spring of 1950, the late Field Johnson, a Yukon Indian guide with whom I hunted on several occasions, was out in the bush near the Indian village of Champagne. He had his beat-up old .30/30 carbine with him and he was probably looking for a moose. Suddenly something struck him a tremendous blow that sent his .30/30 flying and knocked him end over end. He was dazed by the blow, but an instant later he realized he was being mauled by a grizzly. He also knew that his only chance to survive was to feign death—and he did. Presently the grizzly decided Field was dead, so he dug a shallow hole and buried him.

Field was bruised and bleeding and in great pain, but he lay there for about an hour. For a time he could hear the bear shuffling around and sniffing. Then all was quiet. He decided that the grizzly had gone, pushed up through the loose earth and brush that was his grave, lurched to his feet, and started off.

But the crafty bear had been hiding nearby, silent and vindictive, waiting and watching to make sure the hated man was dead. With a roar he was on Field again. Once more he knocked him down with a tremendous blow. Then he chewed on him some more. Again Field played dead, with less difficulty this time, because he had spells of unconsciousness from pain and loss of blood. This time the grizzly decided to bury him in a better place. So he took him by the feet and dragged him a half-mile. Then he dug another and deeper hole and covered Field with brush and loose earth.

When Field regained consciousness he could tell that many hours had passed. He was weak, in desperate pain, and burning with thirst. He once more staggered out of his grave, knowing that if he was to live he must have help. This time, the grizzly certain that he had done his job and that Field was dead, had gone. Field managed to make it to the Alaska Highway, got a ride into Whitehorse, and with the aid of sulfa and penicillin and skillful surgery he pulled through. In spite of good medical care, the terrible ordeal eventually proved too much for him. He went insane and eventually died. He was one of the nicest guys I have ever known.

It is fashionable among hunters who have been very lucky or who have had a very limited experience with grizzlies to scoff at the notion that the grizzly is dangerous and that he has come honestly by his scientific name *Ursus horribilis*—the horrible bear, or his early popular name, the grisly (or terrible) bear.

A northwestern guide and outfitter I know hoots at the very notion that a grizzly can be dangerous. His grizzly hunting experience has been in the states of Wyoming and Montana, where most grizzlies have learned that in spite of their enormous strength and bulk they are no match for white men. Generations of mother grizzlies have taught their cubs that the rancid, sickening smell of human beings means danger, fire and thunder, sudden unexplicable pain. For more than a hundred years white men with rifles have waged war on the American grizzly, with rifles, with dogs, with traps, and with poison. Grizzlies that have survived south of the Canadian border have learned that the white man is his one dangerous enemy.

But this wasn't so in the old days, just as it isn't so in the wilderness today. When the first beaver trappers and mountain men invaded the domain of the grizzly more than a century ago, they found him a very tough and aggressive customer indeed. In the open plains country of what is now Nebraska and the Dakotas, in the foothills of the mountains, and in the high Rockies themselves, the grizzly was the lord of the land, afraid of nothing, just as the lion was on the plains of Africa. Occasionally a big bull buffalo might give a grizzly a tussle, and now and then perhaps a hunger-mad pack of wolves would try to drive one of the great bears away from a kill; but getting accidentally gored by a buffalo was an occupational hazard and one blow from a grizzly's paw would knock a wolf halfway out of the country.

With their puny bows and arrows, the Indians were no match for grizzlies and let them alone. The big bears probably thought no more about the Indians than they did of the bighorn sheep, spry, nimble, elusive, that haunted the rough country. If a grizzly came upon a helpless bighorn lamb, he'd no doubt eat him; but since the ewes bore their young in rough rocky places the soft-booted grizzly did not care for he seldom encountered one. Likewise the Indians lived in large congregations, smelled bad, and were surrounded by dogs and fire. The grizzly didn't bother them except, perhaps, to take a kill away from a hunter now and then.

White men had long been familiar with the shy, timid, furtive black bear of the Eastern woods, and they soon found that the grizzly was another animal entirely. One wrote: "The reddish bears (grizzlies) are mischievous creatures for they fall fiercely on the huntsman, whereas the black ones fly from them." They recorded that the Indians considered the hunting of the black bear a safe and enjoyable pastime, but that the grizzlies played too rough.

If a grizzly smelled something in camp that he wanted, he simply walked in and took it, just as the polar bear is apt to do today. If he could take it without a fuss, so much the better. If he couldn't he was willing to fight. Those early beaver trappers who were the first whites to invade the Rockies, had to kill many grizzlies to protect their meat, a job which soon taught them that their long Kentucky rifles with their small bores and small, light balls were no match for grizzlies, just as they were no match for the buffalo. The grizzly, as much as the buffalo, was responsible for developing the heavy big-bore "plains rifle," like the famous Hawken.

Heavy rifles in the hands of good, cool shots, even though they were muzzle loaders, made the chances of a grizzly distinctly poor in the case of a mix-up. After the Civil War, when powerful lever-action repeating rifles were developed, the grizzly lost what little chance he had against the big muzzle loaders.

Under ordinary circumstances, a cool, well-armed man who is alert and cautious has no need to fear a grizzly. The blow of a modern bullet is as terrible as that of a grizzly's paw, and it can be delivered repeatedly and from a distance. In his dim, animal way the grizzly knows this and the first reaction of the grizzly who lives in settled country today and has been harassed by man is to bolt the moment he smells a human being.

Nevertheless the grizzly anywhere is still a dangerous animal, along with his first cousin, the Alaska brown bear (which is simply a fish-fed grizzly), the only really dangerous game animal in North America. A good shot with a powerful rifle ordinarily isn't in much danger, but the danger is always there. No better hunter than Field Johnson has ever lived, yet he got mauled by a grizzly.

It is rare that the big-game hunter who is out after grizzlies gets into trouble. He is armed. He is looking for grizzlies, and he usually has a guide. He has binoculars that enable him to locate the bear before the bear sees him.

But even the best grizzly hunt can go wrong—and that's one of the reasons grizzly hunting is fascinating. Take the case of a New York surgeon who hunted grizzlies in the Yukon in 1949. He wounded a grizzly and he and his guide went into the willows after it—a wonderful way to get into trouble. The grizzly was lying in wait. He charged the doctor and knocked him down before he could do more than shoot at it from the hip. He had the doctor's right hand in his mouth, tried to chew on it, and the doctor said, "Well, here goes my career." The guide killed the bear and pulled the doctor out from under the great bleeding carcass intact except for some terrible bruises which an Indian told me were "as black as black-bear hide." One thing had saved the doctor's hand—and probably his life. A shot had broken the bear's jaw and he couldn't bite.

Perhaps the most dangerous grizzly of all is the sow with cubs, and the majority of the killings and maulings I have heard about come from someone, usually unarmed, blundering into a female who thinks her young are menaced One pathetic instance happened in the 1930's in Alberta. A Canadian homesteader and his little girl were picking berries in the summer, when they encountered an old female with a cub. The bear showed fight so the man told his little daughter to run for home and that he would hold off the bear while she got a good start. The little girl got home all right and told her mother that daddy was having a fight with a grizzly. Taking a rifle the courageous pioneer women went to the rescue, but she found her husband mauled and dead, a spruce limb with which he had tried to fend off the bear beside him.

On the other hand, an acquaintance of mine got out of a similar scrape much more fortunately. He was photographing big game in Yellowstone Park when he saw a female and her cub eating berries in an open meadow. He stalked them, set up his movie camera, and was letting her roll when mama decided he meant no good and charged. Using the camera on the tripod as a club, he waited until the bear was on him, then crashed it against her skull. She staggered back, then looked around, saw that her cub was getting away, and followed it. The photographer's hide was intact, but his expensive camera was a total loss.

Another bad situation is to find a bear over a kill, particularly if the man has the wind on the bear and cannot be smelled. The eyesight of bears is very bad. They are exceedingly myopic, and I am sure that at more than fifty yards or so they see only masses and outlines. They are also undoubtedly color-blind. Once when I was stalking a grizzly the bear changed his position and saw me in plain sight at no more than 200 yards. He watched me for thirty seconds, perhaps, and then, not the least disturbed, he lay down again. A friend of mine ran across a pair of caribou-hunting grizzlies and drew them up to within twenty-five yards by holding his arms up over his head in imitation of caribou antlers.

Now let us suppose that a human being blunders onto a bear at a kill. The bear is hungry and excited. He has blood in his nose and this impairs his sense of smell. He is on the alert for a rival who may try to take his kill from him. He looks up and sees a human being *standing in an upright position that grizzlies themselves assume in order to see better.*

"Ah," says the bear to himself, "here's another grizzly trying to chisel in on my kill. I'd better deal with him!"

So the bear charges what he has taken to be another bear, and before he has realized his mistake he may have killed a human being.

A hungry grizzly will come toward the smell of fresh blood to see what he can promote. One Alaskan had killed a moose and was dressing it, when a tremendous blow from behind knocked him clear over the moose and against a tree on the far side. His assailant was a grizzly who had seen him bending over the kill and had thought he was another bear. The instant he had *smelled* his opponent he had fled, but the man, though badly bruised, was lucky to be alive.

Once in the Yukon I had shot a big bull caribou and had finished taking off the head and scalp and dressing him when I spied a black speck that looked like a burned stump, except that this stump was moving and my guide and I were far above timberline where there simply were no stumps. It was a big grizzly that had smelled the blood and was hot-footing it toward the kill. He was a grand silver-tip, and the hide of this bear who delivered himself is now hanging on the wall of my study. On another occasion in the Yukon I had shot a fine snow-white Dall ram. Snow was falling and low-hanging clouds covered the ice-sheathed peaks as I slowly picked my way down the steep shoulder of a great mountain through rocks and shale. I was carrying the head and scalp, a load of meat, and my rifle and binocular. I was desperately weary and miserably cold and wet, and the only thing I could think of was to get to my little tent far below to change clothes, to get warm, and to make some hot tea.

Suddenly right behind me I heard a growl. I turned around and there, not more than twenty-five yards away, was a big grizzly. He had smelled the blood and had come to see what was going on. When he got to where his poor eyes did him some good, he had stopped, puzzled. This was very wild country and I doubt if that bear had ever seen or smelled a human being before.

For an instant that bear and I looked into each other's eyes. My hair rose on my neck and my heart skipped a couple of beats. Then I yelled: "Get out of here, you — — —!" At the sound of my voice the bear almost turned a back somersault, and the way he got out of there looked exactly like one of Walt Disney's scared and fleeing bears. I dropped the head and meat, ran to a little ridge where I could watch him run. I didn't shoot. Right then I wouldn't have traded a cup of hot tea and a pair of dry socks for all the grizzlies in the Yukon!

Food + grizzly + human being that the bear thinks stands between him and food is a bad combination. Ned Frost, the famous Wyoming guide and grizzly hunter, was badly mauled by a grizzly once when he was lying in his tent asleep in his bedroll. There was some bacon in the tent and the grizzly felt that Frost stood between him and the bacon. Frost, by the way, hunted grizzlies probably more than any other man when there were many of the great bears in the Rockies of Idaho, Montana, and Wyoming. He believes that when the number of hunters, the number of animals, and the number of maulings are taken into consideration, the grizzly is more dangerous than the African lion. About this I am doubtful—and have hunted both species.

Going into cover after a wounded grizzly is a dangerous thing to do and most northern guides do not relish it in the slightest. Frantic and furious with pain, frightened and desperate, the wounded cornered grizzly is a tough and vindictive opponent. Theodore Roosevelt, who was an enthusiastic and experienced grizzly hunter back in the days when the big bears were still plentiful in the Rockies of the United States, records several instances of maulings in his excellent book, *Hunting the Grisly*. In one case a grizzly mauled a cavalry trooper so badly that he died, in spite of the fact that both the bear's front legs were broken! Roosevelt himself might never have lived to become President of the United States, as he was charged by a grizzly he had stumbled onto and lived to write about it only because he was a quick and accurate shot.

Some years ago in Alberta, an American sportsman wounded a grizzly and he and his guide followed the bear into cover. The bear charged, got the guide down, and was mauling him when the sportsman put the muzzle of the rifle to the bear's head and killed him.

The sportsman got the almost unconscious guide on a horse, managed to get him back to camp, and eventually out of the bush to a hospital. He recovered.

One of the weirdest instances of an aggressive grizzly I have ever heard of had happened in the Yukon only a couple of years before I was told about it. A party outfitted by the late Jean Jacquot of Kluane Lake was on the trail with a full outfit of packhorses. Through some trick of the wind, a female grizzly did not hear the approach of the pack train, and the whole outfit rode right up on her as she and her cubs were feeding on berries. The old bear charged right into the pack train, scattering horses right and left. A hunter from Texas in the party killed her within twenty feet of the muzzle of his rifle. In the majority of cases a grizzly would have run off under those circumstances, but there are enough exceptions to make for occasional excitement in grizzly country.

An amazing piece of information about grizzlies is contributed by the late F. W. "Bert" Rigall, a pioneer rancher and outfitter in Twin Butte, Alberta. Back in the 1890's, he told me, there was a great smallpox epidemic among the Stoney Indians who lived in the Rockies of southwestern Alberta and southeastern British Columbia. When a village would get heavily infested, the Indians who were not yet stricken would ride off and leave the dead unburied and the dying to their fate. Grizzlies found they could invade the tepees to feed on the dead and dying. They got a taste of human flesh, and the next step was stalking and killing live and healthy Indians. So dangerous did those bears become that the tribe completely abandoned the country. When Rigall first settled there he found the trails all grown up and the older grizzlies still man-eaters. He stopped two unprovoked charges within a few feet.

The grizzly is a tough baby, but all reported charges by grizzlies are not charges by any means. The average hunter who goes up against one is in a pretty jittery frame of mind, and if the bear comes toward him he tells the folks back home that he was charged. This may be true and it may not be.

In the first place, all bears see poorly. Let us say that our grizzly is busily and innocently digging up a ground squirrel in a big lonely basin above timberline when suddenly he feels searing pain and hears the crashing report of a rifle. Panic stricken, the grizzly flees, but right in the direction of the hunter. The fact that the grizzly isn't charging doesn't make this entirely free from danger. He might suddenly see the hunter and take a swipe at him as he goes by. If he does, there is a badly hurt hunter.

Once up in northern British Columbia, Frank Golata and I went into a patch of scrub willow to kick out a grizzly another hunter had wounded. The bear spied me first and went straight toward the guide, who in turn was running backward trying to throw a cartridge into the chamber of an unfamiliar rifle. I ran to the side so I could take a pop at the bear without hitting the guide. I shot and the bear turned away and out of the willows onto an open hillside. The guide, who by this time had the rifle working, put a couple of shots into the seat of the grizzly's pants, but did not stop him. I sat down, took careful aim, and killed the grizzly as it ran broadside by me.

Was that grizzly charging? I don't think so. I think he was simply running from me and Frank happened to be in the way. Nevertheless he *might* have taken a swipe at Frank as he went by, and when anyone is swiped by a grizzly he knows he's been swiped!

Above all things, the grizzly hunter should avoid shooting at a bear on a steep hillside above him, as a wounded bear will always roll down hill. One dude I know saw a bear from the packtrain. It was about 300 yards away and 400 feet directly above the outfit. He piled off, shot the grizzly. Bawling and growling the great beast came catapulting right into the midst of the panic-stricken horses. It took the guides the rest of the day to gather up the packs and find the horses.

Once in the Yukon I got my binocular on a grizzly in an open basin about a mile away. I stalked him and finally ended up at the bottom of a little glacial creek about seventy-five yards from the bear and perhaps 100 feet below him. I didn't like the situation. I was too close to him and he was above me. My first two shots broke both shoulders and down that hill he came, propelling himself by his hind feet, roaring, bellowing, bawling. I knew I had the situation in hand, but I must admit that I was scared!

With the hide off, the carcass of a grizzly looks like the naked body of a grotesque and tremendously powerful man. The great ropes of muscle show where the bears get their strength. They can crush the head of a moose or a buffalo with one blow, literally powder the backbone of the largest steer. I once saw a rather small female grizzly uproot the stump of a dead timberline tree with one smooth, effortless pull. Apparently she did it as easily as a tractor would have done. Grizzlies have been known to carry away the entire carcass of a bull elk that would weigh from 700 to 800 pounds, and to drag that of a bull moose for a mile—and a big bull will weigh 1,200 or 1,300 pounds. When a grizzly puts his mind to it, he can break open the door of a trapper's cabin as if he were an animated battering ram. For his size, he is one of the most powerful beasts that walks this earth.

And how large does a grizzly get? They are by no means as large as their cousins the monster brown bears of Kodiak Island or the Alaska Peninsula, which sometimes are reputed to weigh 1,500 pounds. Now and then a wild grizzly may weigh a thousand pounds, and I have seen one that I would guess might weigh between 850 and 900. The average *big* male grizzly will weigh from 500 to 600 pounds and the females from 300 to 400. A hide that will square eight feet is a very large one, and one that will square nine feet is tremendous—larger, probably, than the average hide of an Alaska brown bear. The average adult grizzly's hide will square about seven feet.

At one time grizzlies ranged from Alaska clear into northern Mexico, from California out into the great plains. Now they have been almost exterminated in the United States, and only a few remain in Wyoming, Montana, and Idaho. There are some in the wilder ranges of northern Mexico. In the Canadian Rockies they are fairly plentiful, and the natives of the Yukon Territory believe the grizzlies there to be increasing. They have taken a pretty bad beating in many parts of Alaska, but they are still plentiful. Over most of the Canadian

Rockies, the hunter who packs back on a thirty-day trip in the fall can pretty well count on seeing one or more. He ought to have about a fifty-fifty chance to get one. The most grizzlies I have ever seen on one trip was in the area north of Jasper Park along the Alberta-British Columbia boundary. Between us, Jack Holliday, my companion, and I saw thirty-three altogether, or more than one a day. The most grizzly sign I have ever seen was along the head of the White River in the Yukon. There tracks were so thick along the sandbars of the rivers that it was difficult to put a foot down without stepping on a track!

Probably the majority of the grizzlies killed by sportsmen are shot in the fall when they are come upon by accident while the hunters are above timberline hunting for sheep or caribou. For a short time after the berries are gone and before the bears go into hibernation, they spend much time in timberline basins digging marmots or ground squirrels. They are easily seen then and not too hard to stalk.

The grizzly hunter's chances are better in the spring than at any other time of year, as the bears are then hungry and ranging far and wide to get something with which to fill their shrunken stomachs. They hunt for winter-killed elk or moose or for goats or sheep killed in snowslides. Grizzlies have excellent noses and the smell of over-ripe flesh in the springtime will bring one on the double.

A favorite method of getting bears, either grizzlies or blacks, used to be to bait them. The guide would get two or three old crow-bait horses, herd them back into the hills, then shoot them in spots where a traveling grizzly would be apt to come near enough to smell them. Then when it was found that a bear was feeding on a carcass, the guide brought the dude back, put him in hideout located where the bear would not get his wind. When the bear came back for a snack the dude bushwhacked him.

However, there are dudes and dudes. One chap I knew go so engrossed in a pocket book he had brought along to while away the time that he did not look once at the bait while a big grizzly was finishing up what was left of a horse a little over 100 yards away. Yet another leaned his head back on a log and slept soundly while a female black bear with two cubs had a banquet on a horse he had paid the outfitter $75 for. In both cases the guides had gone up on a hill to watch for the approach of the bears. The moral of this, I suppose, is that for the guide the client is as big a problem as the bear.

Because of the grizzly's liking for ripe meat, the hunter in the North who has to leave part of a carcass in the hills should make it a point to go back to it now and then. With luck he may find a grizzly on it.

Bears commonly feed on the slides where the snow melts off and fresh vegetation comes up. Hunters locate the bears with binoculars, then stalk them. That sounds easy but it isn't. The bear may be seen a mile or two away. By the time the hunter flounders through deep drifts, climbs through thick timber, the bear may have moved off— or he may have heard the hunter and left. Hunting grizzlies in the spring is cold, wet, difficult, and often heartbreaking, but it is the surest time for getting that trophy.

Suppose, just to see what it's like, we go on a spring grizzly hunt. About the middle of May you meet your outfitter at some little railroad station in the Canadian Rockies and pack back into the mountains anywhere from a couple of days to a week. Nights are still very cold and snow lies deep under the trees and in the high passes. Days are bright and fairly warm though, and now and then you hear the thunder of a slide where thousands of tons of snow have broken loose and tumbled down into a valley.

Every day you and your guide climb 1,500 feet or so to a vantage point overlooking several old slides where the snow has melted and vegetation is coming up. When your binoculars show you a grizzly on a slide the stalk begins. You drop off the mountain from which you have been watching, cross the raging creek, then climb through trees, brush, and snow to a point from which you can shoot at the grizzly.

More often than not, the grizzly is gone when you get there. Perhaps he has heard or smelled you—and in the mountains wind can shift often and unpredictably. Perhaps he has simply filled up and gone off to lie down in the timber. If the bear is gone and you cannot find him nearby, the only thing to do is to try to find another bear— and make another stalk.

Eventually, you'll creep those last few yards through the snow and timber, putting each foot down as carefully as if you were walking on TNT, and when you come out you'll see old *Ursus horribilis* rooting around from thirty to 100 yards away. He is big, massive, blocky, 500 pounds of bone and muscle in a shaggy coat of long, dark-brown hair silvered or yellowed along the backbone. You see the hump on his back, the concave forehead that distinguishes the grizzly from the black bear.

He is a big tough fellow and for a moment as you stand there watching him, your breath catching in your throat, you wonder why you're a grizzly hunter anyway, why you've spent all this time, money, and effort for a shot at an animal that may knock your head off. . . .

"Shoot!" your guide whispers.

The grizzly stops feeding, raises his big shaggy head. It's now or never. The crosshairs of the scope wobble around. Sometimes they are on the bear's shoulder, sometimes not. Finally you touch off the shot. It's too high. You see a shower of silvery hair sail into the air. The grizzly whirls, starts up the slide blindly. Now that the chips are down, you're able to shoot almost automatically. The next time you fire you hear the solid plunk of the bullet and the grizzly goes down on his nose. He struggles to his feet. You shoot once more and this time the bear is down for good.

Now the guide grabs your hand. He jumps up and down in celebration.

"Your first grizzly—a big old he-bear," he shouts. "You did fine after that first shot . . . Well, let's go over and skin him!"

But you'd rather not. Your legs are very weak, so you sit down on a log at the edge of the slide, smoke a cigarette, and watch the bear. Now you have forgotten the weary miles by packtrain, the camps pitched in slush, the fruitless stalks through snow and timber. You're a grizzly hunter!

MONARCH

Roger Caras is not a hunter. As a matter of fact there are those who claim he is an anti-hunter and has stated so in his writing.

But it is not my intention to get into this. Whether he likes sport hunting or not is academic. He is a fine naturalist and an excellent writer.

This book, Monarch of Deadman Bay, *published by Little, Brown & Company, 1969, is a marvelous story about a Kodiak bear from birth to death. Caras, unlike Ernest Thompson Seton, who also wrote a book about a grizzly named* Monarch The Big Bear *(Charles Scriber's Sons, New York, 1904), does not attribute human traits to his creatures. But he does put the reader inside his animals in a very workmanlike way.*

The final chapter of this excellent book, about the death of the giant Kodiak bear on Admiralty Island, Alaska, is as good a writing job on bears as has ever been done.

Monarch of Deadman Bay

Roger Caras

The low shale cliffs and meandering shoreline of Deadman Bay became Monarch's stronghold. Perhaps it was the familiar aspect of the area or perhaps it was something else about the region that appealed to him. Most of his early years had been spent on these raw, damp shores, and within a few miles of the sedge tide flats around the Bay's perimeter he had learned some of his hardest lessons. He had feasted hugely on the crystal springs that roll into the Bay from the hills, for here were the rich salmon streams with their pea-sized gravel banks. In this district he had grown from a cub who lost his salmon catch to his elders to the mammoth he now was.

Monarch would have been well advised to leave the area, for it was one of the most heavily hunted on the whole Island. The White Hills behind the Bay were and are known to all hunters who study the Island's potential as a likely spot where a man can get his bear. Yet this was Monarch's country, and although he might wander away from it, he always returned. It was as if he were on a long tether. He might roam in a sweeping arc at the end of his lead, but he always ended up back at the stake in the center.

Familiar and reliable feeding sites are important to a bear. Anything that simplifies his life will attract him. Monarch knew which were the first slopes to be free of snow and knew where the first asparagus-like hellebore shoots would appear beneath the cover of leaves and humus. He knew, too, where to seek the spring harvest of nettle and the beach rye, and the twisted stalk and crowberries under the summer sun. He knew the salmon streams and the high meadows where the sassy ground squirrels could be had. Aside from the probable comfort he found in general familiarity, it was probably this reliable provender as much as anything else that brought him back to familiar trails. It is not always pleasant country and the sun shines no more than fifty percent of the time each year, yet it is that very rainfall, the dampness that is always present, that provides the cornerstone for the vast food store bears must have.

Monarch stumped down through a patch of cottonwoods, crossed a small well-known clearing and entered a stand of evergreens. He was in no hurry; he appeared to be moving almost as the contour of the ground directed him. The area was quiet, for the spring hunting was over and his hide could not be legally sought again until October. He remained alert, however, for the man-smell was always there, frequently encountered. He could not understand that the summer brought only harmless tourists, more each year, who came simply to look and to photograph.

Near the edge of a cedar stand he came upon a well-used tree. The ground around it was worn flat and its bark was badly scarred. Vertical tooth marks were plainly evident where another large bear had recently been at work. As if in defiance Monarch rose to his hind legs and bit into the bark further up the trunk than the other bear had been able to reach. The syrupy sweetness followed by the turpentine aftertaste pleased him and he grunted with pleasure. Thrusting his abdomen against the tree he began moving up and down in a sensual sort of way. He rolled his head back, listened for a moment to reassure himself, and then began rocking back and forth, scratching his stomach and leaving small tufts of his fur clinging to the ragged bark. Satisfied, he sat down heavily on his rump and began scratching every available part of his body that his front and hind claws could reach. He cooed to himself and only occasionally stopped for a quick check of his surroundings. Finally he stood and turned his back to the tree and rocked rhythmically. This was the most absurd display of all. For a full ten minutes he rubbed his enormous rump against the tree. His exertions were so vigorous that before he was done he had worn smooth spots on his hide. With the sheer physical gratification of it all he rolled his eyes, uttered an entire range of contented sounds and drooled pools of saliva onto the ground. It was the hot and itchy time and the hedonist in him dictated his actions. A bear may not be the clown some people think he is, but he can act it at times.

As midafternoon approached Monarch began looking for a comfortable place to lay up for a few hours of rest. As he was settling himself in the damp earth beneath a windfall he heard the unmistakable sounds of a cub in trouble. The bawling and wailing carried to him from an adjacent valley. He could not resist the sounds and, as much a prisoner of his curiosity as he had been as a cub himself, he began heading in the direction of the disturbance. As he passed over the low intervening ridge a growl built up in his throat, an involuntary response to the sounds of the cub. Below him he could hear human voices. Four men were gathered around an eight-foot section of 14-gauge culvert pipe that had been anchored to some stout trees near a stream. A drop-door made from quarter-inch steel sealed the four-foot opening at the end of the pipe and inside, the prisoner, a yearling cub, bawled incessantly. His lament stopped shortly after a nylon syringe was thrust through a hole in the side of the pipe on the end of a pole and was jabbed into his rump. Once he was immobilized, the anesthetized cub was dragged from the pipe, subjected to a series of examinations, and was then finally tagged.

Meanwhile Monarch paced back and forth in the brush just below the ridge and mumbled to himself. He had no sympathy for the cub; indeed, he would probably have killed and perhaps even eaten it if given the chance to do so, but the men angered him, as they always did.

On the far side of the small valley the cub's mother hung back in a stand of trees, lathering herself into a fury, but she did not have the courage to charge. When she had shown herself at the first calls of distress, she had been driven back by firecrackers thrown in her direction. One man had burst a charge under her nose by firing a projectile from a 12-gauge shotgun.

Having grumbled enough, and being unwilling to expose himself to the men below unless forced to a showdown, Monarch slunk off. He grumbled once again when he crossed the familiar spoor of the copper boar that had been his special foe since their encounter on the seaweed flat nearly two decades earlier. The lighter and only slightly smaller boar had survived despite his mutilated right forepaw and the loss of his right ear and left eye, souvenirs of another encounter with Monarch. He always managed to avoid his ancient enemy although they were often in the same territory at the same time and usually about the same business. This was the third time in two weeks that Monarch had come across the antagonizing spoor. It never failed to elicit the same angry response, yet he never really followed it up or attempted to bring about another showdown.

Monarch bred again that year, selecting for his mate a seven-year-old sow of less than average size. Their idyll lasted for three weeks and a few days and was terminated without ceremony or sentiment, just as had all the others. Long before the crisp, early days of fall he was solitary again. His arrival at the salmon stream was leisurely, for he had no need to establish a place for himself or to contend for a better spot. He would take whatever he wanted whenever he arrived.

130

Tiring of the confusion and noise of the salmon stream after several days, Monarch wandered off by himself to the quiet and solitude he seemed to cherish above all else. Other animals, even other bears whom he could easily dominate, made him nervous.

The day after he abandoned the stream he was on the beach. He hung back in the brush for the first day, disturbed by two small boats that were plying back and forth in the inlet. By the second day he was used to the sounds they made and moved out onto a flat of slippery seaweed as the tide rolled back toward the sea. He was spotted at a distance of nearly half a mile, and a 1000-millimeter reflex lens hastily fastened to a tripod with a camera hanging off the back focused on him and recorded his image in color, and then in black and white. At that distance he was not recognizable as any particular bear, only as an animal of exceptional size. The husband-and-wife schoolteachers from Minnesota were thrilled with their "catch" and forgot momentarily about the amount of money their trip was costing them.

Back in the woods, Monarch again came upon the spoor of the copper boar, and again he voiced his extreme displeasure. After casting about for a few minutes he tramped off into dense cover, where he slept for a little less than an hour. He was moving again while the sun was still high and entered a small, stream-cut hollow several miles from the beach. Suddenly, warned by one sense or another, he was up on his hind legs, testing the wind for urgent messages. Men were close, very close. His anger flared.

The winds in the small depression were uncertain and he could not locate the source of his uneasiness. He was unwilling to depart without being able to pick his direction with care. He went down again to all fours and got behind a windfall. The scent was still there, but no noise. He waited, expecting to hear human sounds, but none came. The tension mounted and with it his fury. The scent was so close that he found it impossible to remain still and moved again, out between two trees. He felt the small pain almost simultaneously with the first noise he could distinguish as foreign. He spun to face his unknown foe, but it was too late. His hind legs would not respond, then his forequarters gave out. For the first time since reaching maturity, Monarch of Deadman Bay was helpless. The dart had been fired from a CO_2 powered rifle and had caught him squarely in the rump. Upon contact the automatic syringe had discharged more than 100 milligrams of the drug into his system. It was not a large enough dose to paralyze him completely, but he was helpless.

His hind legs twitched and his shoulders hunched forward, then relaxed. His eyes remained open and he could hear the men talking as they stood off and waited for the drug to take full effect. He could not appreciate their admiring remarks.

Finally, satisfied that the succinylcholine had provided them with sufficient protection, the men moved in. At their first touch, Monarch twitched and fought valiantly to regain his feet, but was unable to so much as lift his head from the ground. He was forced to tolerate their handling and barely felt the second needle enter his intraperitoneal cavity. In a few moments he was totally anesthetized and the biologists began their rapid series of tests.

While one biologist inserted a thermometer into the drugged bear's rectum, another made an impression of his teeth. A third drew a hefty blood sample and then began a gross examination of his general condition. His fur was inspected for external parasites, the wound on his chest was duly recorded on his register card, and he was checked for other wounds or signs of combat. One of his two bullet wounds, the one in his shoulder, was found and recorded, and his eyes, nostrils and ears were checked, again for parasites, and a mucous specimen was obtained. One of the biologists again commented on his extreme size and openly wondered whether or not he was the fabled man-killer so often discussed back in town. He was photographed as he lay and then the team took a break. One, a student on his first big-game survey, sat on Monarch's rump as he lighted his cigarette. A fellow student photographed him in that pose and jokingly offered to sell him wallet-sized prints at a reduced rate for a dozen or more. A senior member of the team suggested that it was time to head back to camp and the students began packing their equipment and specimens into their containers.

When everything was packed and ready, the leader of the team administered the antidote with a six-inch needle. It broke, and was extracted with a small pair of pliers. A second needle was fitted and the drug injected.

The biologists were some distance away before the antidote began to take effect. The leader had been nearly mauled by a bear some years earlier when he remained near it too long after administering the antidote. With the safety of his team members foremost in his mind he was in the habit of clearing out before the bears they examined were fully conscious and usually very angry.

At first, Monarch was aware of a slight buzzing noise, and then light penetrated to the black limbo into which the anesthesia had thrust him. He still could not move, still had no physical sensation of self, but the outside world began to have fractional meaning for him. He heard the brush move, but could not respond. He was neither angry nor frightened. He lay temporarily suspended between the real world and that which had been fabricated for him in distant laboratories and chemical plants. His sense of smell was returning, but he was still too confused by what had happened to be able to make any distinctions. He drooled copiously and made small, ineffectual sounds. He tried to roll his head, but couldn't summon the strength. His limbs twitched and shuddered, but his coordination had not yet returned. He was minutes away from being able to stand. The dose of pentobarbital sodium had been too massive; his great size had prompted the scientist to take too much of a precaution.

The copper male heard the sounds of the departing biologists as they crossed his trail about twenty yards ahead of him. He swung off into the brush and circled around behind them. He came upon Monarch while the giant was still trying to focus in on the world around him. At first the copper male's instincts told him to retreat. He recognized his foe immediately, and his natural response was to withdraw. But something was different this time.

Slowly he approached his hated rival, the great chocolate boar that had condemned him to live his life as a cripple, a secondary force despite his own great size.

Confused as he was, Monarch recognized his arch-enemy. Something between a roar and a screaming whine filled his throat as he managed to extend his forelegs. He pushed the front half of his body up and rocked uncertainly, struggling to coordinate the effort with his hindquarters. Chomping his jaws and drooling, he thrust his head forward and with a deep grunt managed to get the back part of his enormous body into a semicrouch. He wavered for a moment, just a moment, before the copper male struck. Monarch rolled over, first onto his side and then over onto his back. For a moment his four legs pointed straight up. The blow from his eleven-hundred-pound rival winded him badly and he was flailing, trying to adjust his limbs and his senses at the same time. He rocked over onto his side again with a heaving moan but it was too late.

The copper boar had passed completely over Monarch on his first thrusting charge. His momentum carried him ten feet beyond, where he hauled up and turned. His jaws were chomping furiously too; he was in a transport of rage. He paused for a moment, unable to comprehend Monarch's plight. He was waiting for the countercharge that could never come. Seizing the initiative once more, he struck again, this time fatally. As powerfully built as Monarch was, he couldn't withstand the massive blow in the neck, not without being able to brace himself. The huge paw came down behind his ear as the copper boar sank his fangs into his exposed shoulder. For several minutes the huge animal tore at Monarch, clawing and biting, and the noise was horrendous. It was all unnecessary. Monarch had died seconds after he received the blow in the neck. But the last shudders, those last few spastic reflexive tremors that ran through his dead body, served to enrage the copper boar even more. When at last he backed off, his head held low and sounds of fury still issuing from his throat, Monarch was a bloodied, almost unrecognizable hulk. In a last gesture of disdain the copper boar moved forward again and began to feed. Several crows and half a dozen magpies waited on nearby branches. Others began to arrive.

The copper boar did not bother to cache what remained of Monarch. He moved out of the valley and was never seen in the district again.

As for Monarch, he had paid his final debt. In bird droppings and bear scats, between the pincers of beetles and ants, his chemicals were broken down and slowly returned to the land. These chemicals would enrich the soil and help to grow the plants that had nourished the bronze sow when she had carried Monarch and his sister within her many years before. The hunters that came to seek him in the years that followed would miss him, but the life systems of Kodiak Island would not. He was where he ultimately belonged, back in the cycle, back again in time.

OF GRIZZLIES and the RIVER

This collection of autobiographical accounts—one of which appears here—was put together by hunter-writer-photographer Grancel Fitz. In the course of thirty-eight trips between 1926 and 1955, he became the first man to hunt all twenty-four different classes of North American big-game animals.

Grancel Fitz was first and foremost a photographer—and a famous one. He won the Boone and Crockett Club's first prize medal in 1956 for an Alaska brown bear. He collected a number of big game species for the American Museum of Natural History and was a recognized authority on trophy rating. He also wrote numerous outdoor stories for Field & Stream, Outdoor Life, Argosy *and* True *magazines.*

Of Grizzlies and the River

Grancel Fitz

We had tied up the boat to the roots of a stranded drift log, and for most of the afternoon Jim Stanton and I sat behind a thin fringe of brush, watching the riffle that ended less than a hundred yards upstream. It was a good place. At least, it had all the signs of a good place. I could reach out and touch the day-old tracks of a big grizzly, deeply imprinted in the gray glacial slit of the bank.

"That fellow would be just what we want," Jim had said when we first saw them. "No little bear could make tracks like those. Not even if he had big feet. Look at the length of that stride."

Off to our right we could see the spot where one of Jim's hunters had killed a fine big grizzly the year before. Just behind us, where another back channel of the main river had cut through to join the one we had come up, there was a sort of sand bar where the two streams came together. On that bar we had found the tracks of six different bears, all made within the week. I'd been really impressed by that. My experience with grizzlies had been limited to places like the main Canadian Rockies and the interior of the Yukon Territory, where you don't find them in any such concentration. But here, not far from where the Klina Klini River empties into the salt water of Knight Inlet, on the northern British Columbia coast, the bears come down from the mountains to catch the various kinds of salmon that work their way up the river to spawn and die.

As this was in early October, a good run of dog salmon came up the channel throughout the whole sunny afternoon. Every few minutes the calm surface of nearby shallow water showed a sudden bulging ridge as a fish darted a few yards farther up. Sometimes, when his dorsal fin protruded, he left long, narrow ripples in his wake. From time to time a really big one made a great, noisy splashing with his powerful tail. And once, almost beside us, a yard-long, hook-jawed male jumped high into the air.

"The bears can hear those splashes halfway up the mountain," Jim remarked. "That's what makes them come down."

They didn't come in any hurry, though. With the chill of evening the mist began to gather over the water and drift slowly along the banks. It was almost time to start for Jim's house, at the head of Knight Inlet, when he laid a hand on my arm.

"Well, look who's here," he said softly.

On our side of the stream, directly behind me and away down toward the main river, three grizzlies had come out of a dense wall of alders onto a narrow strip of beach. Through the intervening mist they showed up as flat, dark silhouettes, and one of them looked huge. We took our places in the boat, pushed it out into the current, and drifted toward them in perfect silence. But before very long we knew that they were a sow and a pair of very large two-year-olds.

That meant no shooting. I wanted nothing less than the biggest grizzly we could find, and no sow is as big as the old boars from the same region. Furthermore, I've always had personal scruples about shooting female bears. If the sow has this year's cubs at heel, they need her. If they are two-year-olds—born in hibernation two winters before—they are well able to care for themselves, but by that time the sow is already carrying next winter's cubs. Bears breed every other year, and one bullet could wipe out the sow and her probable twins-to-be. The grizzly, nowadays, is much too rare to warrant that kind of waste. So I kept the rifle across my knees and the binocular to my eyes.

The sow was mahogany brown, with a lighter head and a broad, strikingly unusual stripe of orange-buff color that encircled her body behind the forelegs. The other two were uniformly dark brown. As the faint breeze blew toward us across the stream, they couldn't get our scent, and we were well within a hundred yards before the old bear caught sight of the boat. Immediately she came right down to the water's edge to look us over, with the others ranged beside her. At first she obviously didn't know what we were. I'm not sure that she ever found out. But when we had drifted to within twenty-five yards they all began to growl and swear at us, wrinkling their snouts and baring their big teeth. I lowered the binocular and picked up my rifle—just in case. We weren't more than fifty feet away before she said something to the young ones that made them scamper into the alders, and she let us get considerably closer before she strolled after them. Then, just inside the nearest bushes, she turned and kept on berating us. She wasn't looking for trouble, but she made it very plain that she was ready to furnish all we might want.

"The same to you, Mrs. O'Reilly," I told her. "And that goes for Dennis and Patrick, too. Such language! Is that any way to bring up your children?"

At that moment Jim started the outboard motor with a roar, and she faded into the brush.

"Maybe that'll scare her into a little more caution," he said. "When the Indians around here are traveling in their boats, they shoot at every bear they lay eyes on."

Now that the sow was gone, all I could think of was the size of her, and I mentioned something about it.

"She was big, all right," Jim agreed. "Her hide would square close to nine feet."

This estimate gave me plenty of food for thought. Finding a sow that big, on the very first day of the hunt, went a long way toward proving that the theory which had brought me to the Klina Klini country was pretty sound. I was almost as much interested in that theory as in the bears, for the question of where the modern sportsman should hunt for a topflight grizzly trophy is more complex than it might seem.

Grizzly hunting is practically a thing of the past in the United States, for we have almost none left except in a few national parks. North of our border, there are some in Alberta and many in the more remote parts of British Columbia, the Yukon Territory, and Alaska. Which of these game fields offered the best chance? In trying to decide, I first turned to *Records of North American Big Game*, the official record book, and before long I was all tangled up in the question of why the record-class specimens grew so big. A freakishly large animal might be found almost anywhere, but when one region consistently produces bigger animals than most other places, there must be a reason.

In the case of bears, it wasn't hard to find. At the time of my grizzly hunts in 1952 and 1953, the world record skull was in the National Museum in Washington. The measurements of skulls give us the only accurate basis for comparisons, and it is worth noting that this one was inaccurately reported for the 1952 edition of the records. When the figures were found to vary from those on the same bear in earlier editions, the Washington authorities made a careful recheck. The length of that skull is sixteen inches. The width is nine and nine-sixteenths. Combining these gives the record "score" of twenty-five and nine-sixteenths. But far more important is the fact that this bear was shot near the Missouri River in Montana, away back in 1890, and it is highly significant that E. S. Cameron bagged him as early as the fourth of April. As bears may live for forty years or more, unless somebody shoots them, and as they keep on getting bigger until they die, it is a fairly safe bet that this old monster was born in the great days of the bison, at least a century ago.

At that time there were a good many grizzlies in the foothills and plains east of the Rockies, where their usual varied diet was supplemented by plenty of bison meat, fresh and otherwise. The snowfall was comparatively light. These conditions made it possible for the bears to stay out very late in the fall, and to get up early in the spring.

With the passing of the bison and the settling up of the plains, all this was changed. Those huge old buffalo eaters turned to killing cattle, and were wiped out by the ranchers. The grizzlies that survived were in the high mountain country, where the heavy snows and lack of winter feed forced them to hibernate for as much as six or seven months of the year. If a bear can eat for only half of his life, and has to sleep throughout the rest, it just doesn't make sense that he can ever grow as big as one who is out and eating well for nine months, and hibernating for only three.

It was this fact that narrowed down my choice of hunting country. The high Canadian Rockies and the whole Yukon Territory were promptly eliminated, as those bears have to do too much sleeping. East of the Rockies there are still some big grizzlies in the Peace River country of Alberta, where old-time conditions still prevail except that the bison are gone. But the king-sized Alberta grizzlies are too few and far between. Alaska, which demands long hibernation in the interior, has some impressive grizzlies near, or actually in, the country of the giant brown bears along the southern coast. The trouble with them is that they often have an admixture of brown bear blood. This bars them from the record list of true grizzlies, so I wanted to make sure of hunting mine in a country where no hybrids were possible.

The British Columbia coastal region seemed to be the answer. It has the mild, wet climate and light snowfall which the Japan Current brings to the Alaskan brown bear country. It also has the same teeming runs of salmon. If these conditions make big brownies, I figured that they should make big grizzlies, too. Toba Inlet, Bute Inlet,

Rivers Inlet, and a couple of other places were considered. At last, after learning about Jim Stanton, I pinned my faith on Knight Inlet and the Klina Klini as the best bet of all.

After that first evening, Jim and I naturally went back to the same spot, and for three more days we watched riffles in that general area. A couple of black bears showed up. One, with exceptionally fine fur, was big enough to tempt me. But we didn't want to risk alarming the grizzlies, and I didn't shoot. Later I wished I had taken him, for the grizzlies in that neighborhood were too cagey to come out until after dark.

"They have probably found out about us," Jim finally concluded. "All they let us see is the tracks they make in the night. It's time we rested this place. Tomorrow we'll go up the river and camp where we can work on a different bunch of them."

The next morning was perfect when we packed our things into the boat, which was especially designed for the Klina Klini River. It is twenty-six feet long and four feet wide; a square-ended, shallow-draft job which Jim built on the lines of an English punt. Driven by a twenty-five horsepower outboard motor, it is also equipped with both oars and poles. We had with us a logger named Carl Noreen, as a general helper, when we shoved off from Jim's mooring to start a day that I'll always remember.

Several flocks of Canada geese rose with a clamor of protest when we crossed Knight Inlet and entered the river. A little farther up we passed a regular convention of bald eagles, perched in the highest treetops where a steep mountainside came down to the water. An occasional seal took time out from his salmon fishing to pop his dark head above the surface and satisfy his curiosity about us. Dominating all of these was the Klina Klini, a savage, bare-knuckled, brawling river that can be most dangerous where it looks most innocent. The great mountains, some trimmed with hanging glaciers, crowded close along both sides of the narrow valley.

Fairly late in the morning we spotted a big grizzly standing ankle-deep in the water, a good quarter of a mile upstream. He was a spectacular silvertip, in perfect coat. But it is illegal to shoot big game from a power boat, and I wouldn't have felt right about it, anyhow. There is no point in hunting dangerous animals if you deny them any possible chance of being dangerous. I was very anxious for a shot at this bear, but I wanted to be out on the ground with him and he had other ideas. He bolted back into the timber of a good-sized island before I could land on the bank.

"That silvertip has met boats before," Jim said. "Likely as not he's carrying a couple of old 30-30 slugs as souvenirs from some boatload of Indians. But I think he'll slow down when he gets a little way into the brush. We've still got a chance."

The boat roared up the river for half a mile, past the big trees towering over a solid jungle of alders that covered the island right down to the water.

"What makes you think we might see him again?" I asked.

"There's a main bear trail that they use when they leave this island. If we can beat him to the crossing on the other side, he might come right out to us."

The wide channel which cut inland from the river was bordered with silt. Leaving Carl with the boat, Jim and I hurried down this narrow strip of beach, and before long we came to a place where the stream was bridged by a great jam of logs. When we had worked out onto this for about fifty yards, Jim signaled that we had gone far enough.

I began to size up the situation. There is big timber in that part of British Columbia, and spring floods had tossed some gigantic trees into the jam. We stood on one great trunk a dozen feet above the water, but we were fairly well-concealed by smaller trunks piled breast-high in front of us. The claw marks on a number of the nearby logs told me that they had been a highway for a good many bears. I was trying to estimate how far we were from where the silvertip had vanished when Jim heard a stick break, not far back in the brush.

"Get ready," he said quietly. "Here comes your grizzly."

A few seconds later a big bear came out of the alders, but as he crossed the couple of yards of silt beach I was startled to see that he was a lot different from the thickset silvertip we were expecting. This one was long, lanky, and dark brown. When he came up onto the jam, he was hidden so well that I could get only brief glimpses of the top of his back as he angled toward us. Then, not more than forty yards away, he stopped. He didn't see us. His outstretched head, his whole neck, and the top of his withers suddenly appeared in straight profile above one of the logs, and the end of his nose wrinkled as he tested the breeze.

It would have been simple enough to shoot him through the neck. But I wasn't getting trigger-happy about it. Jim knew that I was interested only in a very big bear, and that he was to be the judge of which I should take. So I waited for his verdict, and at that moment, with the corner of my eye, I caught a flash of brown fur inside the edge of the thicket.

Here, I thought, was a fine mess. Could it be that this huge beast in front of me was another sow? Was the new arrival one of her cubs?

"There's another bear in the brush," I said uncertainly.

"Yes," Jim said. "But you'd better shoot this one, now. He's going back."

As he spoke, the grizzly swung his head away from me. Then he began to turn. I had to make a split-second decision. With the bear's shoulder covered by the great log, my only chance was to hit him in the spine. I shot, hurriedly, and hit him too high. He jumped behind the log. I was ready when he appeared again at the narrow beach, but he streaked across it so fast that my next bullet was aimed into the alders, where I hoped his heart would be, just as he disappeared into the cover. We could hear him keep on going, and, slowly, it dawned on me that I was in as nasty a spot as a hunter can get into in North America.

"Don't move away from here. I'll be right back," Jim said. It was practically a command.

He checked the magazine of his .348 Winchester, crossed the logs, and went warily into the brush. In less than a minute he came out again.

"There's a blood trail, but those alders are too thick for a snake to get through," he reported. "Your first shot couldn't have been more than a jab through the flesh of his back, but we don't know where the second shot went. It's a bad deal all around. We'll forget about this one, and go back to the boat."

"No," I said. "I'm going after him."

"I'd advise you not to," he explained patiently. "Maybe this bear is hit hard. Maybe he isn't. But don't forget that other one you saw. That was full-grown, too, and it might hang around with the wounded one. There's no telling how it might act."

"Look, Jim," I said. "Guides have told me, before this, never to follow a wounded bear into the alders. Never. Nohow. And I've never had to try it. I'm going in, though, and so you won't think I'm crazy altogether, I'll tell you why. It's because of a code I learned from Stewart Edward White, a long time ago. That bear wasn't bothering us. The odds were on my side when I started this by shooting at him. I fouled up the whole works by shooting when

I hadn't time to be sure of hitting a vital spot. So the bear is wounded and suffering, through no fault of his own, and it is definitely up to me to finish what I started. If the odds, now, are all on the bear's side, I've got to accept that as part of the game."

"All right," Jim finally agreed. "We'll give him time to lie down and stiffen up. Then we'll circle around and go in against the wind."

At a place much closer to the main river, we entered the jungle of alders half an hour later. We took great care to avoid breaking twigs underfoot. After every few steps we would stop, look, and listen. We worked over to the blood trail without seeing anything, and as we began to follow it I almost jumped out of my skin when a grouse roared out of the brush close behind us.

Before very long we could find no more blood. It became a job of straight tracking under tough conditions, for the wounded grizzly had left the regular bear trail and gone off through the thickest alders he could find. There were places where Jim was hidden when he was only a couple of yards ahead. As we emerged from one of these, he turned and looked me in the eye.

"Keep your head working on a swivel," he said earnestly. "When I'm looking at the ground for tracks, I can't look around at the same time. If we get a few steps past that bear without seeing him, we've had it!"

He needn't have emphasized the risk. I remembered Field Johnson, the veteran Indian guide in the Yukon, who was hospitalized for months by a grizzly that hadn't been shot at. Often I wondered how it would feel to do what we were doing, and now I discovered that I wasn't exactly afraid. Not scared in the way that I've been scared, more than once, when climbing for mountain goats. But I was so tightly keyed up that it almost hurt.

In the thickets it would have been impossible to swing the rifle barrel to the side. So I advanced with my thumb on the safety and with the muzzle pointed up. In that way the barrel could be brought straight down, to point in any direction that I pivoted to face. We worked forward very slowly for what seemed a long time, although we couldn't have covered more than a few hundred yards. Then we came out into an open space, so torn up with bear tracks of all sizes that it looked as if a whole herd of them had been through there. We trailed the wounded one into the middle of it, lost the track, picked it up again, and finally found it so impossible to distinguish from the others that we had to admit we were licked.

It is strange, sometimes, how things work out. We had seen no bear on our trip through the alders. In one way, we had only taken a walk in the brush. But it had all added up to an extremely vivid experience that I never want to repeat. The sheer tension and excitement had lasted a lot longer than when I once crawled into a cave after a mountain lion, and that was the only comparable adventure I have ever had. This bear was the third animal I've wounded that ever got away, and the first in over twenty years. I felt very low about the whole business, yet there was no denying our relief when it was over.

"After about ten minutes, that sort of thing begins to get me," Jim said. "It just isn't worth it. A couple of grizzlies have run over me, and I know how lucky I am to be in one piece."

That is what he said. But we had been in the jungle a lot longer than ten minutes. He had never wavered. And when we lost the track, he had kept searching until we both knew it was hopeless.

The next seven days of hunting turned up five more bears. While it would have been easy enough to settle for an ordinary trophy, none of these compared with the silvertip we had seen in the river, or with the rangy brown grizzly I had failed to bag. So we passed them up. We found enough big tracks to prove that there were several giants around, if we had the time to wait for one. But both Jim and I had commitments that forced us to recess the proceedings until the following season, which I never considered as anything but an interruption.

It was on the fourth day of our resumed hunt, in September, 1953, when we headed the punt up the river to a camp that Jim had put in before I arrived. We turned into Mussel Creek to reach the tent. It was pitched on a high cut-bank facing the main Klina Klini, perhaps 500 yards away, and we were to find, in due time, that this position was highly important.

"If you feel like hiking in the morning," Jim suggested, "there are some salmon riffles a few miles up the creek. We might see if any good bears are working on them."

We went, and in the middle of the afternoon we had a momentary glimpse of a grizzly bear as he plunged into the brush. It is doubtful that he saw us. An eddy of wind brought him our scent. But this bear looked so exceptional that we decided to concentrate on trying to get him. It seemed best to rest him a little before we looked him up again, so the next day was spent mostly in trout fishing around camp, with indifferent success. Those rainbows were too full of salmon eggs to pay much attention to my flies.

"I have a feeling that tomorrow might be the big day," Jim said that evening. "We have a good chance to see that old fellow fishing again, if the weather stays clear. If it rains hard, he likely won't show up. He's so fat now that he'll never worry about missing a meal or two."

The way things turned out, I'd hardly know how to rate Jim as a prophet. The pattern that unfolded was certainly a lot different from the one he had in mind. But in order to understand it, we'll have to take another look at the river, and at the terrain around our camp.

Whenever the Klina Klini is flooding, it has a trick of jamming logs here and there along its main current. Dams are formed when some of these log jams fill up with silt, so the river overflows its banks and scours out a new channel. If the valley is wide enough at that point, other new channels may be cut at the same time, and in this process some huge and ancient trees get swept on down to be stranded along the shores or to jam up somewhere else.

In front of the tent there were several of these minor channels of varying size. Their waters rejoined the Klina Klini by way of Mussel Creek, which they entered from the side, and one of them bordered a fairly wide island, at least half a mile long. This began at the creek mouth and extended upstream along the main river. The lower third of it was heavily wooded, while the upper end was an open sand bar, liberally strewn with drift logs. Between this and our camp, a couple of smaller sand bars rose only a foot or two above the narrow streams which enclosed them.

On the day which Jim's hunch had told him would be fateful, a heavy rain began to drum on the tent roof several hours before dawn. It was still pouring when my little alarm clock sounded, and I reached out from my sleeping bag and turned it off.

"If the bears won't get out of bed this morning, why should we?" I thought, and burrowed deep into the sack.

That is why we were in the middle of breakfast at a little after nine o'clock. While the rain had slacked off considerably, it hadn't stopped. We were sitting just inside the opened flaps of the tent, with our noses deep in our coffee cups. Jim suddenly stood up. And, from that moment on, I was ready to believe that his eyes keep roving when he's asleep.

He had spotted a light brown grizzly wading around near the brushy bank of the island, away down where Mussel Creek emptied into the river. In another few seconds it ambled into the cover.

Breakfast was forgotten. We pulled on our hip boots, grabbed our rifles, and hurried across the various channels to the sand bar nearest the shore where the bear had disappeared. There was a single drift log on this one. We concealed ourselves behind it and waited a few minutes for the grizzly to come out. When he didn't, we went back, untied the punt, and poled it to the island bank for a close look at his tracks where he left the water. They were big.

"He's a good bear, all right," Jim said. "If he isn't going to bed down in there, he'll either go on up the island or cross the main river. We'll pole along the channel and go ashore where the timber quits."

When we began to skirt around the jungle of brush and trees, we kept about ten yards out. It was easy to move silently in the soft sand. But when we had gone possibly two-thirds of the way across this broad end of the island without finding any fresh tracks, the edge of the forest began to swing downstream. We didn't dare to follow it any farther, for the wind was blowing inland from the river.

The bank of the Klina Klini was almost barricaded with stranded driftwood, and Jim turned toward this on a course that would keep our scent from being carried back into the cover. There was still a short way to go when he pointed to a tiny rift between the logs piled high along the shore.

"I caught just a flick of something dark, through there," he told me. "It was heading up the river. Could have been an eagle."

That should have prepared me for anything. Jim doesn't sound off unnecessarily. But I failed to give it much thought, and he may have seen that I wasn't properly alerted. He led the way for another fifty yards and paused again.

"It might have been a black timber wolf," he mused.

I nodded, waking up a bit. We kept on for another ten steps and he halted abruptly. This time he was looking toward the upper end of the island.

"There's your grizzly," he said, "but it's not the one we came over to find. This one's a lot darker. And he's too far away to shoot."

We were almost beside a stranded log, so big that its top surface was shoulder-high. I took a couple of swift steps, rested my forehand on the trunk, and looked at the bear through my rifle 'scope. He didn't know that we existed. As he wasn't much farther than 200 yards when we first saw him, the range was hardly extreme. But he was rapidly making it longer as he traveled straight away from us, just inside the heavy driftwood along the river. He walked with that head-swinging, shoulder-rolling stride so characteristic of big bears. It is a gait that may seem clumsy. Actually, it is silky smooth in its own peculiar way. I knew that we had no chance of getting closer. In less than a minute he could cross the channel at the tip of the island and be swallowed up forever in the heavy underbrush beyond.

"That's one whale of a big bear," I said, suddenly convinced that this was the biggest grizzly I had ever seen.

Jim nodded, and his face was troubled. "Take a chance, if you want to. But wait for him to turn around."

"Don't worry. I'm not going to shoot him in the rump," I said.

A lot of things can flash through your mind in a few seconds. We both knew that my rifle was properly zeroed for 200 yards, for I had targeted the 'scope when I arrived at Knight Inlet. The green light that Jim had just given me was based, I suspected, on those tightly grouped bullet holes. But, beyond that, I knew what was troubling him.

There is one point in dealing with dangerous game that is just the opposite of what a novice might think, for it is much safer to start shooting at close range than at any considerable distance. At forty or fifty yards, in a place that wasn't too brushy, there would have been an excellent chance of killing the grizzly outright with my all-important first shot. Even if he might have had enough left to charge us, I think I'd have almost welcomed it for the thrill, for I had a lot of confidence in the 220-grain loads in my 30-06.

In contrast, the situation that confronted us could be downright dangerous. The bear was already so far that I could hardly count on hitting a vital spot precisely. If I wounded him and he managed to get into heavy cover, there might be hell to pay. I'd have to follow him. And if I went in, I knew that Jim would go in, too. So, entirely aside from personal safety, I'd have no business to let Jim in for any such risk unless I could be reasonably sure of a mortal shot. Much as I wanted the trophy, I wouldn't have thought of shooting if Jim hadn't given me the word, and I hope that my answering nod expressed my appreciation.

Meanwhile, as the grizzly continued to offer a no more vital target than his huge stern, I was just about ready to give up on him when the gods decided to smile. At a range that I judged to be 300 yards—it later measured out at 272—the bear turned sharply to his right and stopped. With the rifle rested on the tree trunk my 'scope picket settled steadily, a trifle behind his shoulder and high enough to allow for the added range. The bear kept still, and at last I could feel sure enough as I carefully squeezed the trigger.

That bullet knocked him flat, but it didn't keep him down. In an instant he was up and galloping unsteadily across the sand in the direction he had faced. Then he was down and up, down and up, as I shot again and again. I felt certain that at least two of those bullets had smashed through his lungs, and was sure that I had him until a new danger occurred to me. If the bear got as far as the channel we might never see him again, for he might die in the middle of it as he tried to cross. He would sink far enough for the current to slide him along the bottom like a greased pig, and he'd probably end up under some log jam down the river. So the fourth shot was aimed at his flank, in the hope of breaking a leg, as he suddenly turned away and was lost to my view behind some thin brush. I turned to Jim. He wasn't there.

A moment later I caught sight of him, just as I heard a couple of blasts from his .348, and I understood why the local Indians have given him a name which means "White man who travels like a wolf." He know the danger of the river better than I did, and though the bear was down when Jim approached him, it was no time to take chances. I walked over to where Jim stood. The grizzly just managed to raise his great head from among the drift logs where he lay. Taking care not to damage the precious skull, I punctured him again. He died, close to the channel bank, more than fifty yards from where the first fatal bullet had dropped him.

What did he weigh? Everybody asks me that, and I have no more accurate knowledge than the overwhelming majority of other hunters. You just can't pack scales to weigh such big animals. The usual formula is to take a deep breath, remember what the last liar reported, and then add a hundred pounds for good luck. But the very biggest true grizzlies are considered by the authorities to weigh around 1000 pounds, and mine must have approached the top figure, whatever it may be. I only know that he weighed entirely too much. Under Jim's expert supervision, an hour and a half of our combined hard work was spent in levering the bear about six feet, so that we could skin it.

The measurements are on more solid ground. From the tip of his nose to the end of his tail *bone*, before skinning, my bear measured seven feet nine and three-quarter inches, and the hair on his tail would have made him an even eight feet. Don't let anybody tell you that grizzlies ever get much longer. The biggest Alaskan brown bears aren't more than a trifle over nine feet, if this measurement is properly taken.

It wasn't until the following day that I measured the hide. Laid out casually on the ground, I taped it at nine feet nine inches wide and eight feet seven inches from nose to tail.

"What do you want to write that down for?" Jim demanded accusingly. "I don't ask you to stretch it, but this hide will square ten feet if you just pull the slack out. You don't even have it spread flat."

"The Records Committee isn't worrying about green hides, stretched or otherwise," I told him. "Only the skull measurements count, because those are figures that nobody can cheat."

We cleaned the skull. After that there was nothing more to do but hold my breath until the two months had elapsed before official measurements could be taken. Finally word came from the chairman of the Records Committee. With lower jaw removed, the skull was sixteen and four-sixteenths inches long. The width was nine and five-sixteenths. The official score was twenty-five and nine-sixteenths. And as that is the identical score of the old Montana buffalo-eater killed sixty-three years earlier, my grizzly became, for a while, at least, the recognized co-holder of the world record.

BEARS THAT MAKE MY MEMORY SWEAT

Slim Moore is a fine writer and this story, done for True's Hunting Yearbook *in 1959, did justice to some big, mean and scary bears he had hunted. His powers of description are good enough to make the reader feel just as frightened as he must have been on several occasions with the big Alaska bears.*

Bears That Make My Memory Sweat

Slim Moore

The grizzly walked in the loose-jointed, hump-backed about-to-fall-apart way of its kind. The great amber coat rippled with each step as it leisurely moved across the autumn-reddened hillside. We were above timber line, but a slash of frost-yellowed willows filled the draw directly beneath the bear. I don't think the hunter I was guiding was really nervous, but when he squeezed a 250-yard shot off at the animal he hit too far back; the bullet slammed through the back ribs to kick up dust on the hillside beyond.

The grizzly dropped and rolled limply down the hill into the head-high patch of willows. There was time for only the one shot—after the bear started rolling just a flash of yellowish fur flashed through the brush now and again.

It was the kind of a situation that could have caused trouble. It almost did, but in an unexpected way. I posted the hunter on the hillside above the willows, then went down to find the bear. As I neared the spot I heard it groaning, so, rifle ready, I went on in.

I spotted it at about 50 feet—an indistinct patch of fur amidst the thick willows. It lay flat on its back.

"You want me to finish it off?" I called to the hunter.

"No," he yelled back, "I want to."

I should have known better, but I told him to come on down and get to it.

But every time he tried to center his low-mount scope on the groaning and threshing animal all he could see was a blur of brush. And the brute was rolling back and forth more and more forcefully.

"That bear's going to make his feet," I warned. "You'd better shoot."

After another attempt he gave up and turned to me. "Here. Take this hard-point and shoot it in the head. I'd like to save the skull."

Glancing warily at the still-prone bear, I decided to try it. After all the hunter was paying me to see that he got the trophy he wanted. But just as I started to pull the bolt back to put the hard-point cartridge in, the grizzly heaved to its feet and somehow found the energy to streak through the brush toward us.

My hunter heard it coming and didn't even look. He reminded me of an old Fatty Arbuckle movie when he took off. I'd swear he jumped into the air and made about three steps before his feet hit the ground and he left.

I rammed the bolt home on my '06 and snapped a shot—the soft-point I had started to extract. The bullet struck the nostrils, ranged through the nose and into the brain. The bear skidded and rolled to a limp stop 15 or 20 feet away.

Turning I watched the hunter come back, rather carefully, peering suspiciously at the dead trophy. I asked him where he had figured on going.

"I was getting out of your way so you could shoot," he explained.

This incident illustrates a couple of facts. Obviously it's possible to get hurt while hunting bears—they're different from most big game in that they sometimes try to fight back. I didn't blame that hunter in the least for sprinting. And bears are often hard to kill. I've seen many a bear drop and roll at a shot, seemingly a trophy in the bag, then suddenly climb back on those powerful legs and charge. Or if it didn't charge it would get into the brush and scare the adrenalin out of both me and my hunter before it was all over.

I've hunted Alaskan big game for 30 years, 26 years of that time as a registered guide, and I think I've had more fun on bear hunts and have seen more interesting incidents than with any other single species of game.

Bears are individuals. You can't depend on any two of them behaving alike. One reason for this is that a bear can think a little for himself, which sets him apart from most other big game. Such individuality makes for a lot of uncertainty on a hunt. You never know just what is going to happen when you're in good bear country.

One of my biggest surprises on a hunt came on the Alaska Peninsula, shortly after a hunter I was guiding had killed a beautiful big brown bear.

It was a hot day—one of the two or three that come to the Peninsula every year. The hunter, his teen-age son, and I, spent the day moving slowly and glassing. We paid particular attention to the snow drifts. Bears, of course, rut in the spring. Apparently part of the brown bear's courtship activity includes sliding down steep snow-drifts. I once watched a female, lighter in color, as is the rule, as she stood at the top of a steep drift where a big dark boar swiftly skidded down on his rear end, then walked back to the top to repeat the maneuver. She seemed impressed.

New slide marks on the old dirty snow are clean and white. We were looking for these when we spotted a big bear about 4 in the afternoon, a good three miles away. He was alternately feeding on skunk cabbage and plunging enthusiastically into a little stream, trying to cool off. He looked big and dark, so we started for him.

He wandered far and fast enough so that by the time we got him it was 7 o'clock, and we were a long long way from camp. To make it worse the killing shot dropped him into a snowbank where he doubled over and broke through. When we reached him his hind feet stuck up in the air and his head was between his hind legs. After we trampled the snow down he dropped yet another four feet to where the snow was hollowed out. I had a long difficult time skinning him. His hide squared 10½ feet, that is the total of the distance from the nose to the tail plus the maximum distance between the forepaws was 21 feet.

So it was late when we started home. I led, packing the hide. We reached a spot on a creek where I thought I could bring a rubber boat to float the hide on out—a big green brown bear hide weighs anywhere from 125 to 175 pounds, and I couldn't have packed that one much farther.

After caching the hide we walked on down a bear trail, which, like most old brown bear trails, was worn deeply into the tundra. This one was knee-deep most of the way. It was almost dark, for it does get dark on the Alaska Peninsula, even in June. We were tired, hungry. It was one of those times when a guide wonders if there's maybe an easier way of making a living.

Just before midnight, ahead and below us a short way, five moose broke out of a valley and hit the trail we were following. A moment later they got our wind, which was at our back, and ran, following on down the deep bear trail.

A few hundred yards farther a side creek came in. As we reached it the youngster, directly behind me, called out excitedly, "Look, look, bear!"

I whirled, and there out of the deep dusk, not 50 yards away, came a charging big brownie. He was whipping through the heavy alders as if they were nothing but grass.

I jerked my rifle off the packboard, pointed it, and threw a shot his way; I couldn't see the sights in the dark. Fire streaked from the muzzle and the report echoed loudly in the little canyon. The bear stopped and stood on its hind feet, growling, I slammed another cartridge in, pointed against black, and fired again. This time the bear bawled loudly, stuck his big head between his hind legs and rolled over two or three times and disappeared into the heavy brush.

We couldn't see him then, though he was a scant 30 yards away, bawling loudly and thrashing about in the brush. I fired twice more into the thicket where he had rolled, and yelled at the hunters to run backwards, with rifles ready. We had crossed a small meadow a short way back and I felt we'd have a better chance to fight him there.

As soon as the hunters had gone a short distance I followed, also running backwards, reloading at the same time. I doubt if I could do that on level ground in the daylight under ordinary circumstances.

We gathered in the center of the meadow and tensely listened to the awesome noises of the angry and wounded brownie. Presently he recovered a little and continued his charge to the trail. When he reached the point about where we had stood when we first saw him, he turned sharply and crashed through the alders back up the little side creek. He didn't run around the brush—he ran *over* it. And he groaned loudly all the while.

We arrived back at camp at 5 a.m. . . . .

That bear probably didn't realize we were humans when he charged. Those five moose had preceded us only a short distance, and all he could see was our heads sticking out of the brush as we walked. He had come down a side draw so he hadn't winded us. Of course, he could easily have slapped one or two of us down before he learned his mistake.

The next day we tried to locate him. We found a little blood and plenty of tracks, but no bear. From his tracks I estimated that he was a 9-footer (that is, his hide would have squared about 9 feet).

Track size, I have found, with some exceptions, is a good indication of hide size of an adult brown or grizzly bear; for every inch of pad on the hind foot, not including toes, they pack about a foot of skin.

Until you have actually seen the size of a good brown bear's feet it's difficult to imagine their size. Hunters seeing brownie tracks for the first time—get goggle eyed, their mouths drop open, and they look around nervously when it dawns on them that the critter that made those tracks is running around loose. I know how I felt the first time I saw a brown bear track. I also remember one brownie whose huge feet I looked at longingly.

155

A hunter and I had stalked the bear for some distance. We finally topped a hill and there he was at about 50 yards, flat on his back in a snowdrift, sound asleep. Both of his hind feet were in the air. We were slightly above those big paws, and when I saw them I suddenly had a crazy desire to give him a hotfoot.

Now I like dogs, goldfish and kids, and I don't think I'm any more sadistically inclined than the next guy; but I wanted to skid a bullet across one of that sleeping bear's feet so badly I could hardly keep from it. He was at just the right level. But my hunter had no sense of humor, I guess. He insisted on shooting to kill. I'll bet that brownie would have stomped his foot in the snow if I'd had my way.

In my experience the bears that don't follow true on the foot-hide-size relationship are those on Montague and Hinchinbrook Islands, in Prince William Sound. The bears there are small, but their feet aren't. They walk on mud flats a lot, so maybe they need those near-snowshoe-sized feet.

I have found that areas that produce big grizzlies, as distinguished from brownies, are generally good salmon country.

I try to keep a bear's habits in mind when I hunt him.

When on the move bears like to follow valleys, where, if they can find it, they feed on wild peavine along rivers and on big gravel bars. They also dig and eat willow roots, which may be as big around as a man's thumb and several feet long. During berry season they are likely to be in berry patches. But the best place to look for bears is where there are fish; they will travel miles to concentrate on a good salmon stream.

Bears have poor eyesight, but they have awfully good noses and ears. I have found that they will often move out of an area in a hurry if they smell humans. For that reason when I hunt them I keep high, move little, and use glasses a lot. It doesn't pay to run all over the country and scatter your scent—and especially it doesn't pay to get right down where you expect to find a bear, as along a good salmon stream.

I have said that bears can be hard to kill. I'll never forget the 11-foot brownie one of my hunters shot a few years back. We saw the animal shortly after leaving camp—it was walking towards us. We sat down and watched as it fed to within about 75 yards of us, hit the trail, and started walking.

As the big hump-shouldered beast started to shamble off the hunter shot and knocked it sprawling. Then it lay still. I thought to myself it was an unusual shot—one-shot kills aren't common with brownies. We wanted to take pictures before we started skinning, so we sat down to await the arrival of Warren (Tillie) Tilman, another guide who was along on the trip, and his hunter, who had the cameras. They were in a boat on a lake nearby where they had seen us shoot.

After five minutes or so one front foot of the bear started to twitch.

"Reflex action," I thought to myself.

Then the other front leg started to move a bit—and the hind legs started to twitch; next they started to move strongly.

"That's funny," I remarked to the hunter. "I thought he was dead." The bear had been lying there for perhaps 10 minutes.

Next the bear rolled over and kicked all four legs—hard. He got to his feet, only to fall down again promptly. We were still so surprised that the hunter didn't think to shoot. A moment later the bear got up and walked into a little patch of brush. Still we didn't shoot.

We got on a little knoll where we could see. After a bit the bear came out of the brush and started off cross-country—and he was walking as fast as a man could move. My hunter shot again, breaking the animal's back. We moved closer to finish it off, and by then Tillie and the other hunter had arrived with the cameras. In the party was a youngster who was carrying a .270. He wanted to shoot a bear, so my hunter suggested that he finish that one.

The boy nervously approached the animal, with all of us right behind, backing him up. The bear was on his front feet, hind legs dragging. He fired a shot into the animal's neck. It didn't even knock the bear over. A second shot had the same result. Finally the third shot broke the bear's neck. But every one of those three 130-grain .270 bullets, fired from close range, stopped in the bear's neck. The first shot my hunter fired had struck the small of the back, paralyzing and knocking the bear senseless.

One brown bear a hunter and I stalked had me completely puzzled over its peculiar actions.

It was a long way off when we first saw it feeding on salmon. As we followed up the stream toward him an old sow with two cubs charged out onto the opposite bank, snarling. She was only about 40 feet from us, but between us was a six-foot-deep hole in the creek. The cubs were curious, and they came out to look too. She batted them, and then ran back into the thick alders with them, where she stayed for perhaps half a minute. Then she came back to the edge of the bank, still snarling. She ran back and forth from the brush to the creek bank about six times before giving up. I was sure relieved that we didn't have to shoot her. Even as we walked on, watching over our shoulders, she continued to blow and snort at us.

Finally we could see the bear we were after, and it was then I became puzzled. He was fishing, but he operated differently from any bear I have ever seen. Bears normally grab salmon with their teeth, even when the fish is fairly deep in the water. This one was trying to put his foot on a fish. Another peculiar thing about him— when he turned sideways to us now and again I thought I could see his tongue hanging out.

When he did manage to catch a fish with his feet he ate it by holding his head real high and shaking and chewing—like a seagull eating a herring.

"That bear must be crazy," I told the hunter.

As soon as we had stalked near enough, the hunter shot his .375 Magnum when the bear came out on the bank. Water sprayed in all directions when that big fast bullet hit wet hide, and the brownie was knocked flat. He struggled, rolled and fell back into the creek and got down into a bunch of drift-wood in an eddy hole.

The water there was five or six feet deep, and I yelled, "Don't shoot him there," thinking about the difficulties of trying to get a dead bear out of deep water. Two of us couldn't drag him very far into the shallows, either.

The bear tried to climb back up the steep bank, but he had a broken front leg and couldn't make it. I decided to lure him out on the other side—I was afraid he'd drown where he was.

"Wait there," I told the hunter. "I'll run over and try to get him to charge me. If he does he'll get out on that gravel bar where you can shoot him."

The hunter looked dubious when I said that. As I left I kidded, "And don't let him chase me too long."

Before I got into position to lure the bear out he gave up trying to climb the steep bank and splashed across the stream to where we wanted him. I got out of the line of fire and the hunter finished the job.

When we looked him over we learned the reason for his peculiar fishing and eating behavior. He had been shot in the jaw some time previously and the tip of his lower jaw had been completely cut off just behind the tusks. Both tusks and all the lower incisors were grown to his lower lip, the teeth pointing almost straight ahead. The lower jaws had grown together, but out of line, and all of his molars had worn to almost a razor edge. He must have been shot in the late fall, and the jaw healed while he was hibernating. I don't see how he could have survived otherwise.

Interestingly, another hunter I had out on a later trip killed a brown bear that had also previously been shot in the lower jaw. The bullet has struck about center and had cut out one tusk and several other teeth. This bear too was in good condition.

They're a tough animal.

I've said that it's possible to get hurt while hunting bears. To my knowledge, however, no *guided* hunter has ever been mauled or killed by a bear in the Territory. It seems that someone is either killed or badly mauled every year in Alaska, usually by a brown or grizzly bear. One of the closest escapes that I know of personally happened a few years ago not far from my place at Summit Lake, on the Richardson Highway, where it winds across Isabella Pass in the Alaska Range.

It happened in October. Snow was falling, and the lone hunter trailed the grizzly over several hills, above timberline. After a mile or so the tracks went into a little draw which was thickly grown with head-high willows.

Instead of going around the brush patch and getting above, the hunter followed the tracks. Most of the snow was on top of the willows, and he was working alone, parting the brush with his hands, when he ran out of bear tracks—at the bear.

The animal was scarcely 12 feet away when it reared up and leaped. The hunter tried to shoot his .351 auto, but it didn't fire. The first swipe the bear made caught his binoculars, which were hanging from his neck, and flung them cross-country. The great claws left raking gashes on his chest.

Before he knew it the grizzly had him down, and grabbed the top of his head in its mouth. The bear was rather small, and couldn't get purchase on his head. But it did cut his scalp to ribbons, and also hung a tusk in one eye socket, which caused a clot and the eventual loss of the eye. The bear also chewed one ear badly, and one arm was bitten deeply from wrist to shoulder.

While the animal mauled and scuffled him about the hunter clung to his rifle, trying desperately to clear the action. Finally he doubled up and got his feet in the bear's belly and gave it a kick. As he did, the great teeth closed on a foot and it started to drag him.

By then the rifle was in working order, so he fired point-blank into the bear's chest, killing it almost instantly. Luckily he was near the highway, and managed to totter to it, stop a truck, and get a ride some 60 miles or so to a doctor.

A few days later I went over to look at the spot where the fight had occurred. It looked as if two bull moose had battled there. Bark was peeled from willows, and a lot of them had been uprooted. Moss was torn up, and blood and hair was well scattered over the site. Some of the area looked as if the man and bear had been over them two or three times. The torn-up area was about 20 feet square.

The bear had had a cub, which, when I was there, had been eating on the sow's carcass. I couldn't find the cub or I'd have shot it— it was less than a year old and probably didn't survive the winter.

From incidents I have recounted, it might sound as if all grizzly and brown bears are hell-roaring to charge, given even the sight of a man. Actually this is far from true; perhaps 95 percent of these bears will run, even when wounded. The 5 percent that don't are those that stand out most vividly in one's memory. That 5 percent is part of the reason that big bear hunting is such grand sport.

I've had quite a number of bears come at me, but none of them have quite made it. One might have if it hadn't been for a big deadfall. I was hunting with Doctor Gillespie, who was a Fairbanks, Alaska, physician at the time. We found where a nice grizzly had been fishing near Paxson Lake on the Richardson Highway, and trailed it up the hill where it had headed for a sleep. There was fresh snow on the ground and the going was miserable. We got up the hill and found where the bear had moved into a thick brush patch.

"We're about ready to rouse that bear, Doc," I warned. Doc had been kicking about the deep snow. He thought I was just trying to encourage him and didn't take my warning seriously.

Suddenly the bear got up out of the willows about 25 feet away, snorted, and crashed through the brush up the hill. About 80 yards from us was a little opening that I hoped he would cross. Before long I saw he was going to miss it, so I told Doc, "Get ready, I'm going to try to jump him into that opening."

We couldn't see the bear, but we could follow him by the snow he knocked off the willows. From the tracks we had followed we knew he was a big one. As he got opposite the opening I drove a shot into the brush next to him. At that the bear leaped into the clear.

He had no sooner landed from his startled jump when Doc shot him right in the fanny—a flesh wound. That bear whirled and headed right for us on a dead run. There was no doubt as to his intent. A bear can gallop along an open ground at 30 to 35 miles an hour—I've clocked them in my car several times.

One jump and that big grizzly was in the brush, out of sight. But we could hear him, and we could see the snow flying from the branches as he crashed toward us. It was impossible to judge where he was—he could have been four or ten feet under the tops of the willows. And we were right in the brush ourselves, downhill from him.

I jumped on a small, half-rotten stump, praying it would hold me, and tried to find the bear with the sights. In moments he was frighteningly close, and I still hadn't managed a shot. Suddenly about 40 feet away, a big bear head loomed in my sights. I didn't squeeze that shot—I almost jerked the trigger off. As I fired the head went out of sight and we could no longer hear the bear. It was an awfully loud silence.

We stood for a few moments listening—and shaking—and then went around and up on a knoll. Doc covered me while I went down to see what had happened. I found the bear, dead, by an old windfall over which he had started to leap when I had seen and shot him.

That bear's hide stretched 8 feet 8 inches, big for an Interior Alaska grizzly.

I've always felt pretty safe in bear country as long as I had a rifle. Though a bear may be hard to kill, and a charging bear seems especially so, it's not hard to cripple and slow one down. A shot in the head or anywhere up and down the back is best when one charges—and a good shot in the hump is probably the surest. But sometimes you have to take whatever you can get in the way of a shot.

When you don't have a rifle and a grizzly faces up to you, it's a pretty helpless feeling. The bear is pretty much boss.

Three of us had returned to pick up a ram that we had killed the previous day; we had shot two, had packed one in and left the other.

It was a long hard trip from camp. We had seen no bear sign so we left our rifles.

When we got to the rim, about 50 feet above the sheep, and looked down we were surprised to see a small grizzly lying on it.

We yelled but it simply stood on its hind feet and snarled back.

We walked back up the hill and gathered arms full of rocks and piled them on the rim, then started heaving them at the bear. He was only about 75 feet distant, and some 50 feet below us.

Instead of running away, he started toward us. As he came up the cliff we poured it on him—rocks really bounced from his hide. But he kept coming. By the time he reached the top we had vacated and high-tailed it another 50 yards up the hill. He stopped on the rim, luckily, stood up, and snarled.

Art Smith, one of my companions, was the pilot who had flown us in, so he went back to camp, rolled my rifle in my sleeping bag, then flew over us and dumped it out. But he neglected to splint the rifle, the sleeping bag hit lengthways and the stock broke off at the trigger guard.

We used some willow splints and rope to lash a stock to it and then headed back to settle with the bear. Because he had run us off once he thought he'd do it again, so he started for us. My first shot rolled him for a good 100 yards, where he stopped at the edge of a cliff. The second shot dumped him over the cliff. We were amazed to see eight big rams spurt out from where he had dropped —he must have landed right amidst them.

Anyway we got our sheep—or what was left of it, plus a bear hide. The bear was small, but then it didn't have to be very big.

We were lucky, for the reluctance of hunters to carry seven or eight pounds of rifle when packing meat is the cause of many grizzly attacks. Scarcely a year goes by but what some hunter gets into real trouble that way in the Territory. Once a bear finds meat, if he's hungry, he's likely to be willing to fight to keep it.

John Pettijohn, who at the time was an assistant guide for me on a bear hunt on the Alaska Peninsula, still talks of a little misunderstanding he had with a bear over meat. We were camped near the beach, close to a huge acre-sized jackstraw pile of driftwood. The hunter we were guiding killed a small moose for meat, and we put it in a pup tent in camp.

One evening, after hunting with us all day, Pettijohn hurried back to camp, ahead of us, to get the grub ready. The hunter and I ambled along behind. Shortly we heard nine shots, fired almost as from an automatic. There was no noticeable pause between any of the shots. I remarked to the hunter that there must be another party in there. Certainly no one man could fire a bolt rifle that fast.

When we arrived at camp Pettijohn hadn't made any progress toward supper. I guess he had bad nerves. Anyway he was standing there looking at a very dead brownie that had torn out the end of the pup tent and gotten at the moose meat. It had charged him when he arrived in camp. He went into great detail, telling us how it had rushed toward him, snarling. As he talked I examined the bear—he'd hit it every shot and it looked like a sieve.

In Alaska, except for emergencies, it is illegal for a guide or an assistant guide on a hunt to shoot any game. This obviously had been an emergency, but I decided to have a little fun. Assuming a severe expression, I looked up from the shot-up bear, stared the still-shaking Pettijohn in the eye and bawled him out, good.

"You know the law just as well as I do," I told him. "You weren't supposed to do any shooting on this trip."

His jaw dropped and he eyed me as if I were crazy. I went on.

"You knew we were only a few hundred yards behind you. Why, you could have outrun that bear in the drift pile here until we got back. That way the hunter could have done the shooting."

If there had been an airplane handy I'm sure that Pettijohn would have quit me right there. That's one bear *he'll* never forget.

THE DAY THE BEARS COME OUT

Peter Barrett was for many years the hunting and fishing editor of True. *Its publisher was Roger Fawcett, who loved to hunt and fish all over the world. So it was natural that Peter and Roger hit it off right from the start. Roger traveled all over the world in search of big game and it was made to order for Pete, who is excellent with a rifle and shotgun and an avid fisherman. In addition he is a fine writer and still at it today as senior editor of* Field & Stream. *Pete has killed the big five of Africa and many another exotic big-game species all over the world, but it is doubtful if he had any more fun writing about his other hunts than he did about this one—hunting with Roger for brown bears in Alaska.*

The Day the Bears Come Out

Peter Barrett

A hunt for brown bears! Something I'd dreamed about since I was a boy, never quite believing it would happen but dreaming about it just the same. And now I was in Alaska with two hunting friends —Roger and Gordon Fawcett—with the old dream about to come true. But not in the way I'd planned. Or hoped. In no single instance did this hunt turn out as I'd imagined so many times.

To begin with, we were fishing.

Back in Anchorage, our guide and outfitter had given us some bad news. "Spring's late and it's too cold for the bears to come out," Tommy Thompson told us. "Why don't you rent some fishing tackle and I'll fly you down to a camp I have at the outlet to Lake Iliamna. While you're fishing, I'll fly down the peninsula and double-check on the bears."

So here we were on the Kvichak River. The two Super Cubs sat on a gravel bar near the camp. Across the river on a high bluff were the few Eskimo houses of the tiny settlement called Igiugig. Snow lay in two-foot drifts against the front of the camp and a shelf of snow-covered ice extended for yards from both river banks. The thermometer stood at 20°.

Presently Tommy took off and disappeared to the west. We shivering fishermen climbed into a long wooden work boat with Lynn Stephan, our other pilot and guide. We headed downriver to a certain long pool where we'd spotted some trout from the air on the way in to camp.

"Spring!" said Roger, settling the fur-trimmed hood of his parka snugly around his face. A stiff breeze laced down the river.

Talk about bitter-cold fishing! The water was 36°. I crept out on the shelf ice until it broke under my weight, then sloshed through ice cakes of my own making into clear water. Though I'd protected my legs with heavy wool pants, down underwear and several pairs of wool socks under my rubber boots, the river's chill bit through so strongly in 20 minutes I had to get out and run up and down the bank where a moose had left a trail in the snow.

Meanwhile a stiff breeze whipped down the river unceasingly. The guides froze solid every three casts, forming weird flowerlike icicles at the rod tip and the first few guides. I became quite adept at snapping the ice free without removing my gloves.

I did not believe that trout would feed when the water was only 36° and was fishing mostly for something to do. Suddenly Lynn yelled from 200 yards upstream and I saw a fish splash. He was using spinning tackle. Presently he slid a still-lively fish upon the shelf ice.

Then Gordie yelled. And along about that time I found myself yelling. A rainbow had grabbed my fly during a slow, deep drift and now actually leaped clear.

Considering that the water was only four degrees above freezing, the trout were magnificent. These rainbows ran from 2½ to 5 or 6 pounds and each was good for a couple of strong runs and sometimes a low jump or two. We didn't murder them—we each caught one apiece that afternoon—but as a prelude to spring it was a great experience.

That evening, over a dinner of steaks from a moose that Lynn had shot the previous fall, Tommy filled us in on our bear prospects.

"Saw only two dens," he said. "Both abandoned, but that's not enough activity to warrant going way down to Port Heiden and putting up a tent camp. We need a few mild days first."

"How can you tell a den from the air?" Gordie asked.

"Easy. The bear breaks out through the snow and there are his tracks. If he gets discouraged and goes back in, you can tell that too. Both the dens I saw were in high country. The bears came out and headed straight for the coast, where it's warmer."

"What do they do on the coast?" I asked. I'd heard that brown bears eat fresh green grass in early spring but it seemed too cold for any greenery yet.

"They beachcomb," Tommy explained. "A bear might find a dead seal or fish. You see their tracks following a beach for miles."

The gas lanterns hissed and the wood stove popped. This had been a homesteader's cabin. He'd trapped some and traded some. When he married two bedrooms were added, and maybe that was when the wallpaper got on the walls and the linoleum on the floor. The place was snug, a good spot for waiting out a break in the weather.

But it was slow in coming. And so were the trout. I finally decided that what they wanted was a dark fly fished deep and proceeded to make one from odds and ends. I tore apart a bright streamer I'd bought in Anchorage for the hook and weighted the body with one of those wrap-around lead strips normally used to weight a leader. The body itself I made by cutting a strip of dark-gray wool cloth from the inseam of the seat of my pants—the kind of heavy wool pants that Mr. L. L. Bean wouldn't be caught without on a cold day in the woods. A bit of dark hair from the trim of an old mouse-chewed parka I found in the tool shed topped it off.

They laughed when I cast this thing into that long pool of the Kvichak. But it caught fish consistently and we named it Pete's Pants.

Days slid past. Gordon and Tommy flew 250 miles down the Peninsula to Port Heiden on the Bering Sea side in the hope of making a quickie bear hunt but ran into bad weather.

A couple of days later the bear hunters returned.

"If that bear had only been bigger!" Gordie said as he struggled out of his warm clothes in the cabin. "Walking right out in the open on a beach, just like Tommy said! But it was a small sow."

"Could you have shot it?" Roger asked.

"Easily. What a sight though! She was quite light colored."

"The hide was perfect," Tommy remarked. "Often as not a bear fresh from its den won't have a blemish on it and the hair will be at its thickest."

"What happened then?" Roger asked.

"We watched the bear for a while, then had to go back to Port Heiden because a storm was coming up," Gordie said. "Well, I guess I'll head for home tomorrow—my time is up."

And we couldn't talk him out of it. Weeks earlier we'd all had a successful polar bear hunt with Tommy far to the north. The time remaining for all of us was short.

Next morning Gordon flew over to King Salmon with Tommy to catch an airliner to Anchorage. There isn't a highway on the entire Alaska Peninsula, incidentally—you travel by boat or air. Sometimes you'll find a small network of roads near an airport, especially if the military has an installation nearby. But they are roads for trucking supplies and don't go far.

We had our last day on the river. The air temperature broke into the 30s and it almost felt hot. But the big ice cakes still sailed down the river implacably, some of them 20 feet across, and the ice shelves still extended from the banks. Only now they were dripping. Big pools of water gathered upon the frozen ground at the cabin.

I cast a thousand times and more on the long pool, keeping an eye on the brushy far bank for a bear, without ever getting a touch. Then I made my last cast. Nothing. I decided on a second last, final cast. Nothing. Well, what was the hurry? I made an absolutely, this-is-really-the-end last cast.

When no fish struck there was only one thing to do—make one more irrevocably last cast and guarantee to wind in when the line straightened.

The line straightened. With a sigh I grasped the reel handle and began to wind. Instantly I felt a tug. Then a beautiful rainbow burst from the river and brought me to life.

"Keep him for supper!" Lynn Stephan shouted.

I was glad to. Furthermore, I got smart and quit right then. On the way back to camp I laid the trout out on the boat's planking— he was a 24-incher, deep-bodied with silvery sides yielding suddenly to a dark-green back—and thought what a wonderful river this would be in a couple of weeks. Rainbows two and three times as heavy as this one, according to Tommy. Plenty of grayling. And only a few hundred yards from the cabin door lay Lake Iliamna with a broad beach ideal for casting to the lakers and rainbows that would congregate there at the outlet.

But the object of this trip was brown bears. Next morning, it still being "warm," we took off for Port Heiden . . . and landed there in a snowstorm. Next day was cold and mean, though it didn't snow. Here we were, only about 60 miles from our destination and it was still long-underwear weather. A 500-foot overcast blanked out nearby mountains, making further air travel impossible.

That night we laid into more of Lynn's delicious moose meat. We were staying at the transient quarters in the Reeve Aleutian Airlines building and thanks to Ed Harris, the station manager, had access to the latest weather information. It sounded as promising as it ever does in Alaska for the following morning.

"No matter how cold it is," Roger suggested, "if we have flying weather tomorrow let's get out of here and set up our hunting camp. We only have three-and-a-half days left."

By noon the next day we'd been transported to a new world. The boys had flown the tents and gear in first with Karl Hein, who had cooked so ably for us at Igiugig. Now as we flew in through the snow-covered peaks, I thought suddenly that some of this country was as rugged as the Alps. Then the two Super Cubs flashed through a pass and there below us was a broad flat valley, snow free. The tents were a pair of white dots in the willows at the edge of a cinder flat.

It seemed almost warm as we stepped from the planes into the sunshine. Karl had set up a spotting scope on a tripod.

"Haven't seen a bear track in the snow yet," he said in greeting, "but the stew's ready."

Not long afterward we were climbing through willows up a long slope to gain a vantage point from which to scan this big country. A moose ran out of the brush ahead of us, its mane abristle.

Presently we topped out and scattered to find comfortable spots for a session with binoculars. Two creeks snaked through the willows below and emptied into the Pacific at Kujulik Bay. We were about a third of the way down the Alaska Peninsula, beyond Kodiak Island, in the Aleutian Range.

"Most of this area has been closed tight for two years," Tommy said. "How do you like that herd of caribou down there?"

Eight specks of grayish white suddenly became caribou feeding on a flat when I stared through my binocular.

We spent a lazy afternoon looking and changing positions on the mountainside without glimpsing a bear.

"What will a bear be doing when we finally see one?" Roger asked that night in the big cook tent.

"Just walking along, probably," said Tommy. "This early, when the country is all shades of brown, a bear standing still is practically impossible to see, unless he's on a flat or a beach."

"When we came in for supper, the temperature was 19°," I said. "And it'll probably get colder in the night. What'll that do to the bears?"

"Well, this *is* pretty cold. But it was thawing all afternoon in the sun and I'll just bet you—though we didn't see him—that a good-sized bear was prowling around in this area. For some reason, the big boars usually come out first and that's what we're after."

"Amen," said Roger. "A big one."

We drank a toast to big bears and went to bed . . .

Some ptarmigan in the willows nearby woke us next morning with their whistling and calling and when we got dressed and outside it was plain to see why the birds were happy—a bright sun shone from a cloudless sky and set the snowy peaks to glittering.

Every puddle around camp was frozen tight and I had to use an ax to chop through to some wash water. But the brilliant sun soon took the bite out of the air and warmed the tents.

We separated by agreement after breakfast, Roger and Lynn and Karl heading for the snowy slopes at the head of the valley, Tommy and I going across the big flat to the beach.

I saw huge tracks where a bear had punched through soft moss to leave a series of staggered holes somehow reminiscent of an old battleground.

"I call these traditional tracks," Tommy remarked. "All bears walking this trail in this spot will step in those tracks, just like a kid stepping on cracks in a sidewalk. It's quite a sight to watch."

We came at last to the beach and scanned it anxiously. It was trackless as far as we could see. Offshore a pair of sea otters played and a great bunch of black brant paddled away from us, keeping at a distance of about 100 yards as we went down the beach.

Tommy spotted a bleaching moose skull with antlers attached and we went over to look at it.

"Bet it'll go over 60 inches," I said.

"Easy," said Tommy. The tape from my pack proved us shrewd judges of moose spread.

But we didn't seem to be such hot bear hunters that day. Not a track was found. Not a bear glimpsed. Not a fresh pile of dung.

"They've got to be out," said Tommy as we headed at last for camp and supper. "If Roger and the boys didn't connect, then a bear hasn't crossed this valley yet and we'll have to hunt the next one over tomorrow."

"Be quite a hike," I said.

"Shucks, we'll fly down to the beach and walk in."

Eventually we made it back to camp and when the cross-questioning had died down it was plain that Roger was bearless. They'd seen only a moose and a red fox.

It was a gloomy camp that night. Roger's back was bothering him but that wasn't going to keep him from hunting, for tomorrow was our last whole day; we'd have to pack up and get out by midmorning the following day.

"I can't see my breath in this tent," Roger remarked as we climbed into our sleeping bags half dressed. "Must be damned cold again."

"It's fifteen," I said. "But it's a starry night so let's hope we get another mild day. . . ."

171

The excitement began when the planes left our valley after breakfast and swung left over unexplored beach. This next valley we were about to hunt was separated from ours by a mountain ridge deep in snow but was easily accessible from the beach.

We'd hardly hit new beach when Lynn shouted over the roar of the engine, "Look at that fresh track!"

My heart jumped. In places the bear had walked only a yard from the receding water.

"Good big track," Lynn yelled as he swung out over the ocean to come in for a landing.

Just before we touched down I happened to see a bear running through a long, narrow stand of willows that fringed the land above the beach. The bear was only about 100 yards away but going fast. We piled out of both planes almost simultaneously and began to run up the beach hoping for a clear view of the animal.

The soft sand made it slow going.

"A good bear?" I gasped at Tommy.

"Hell, yes! Good boar trophy."

I had only glimpsed the bear that once. If it still held the same direction, it was running parallel to the beach toward a small but steep hill that was clear of brush at the top. The four of us panted and struggled through the sand, then clawed our way up a 15-foot cliff of the miserable stuff.

Just as we topped out, breathless, the bear hit the skyline of the hill about 200 yards away. For a long moment the bear looked back in our direction, then ambled over the crest.

"I think he was just spooked by the planes," Tommy remarked. "I doubt he knew we were after him or that he winded us. So he ought to slow down in about half a mile and if we cut back over that mountain, maybe we'll come out above him before he disappears."

For a long time after that no one spoke because we were climbing steadily in the sort of daydream that befalls hunters wherein your imagination leaps ahead to the moment—always better as you dream it up—when you see the quarry and drop it with a single well placed shot.

Finally we rounded some screening brush and could see down the mountainside and into an arm of the valley we'd intended hunting.

And there were two bears! One was a dark brown, the other more cinnamon colored with a lightish streak down the back. Even at several hundred yards their coats looked long and the ripples caught the bright sunlight almost like wind on summer wheat.

"I believe they're both boars!" Tommy said. He'd been studying them through his binoculars. "Now, if they both stop in the same area . . ."

Presently one of the bears crossed a snow patch and sat down in it.

"He wants to cool off," Lynn remarked. "Maybe he'll stay."

But the bear was soon moving.

"Which one do you want?" I said to Roger.

"I'd be happy with either."

After a time both animals went over a low hill perhaps a quarter of a mile apart. This hill gave onto the valley floor and a big willow patch through which a creek twisted.

"The wind is perfect for a stalk up the valley," Tommy said. "With a bit of luck, we'll have a bear killed by lunchtime."

But a few hours later we gave up the search and walked out to the planes to return to camp for lunch. We never glimpsed them again and there was no way to track them.

"I'm convinced those bears are right around where we were looking for them," Tommy said at lunch. "Now, if that wind keeps blowing down the valley, we could go in over the high mountain and come out farther up the valley. This would put the bears downwind of us and we might just run one out into the open long enough for a shot."

That's why I found myself climbing again a little later. Roger's back was bothering him to such an extent he decided to try a short hunt in the valley of our camp—for that was the direction the bears had taken.

Now, in late afternoon, we came down off the high mountain under a cloud-streaked sky. The wind still held in our favor, however, and we set about searching the slopes, slowly working down the valley toward where our hunt had ended in the morning.

No bear.

Two hours later. No bear.

"If we keep working toward the beach, something's got to give if they're still here," Tommy said. "Let me go on ahead and circle back—maybe I can drive one past you on this big slope. A spooked bear will probably run upwind and there you'll be."

Another hour passed. We'd made no plan for doing anything further since Tommy either expected to hear me shoot, or I would see him at the end of his drive.

Suddenly I heard a single shot from around the bend.

In the half hour before I heard Tommy crashing through the brush I imagined a thousand things and thought I saw the bear twice, but didn't.

"What happened?"

"I finally decided to fire a shot to see if I could smoke one of them out," Tommy said. "Damn if one of them wasn't down the slope from me. I could have hit him with a rock when he showed. The bear went straight downhill into the big willow patch."

We were hurrying around the mountain as he talked. It was 6 o'clock but at this latitude, even though it was late April, we'd have light enough to shoot by until nearly 8.

At last we came to where Tommy had stood when he shot.

"The bear went in right there," he said, pointing to a spot on the valley floor a quarter of a mile away.

We could see nothing with binoculars. It was decided that I would go downwind of where the bear was last seen and station myself on a little ridge overlooking the willow jungle. Tommy would wait until he saw me in place, then attempt to drive the bear toward me with his scent. He was going to crisscross the willows, working toward where he thought the bear was.

Half an hour later I climbed out on the ridge and waved my cap. Tommy disappeared. I put a cartridge into the chamber of my Winchester Model 70 .375, a rifle that I'd been lucky with in the past. I had a fine view of the beach side of the willow jungle edge, which was bordered by an open field of tall, dead grass. From my elevation I could see fairly well into the willows too, and make out a stretch of the creek that came snaking out of them.

I stood there getting more and more excited. I tried to figure where the bear might appear and estimated the edge of the willows was just about 225 yards away. I was zeroed for 200.

A shot rolled and echoed in the valley.

Then all of a sudden I saw the bear, running broadside to me in the willows but crossing away from me. When he came to a little clearing I led for a shoulder hit and pulled the trigger.

The bear kept right on going as if nothing happened. A moment later he passed through some thin brush and I shot for the shoulder again.

Then the bear disappeared and I thought he was down. Instead, he was only swimming the creek. But now he turned and headed straight for me, through the willows.

He was on a bear trail that was going to take him right out of the willows and into the field!

I thought, *If he follows the trail, he'll be head on and the shot will ruin the skull.* As every bear hunter knows, only the width and length of his trophy's skull is used to determine its "score" and standing in the all-time records.

The bear kept coming. I could hear him complaining now. He was head on in the willows and still coming. I put the rifle up hurriedly and swung the scope to cover the edge of the field.

On he came, only now he was in the scope. The head looked as big as the front end of a bus and I thought, *The hell with the skull if he comes.*

The bear reached the opening and trying to hold the crosshairs steady a few inches above the eyes, I shot. The bear fell flat!

Man! I threw my cap into the air. I shouted at Tommy, whom I couldn't see. Meanwhile the bear didn't move an inch, so far as I could tell and I started down the hill.

We met near the bear, watched it, then walked over. The bullet had struck a little above the right eye and killed instantly.

After the back pounding and examination of the bear, I asked Tommy about his shot.

"Was that a scare shot?"

"Yes. But not the kind you think. I'd just crossed the creek on the bear's trail when he suddenly reared up about 50 feet from me."

"I'll bet that was a sight."

"It sure was. He just stood there and blew at me a couple of times. I decided to throw a shot over his head real quick. Well, the bullet hit a dead branch which fell on the bear. He turned and beat it, then you started shooting."

It was now 7 p.m. We started the skinning. It was the cinnamon bear, about average sized, according to Tommy. The pelt was flawless and thick and I was mighty happy. One shot—probably the first —hit the lungs just behind the shoulder. The other hit the shoulder but made a tiny wound such as a .22 might. Apparently the bullet had blown up on brush and only a fragment reached the bear. The skull was a ruin; I left it right there.

At 8:30 we finished, washed and drank in the creek, and tied the hide to Tommy's packboard. Halfway to the beach, I relieved Tommy of the load which was over 100 pounds.

"This is the hardest part of bear hunting," I remarked.

"All bears should be shot right in camp, but they never are."

When I staggered to the plane finally it was full dark and snowing lightly. We loaded up and took off. Tommy flew down the beach toward our valley. Presently we came to the little island off the camp beach . . . and a raging snowstorm. . The valley's outlines were completely obliterated.

Muttering, Tommy turned back and soon landed on the beach we'd recently left. He had a pup tent aboard, one mummy sleeping bag, some dried apricots and candy.

So we siwashed it on the beach, out of the wind's reach in the tiny tent. A driftwood fire flew sparks out to sea and threw a little warmth into the tent.

The wind roared all night as we half slept and shivered in the tiny tent. By 4 a.m. it was light enough to see and we tried it again. A beautiful day was dawning as we landed on the cinder flat and taxied up near the tents. We told our stories, took a jolt of Scotch and crawled into our sacks.

Roger hadn't seen a bear but was mighty pleased my luck had changed. I fell into a dream-filled sleep hoping that by some miracle he'd get a trophy before we had to break camp at noon . . .

At breakfast we had a sober discussion of Roger's prospects. The boys had combed our camp valley again yesterday afternoon and found nothing encouraging. Tommy didn't feel there was time for a hunt where I'd got my bear if we still intended to make our airline connection at Port Heiden, which we did.

"Guess I'm done then," Roger said.

"Not exactly," said Tommy. "If we should happen to see a good big bear from the planes en route to Port Heiden—and there's a spot where we can land nearby—there is nothing improper about our going after that bear."

"Is there a chance we might?"

"Fair chance. But can you run with your back the way it is?"

"My back will just have to make out somehow."

And so we broke camp quickly, leaving Karl Hein with the tents and gear to await a return trip. Our little planes lifted off the valley floor at full throttle and circled to gain altitude to get over the mountains.

What a view of hunting country! We passed three moose, antlerless of course and looking as big as horses.

Where could a plane land here? I wondered. It was rocky and brushy in every direction. But at 100 miles an hour we were covering a lot of ground and soon the character of the valley began to change. Here came a winding river, deep between cut banks and precipices. We were coming onto a volcanic plateau with now and then the gray of small cinder flats.

There was another moose, looking worried at the edge of a sharp dropoff. Lynn shouted something and then I saw the bear.

"I think the bear's after that moose," he shouted.

We made a wide circle, watching. The bear did seem to be crowding the moose toward the rimrocks above the river.

"How big is the bear?" I asked. I found myself completely unable to judge its size from the air.

"Not bad."

I looked for a landing spot. Why not on the flat over there? But Tommy in the lead plane flew on. The country became even more open and we suddenly saw an almost white wolf loping along and watching us over one shoulder. There were snow patches on the ground and the beaver ponds were still frozen over, but somehow there was a look of spring in the sparse willows.

A pair of ptarmigan, still a snowy white, flashed across a flat under us. And then the planes started to slow suddenly and go into a turn. Looking about wildly, I suddenly saw a bear in the middle of a flat. He must have been dead on course before Tommy turned aside.

"Big bear!" Lynn shouted excitedly. "We're going to land."

Tommy made a single circle so as to come in into the wind and dropped to the flat with us tight behind and to one side. The bear had reached the willows by now and disappeared.

We burst out of the planes and half ran into the willows. It was as flat as a table here and very difficult to see more than 100 yards in the stuff we were traveling in.

We crossed a snow patch and Lynn pointed wordlessly at a huge fresh track of the bear. Roger was running well and if his back was troubling him it didn't show. I guessed that Tommy was making a circle in the hope of intercepting the bear.

Maybe half a mile from the planes, we pulled up for a quick look around and to catch our breaths. Ahead the willows became quite thin for 200 to 300 yards. We hadn't stood there a minute before Tommy was pointing into the willows.

"There's your bear, Roger!" he whispered. "Wait him out till he hits a clear spot."

The bear looked huge. He was about 175 yards away, walking quickly through the willows and broadside to us. His back showed clear above the brush every so often.

Suddenly Roger fired and the bear went down. But a moment later the bear got up and continued, slower now. Roger belted him again with his Winchester .375. Still the bear went on. A third shot dropped the animal at the edge of a half-frozen creek.

We advanced cautiously. The bear was kicking spasmodically and when we got to about 30 yards Roger killed it with a final shot though it seemed nearly dead anyway. I glanced at my watch—11:45.

"He sure looks big now," Roger said in an awed voice as he picked up one of the huge paws.

"He *is* big," Tommy replied. "That bear ought to square better than ten feet."

We were standing around just grinning and looking at the bear.

"For a guy with a sore back, you can run pretty good," I remarked.

"You know, I forgot all about my back the moment I saw that bear."

Roger had aimed for the spine with his first shot and just missed it. Either of the two lung hits that followed would have killed the bear soon.

With three of us skinning, we had the hide off in just under an hour and a half. It squared out at about 10½ feet without any hauling on the pelt and Roger was delighted. We lashed the skin to a packboard and Lynn went staggering toward the planes with it.

It had become cloudy. A cold wind swept the plateau.

"I still can't quite believe it," Roger said as we came to the planes parked there on the wild, deserted cinder flat. There was no room aboard for the hide and skull, so Lynn covered them with brush for retrieving later.

"Same here," I said. "For today *and* yesterday."

Tommy Thompson permitted himself a small smile. "In bear hunting," he said, "it pays to never give up."

POLAR BEAR—1966

Nobody who has ever spent any time with Fred Bear, the famous archer and hunter, would have any doubt that he could kill a polar bear with an arrow. He is a consumate hunter and one of the world's greatest bow hunters. Not only has he taken just about every species of North American big game, but he has also killed many species of African big game with arrows.

Founder of Bear Archery Company, Fred is a mild, modest man who is not given much to talking about his many great exploits. But he has done it all with a bow and until one has faced the big bears with a bow and arrow, he ain't lived, says Fred. Amen!

Polar Bear–1966

Fred Bear

Five hundred miles by air north of Fairbanks, Alaska, lies the Eskimo village of Barrow—the largest Eskimo town in the world, boasting twenty-one hundred inhabitants. It occupies a small segment of Point Barrow, which juts into the Arctic Ocean 350 miles above the Arctic Circle. The most northerly tip of Alaska.

Twice in previous years I had hunted polar bears from this point. Both times I had failed to get a bear with a bow and arrow. Bob Munger of Charlotte, Michigan, was my hunting companion again on this trip.

In this third attempt we made arrangements with the outfitter to camp out on the ice pack and hunt from motor sleds instead of planes. The location chosen was the mouth of the Coleville River, in Harrison Bay, 150 miles east of Barrow.

The American Broadcasting Company would film the hunt for their "American Sportsman" series. Cliff Robertson, cinema star, would hunt with a rifle and I would hunt with the bow. We had much to learn. . . .

The hunt began late in the season when we hoped to miss extreme cold weather.

During the winter the Arctic Ocean is almost covered with ice— usually referred to as the ice pack, and correctly so. Not the smooth sheet of ice we find on a frozen lake or river but of jumble of broken pieces, many of incredible thickness and breadth, scattered about or piled in ridges many miles long.

The action of wind, current, and tide may break a great chunk apart and drift it out into open water. Later this island of ice, that could be many square miles in size and up to five feet thick, might start back to its original source again by a change of elements. Its velocity will be slow but the tremendous energy behind its millions of tons meeting shore ice results in such awesome grinding and churning that pieces are tossed about like feathers.

Pressure ridges build up like small mountains and the whole thing is welded together by the excessive cold until the wind changes again and the sequence is repeated.

Walking around on this frozen ocean is like traversing small valleys and climbing up mountains. This frozen salt water is not brittle as frozen fresh water is. It is somewhat rubbery and milky in color. In very old pieces, however, the salt has settled to the bottom leaving the ice a clear, cold aquamarine blue. It is from this ice that we get our drinking water supply.

The ice pack is mysterious, challenging, beautiful, and moody. It permits few errors in judgment. . . .

April 13, 2 p.m.—The plane from Chicago had a group of priests who were traveling with The Most Reverend Joseph T. Ryan, Archbishop of the Diocese of Anchorage. Consequently, the plane was met by the governor and senators plus a band, so we had a royal welcome here in Fairbanks. Hope to be out on the ice sometime tomorrow.

April 15, Friday—We met the ABC crew in Fairbanks on Wednesday and got here to Point Barrow by DC-3 charter plane last evening. . . . Waiting for the bush plane now to take us to Colville River where the guide and outfitter, Bud Helmericks, lives. It will take three trips to get us all out. Burr Smidt, Cliff Robertson, and I are going on the first flight. The film crew is griping about the weather.

Barrow has changed from when I was here three years ago. Motor sleds replacing dog sleds and motorbikes replacing bicycles. Main Street is rerouted for two blocks because of abandoned vehicles half buried in the snow. Kids noses are still running. . . .

The bank, opened when we were here in sixty, has burned twice. Natural gas has replaced coal and General Telephone has dial phones in many places.

We are renewing acquaintances with local people. The hotel is full of guides and hunters. Ninety-three bears have been taken to date. Also a number of wolves. Snow sleds are spelling the doom of caribou, wolves and wolverine, as they travel faster than the animals can run.

The movie at the local theater last night was *A Thousand Clowns*. The theater is converted to a dance hall when the movie is over at midnight.

Whalers around town are gathering gear since a whale has been reported offshore.

I talked with Helmericks by radio last evening. Everything in fine shape, he says. Expect to have camp established out on the ice in about four days. Robertson has to leave on the twenty-sixth, so the first bear is his.

Later, Same Day—We are still delayed by bad weather. The small plane can't take us until it clears. The hotel lobby is crowded. Some tall stories going around. . . .

April 16, Saturday—We left the Top of the World Hotel in Barrow by a Beaver plane on skis. It was late afternoon before swirling snow, reducing the Colville River area visibility to zero, let up. Our first sight of Bud Helmericks' home reminded us of a lonely lighthouse squatting in a vast expanse of space, a never-ending sea of white. The ocean ice pack was to the north and the prairie sloped gently south to the Brooks Range of mountains fifty miles away.

The home is fitted with modern conveniences. A diesel generating plant churns night and day while a radio transmitter sputters its messages.

Burr, Cliff, Jerry Kaligeratos, and I, together with some of our gear, made the 160-mile flight in two hours. We will sleep here tonight.

April 17—Bud and his son Jim took us out to the ice camp this morning by bush plane. Two of our tents had been erected the day before but a bear had come through and ripped some canvas. One tent was partly down and both were torn. We sewed them up with a bag needle and thread. The rest of the camp will consist of more Thermos tents. Two Prairie Schooner types and two Giant Thermos Pop Tents. We will put one tent inside another for extra warmth.

April 18—Bob Munger came out from Barrow today with one thousand pounds of camera, film, and gear. The pilot set the plane down on the ice beside camp. Another load of the crew is expected later today if some engine trouble with the plane clears up.

April 19—The Beaver was not repaired so Mike Scott, sound man, and Steve Goldhor, cameraman, chartered George Thele and Joe Vanderpool who are Polar Bear guides, to bring them from Barrow in bush planes.

Our cluster of tents is about forty miles out on the ice pack. This is about the limit of what the natives call shore ice which is not expected to break up for another thirty days or so. Leads (open water) will be opening up farther out, however.

A mountain of ice, about thirty feet high, fifty feet wide, and three hundred feet long, rises immediately behind our camp. This serves two purposes—one, a windbreak, and the other an attraction for bears. Deep, hard-packed snow has drifted around the edges of this outcropping and seals, wanting to hide their breathing holes, come up underneath this snow. When it is time for young seals to be born, the mother enlarges the holes with her teeth and claws until it is big enough to allow her to emerge completely and make a den in the snow nearby, which serves as an escape in times of danger. The young seals are kept in this den until they can go into the water and learn to swim.

The polar bears are completely aware of this routine and prowl the ice packs sniffing for seals. If the camera and sound men had been here the first day when the bears came through, they would have had a great opportunity for pictures.

Another purpose this large ice pile at the campsite serves is to provide our water supply. Some of the large chunks are many years old and the salt has completely settled out of them. With a steel tent stake and hammer we can flake big pieces off and melt them down over our propane gas cookstove.

One of the eight-by-twelve Prairie Schooner tents is used for the kitchen and dining room. It is heated by the cookstove fed from a small propane gas tank. Another eight-by-twelve tent is heated by an oil burner. The two Giant Pop Tents are heated or, I should say, partly heated by catalytic heaters burning white gas. In one of these Bob and I sleep. Because there is so little space, most cameras and gear are left outside covered with a tarpaulin. Our lowest temperature to date was eighteen degrees below and the hightest eighteen degrees above.

We arrived here on the ice, which is five to seven feet thick, on Friday. Today is Tuesday the nineteenth. No hunting has been done, since our outfitter has had three other clients who will not finish until tomorrow. In the meantime, we have been shooting camp scenes and getting acclimated.

Wednesday, April 20—The label on a bottle of wine we had for dinner last night read SERVE AT ROOM TEMPERATURE. This brought on some reflection since it had to be thawed before pouring.

Yesterday was a beautiful day. It was snowing but the wind was mild. The temperature was ten degrees below at early morning and up to ten above at midday. We spent the morning shooting film and in the afternoon we had an archery contest, a card game, and hiked around on the ice pack.

This morning we shot film again. Helmericks still has a client and they are out now to get him a bear. Jim Helmericks is in camp with us, doing the cooking. He is repairing a landing strut for his plane that sits on the ice nearby.

We have soaked a burlap bag of fish in seal oil with which Jim, with his snow sled, had made a drag trail around a three-mile circle here. We hope a bear will pick up the scent and amble into camp.

Thursday, April 21—Bud flew in this morning. He advises us that he has hired Dick MacIntyre with his 185 Cessna to replace Jim and his broken plane.

This is good news. Mac is a good pilot and has good equipment. He might be of great help in locating bears. Another day of shooting film. There is much trouble with camera equipment in these low temperatures.

Friday, April 22—Helmericks flew in at ten-thirty this morning to say that MacIntyre developed engine trouble and had to turn back to Fairbanks. . . .

More film work. Mac radioed that he would be in tonight and this is none too soon as Cliff must leave on the twenty-sixth.

Bud and Cliff and I flew over the ice for two hours today trying to find bear tracks. The number of tracks was encouraging—some just three miles or so out.

Our problem is to find seals for bait. This is not likely to happen until a lead opens up. So far there has been no open water. The temperature last night was twenty degrees below zero. The high today was twelve degrees above.

Writing my notes is difficult. Our sleeping tent is too cold. The camera tent is full of equipment and the cook tent, where I am now, is crowded and heavy with cooking and gas stove fumes.

Sunday, April 24, 6 p.m.—We are weathering a storm. It was twenty below last night. It is twelve below now with a twenty-knot wind. Impossible to remain outside for long. A card game is going on. There are seven of us in this eight-by-twelve tent. The oil burner keeps it fairly comfortable.

Three bears passed by camp a few miles south sometime yesterday. I found the tracks on an exercise hike while waiting for Helmericks to come in. We then flew for two hours, Bud, Cliff, and I, and saw many tracks—quite a concentration of them just two or three miles north of camp. No open water that we could see.

Bud came in about noon today bringing fuel and groceries. Cliff has been staying at Bud's house the last two nights. MacIntyre finally got in last night but we can do no hunting in this weather.

The snow is blowing in and drifting around the tents. We have put up snow walls (blocks of snow) for a windbreak. Bob and Mike have been building an igloo in odd moments but the storm put an end to that.

The main reason we need Mac's plane is to get Cliff a bear. No one can guess as to when this gale will stop but when it does we will go out and do the job. This will wind him up and his part of the film will be finished.

In our plane hunts to date we have seen many tracks and ordinarily one just follows the track until he comes to the bear. Unfortunately, there has not been enough snow for tracking. We can see the tracks now only where snow has drifted up against an ice pile. What we need is snow without wind so we can see bear tracks in the open. The weather is colder than it should be at this time of year. Bud says they had three days straight of sixty-five below in early March.

This hunt is a great hardship for the camera crew fresh out of New York. Bob and I had a general idea of what conditions would be since we have hunted up here before. Burr Smidt, ABC director, is doing a masterful job in keeping harmony, however, and everyone is being a good sport to the best of his ability. There are four days left for the ABC crew.

Cliff's bear will have to be shot in the next two days. If weather permits. It will take another day to film his kill and departure. This will leave five or six days for my show, none of which has been shot. We will start with arrival, assorted camp shots, snow sled pictures, etc. When this is finished, the ABC people will probably leave and Bob and I will finish the film.

I am determnied to kill a bear without the use of a plane. It is not that we have been neglecting opportunities to do this to date but the elements have been against us. Only two seals have been sighted up to this point. The weather must be warmer before they will come out on the ice to sun.

Helmericks is not much help in figuring out my problems of bow versus bear. But in these nine days I believe I have learned how to do it—but we need seals.

Wednesday, April 27—I am three days back on my notes. It has been very cold. Usually twenty below at night and yesterday ten below all day with a fifteen-knot wind. It is 5 P.M. now as I write this. We have just come in from five hours of flying.

This was an exceptional day in temperature—plus twenty-four at noon. We were able to stay on a bear track for half an hour because the temperature softened the snow and tracks could be seen better. But it was not quite good enough. We tracked a good bear for almost an hour but ran too low on gas and had to return to camp.

Cliff was supposed to leave yesterday but canceled a TV contract and is staying tomorrow also, for what is to be his last day. He could possibly extend this by an additional day as he is very anxious to get a bear. If we have snow without wind, we could get Cliff a bear in half a day.

Jim got a new strut and left for Fairbanks today to have the wing tip repaired. Bob is taking over as cook. We don't object to Jim's departure as it makes one less for our crowded quarters. It is not likely that he will be back for a week or ten days.

On Monday we sighted an ugrug (bearded seal) sunning on the very edge of the ice beside open water. Bear hunting was not good because there was no tracking snow, so we decided to have a try at him.

We landed both planes a mile and a half from the seal and did a stalk; Cliff and I and Steve with his camera. We were lucky to get to within a hundred yards and find cover behind a chunk of ice.

I had my camera running on long lens with the seal centered. Steve was wider and back of Cliff who successfully shot the animal.

Yesterday we hunted all the way to Barrow, gassed up there and hunted all the way back. We saw no bears.

Because of this warmer weather I feel confident, for the first time, about the hunt tomorrow. Some snow would guarantee success but warmer temperatures would be almost as good. Most bear signs are near camp. They are cruising this so-called shore ice sniffing snowdrifts for seal dens.

It is difficult to write. I am in the cook tent and everybody is talking. Have just finished a rundown on my part of the ABC show. As I have said, nothing at all has been done on it execpt to outline the script. If Cliff does not get a bear, we have prepared a double ending. It will be a good film even without a bear. The ugrug hunt was terrific.

Mike and Bob are still putting finishing touches on the igloo. Eskimo men put one up in just a few hours. Our contractors worked two days. . . . It stands fifty yards from camp, flying a yellow towel from atop a staff. We call it "Camp Yellowbird."

Since we are outside the continental United States, we are preparing a charter to become eligible for foreign aid which is badly needed.

Jim and Bob dug a fishing hole today. The ice was seven feet thick and, when they broke through, water rose so rapidly that it threatened to swamp the tent where Burr lives. A hastily improvised dam of snow is holding the water back temporarily. We have caught no fish to date.

Thursday, April 28, 7 p.m.—It is hard to believe that the temperature was eighteen above at 7 A.M. After the cold weather we have had, it was like a heat wave.

We went flying at nine-thirty—Cliff's last day. I had great hopes for good tracking snow.

While tracking might have been better, apparently the bears could not stand the heat wave and were not moving. We could find no fresh tracks but there were quite a number of seals out sunning.

Back in camp at 3 P.M. Cliff took off with Mac for Fairbanks and home. Temperature in camp at noon was forty above.

We were surprised to learn how quickly one can get acclimated to the cold. Twenty above is almost hot. I sat on a snow sled outside a half hour ago and shaved very comfortably in that temperature.

We finished Cliff's show with no bear.

Mike and Steve have been fishing through the hole Jim made. Meat bait brings up small shrimp.

Tomorrow we start production on my show. Ours is to be a snow sled hunt. Bud has been detailed to bring in seals for bait. We are finally in business.

Friday, April 29—Another beautiful day. Twenty above at 7 A.M. and up to forty at noon. I can understand how Eskimos can get used to cold weather. I was quite warm in a light outfit.

We shot fifteen hundred feet of film today. All of it traveling with the two snow sleds. What great machines they are.

We have a new campsite, a big, blue hunk of ice that rises about forty feet above the ice pack. It has straight walls on two sides and is about fifty feet square. We will pitch our tents tight against one wall. This will be our hunting camp. It is a half mile from main camp where we are now.

We will lay trails both north and south from the hunting camp (bears here move east and west) by dragging seal or seal oil scented

189

bags for about ten miles each way. When seal blubber is available we will put a scent in the air by burning the blubber twenty-four hours a day.

Bud flew in about 11 A.M. with groceries and then went seal hunting. He came back at 3 P.M. without a seal.

Saturday, April 30—The fifteen hundred feet of film we shot yesterday was all on snow sleds going across the ice and past picturesque places and over and through drifts and piles of ice. The snow sleds are SKI DOOS made by Bombardier in Quebec and have eight-horsepower four-cycle engines.

I tow a freight sled which is about twelve feet long, loaded with all kinds of duffle and with a thirty-inch target at the very back. The duffle is covered by two caribou skins and the whole thing is lashed down by ropes.

It was twenty above again at 8 A.M. We set up camp at the west ent of our big ice cube—two Thermos Pop Tents and a sled garage and blind made of blocks of snow. From this blind we hope to shoot a bear if, and when, we can lure one into camp.

We shot film of building the camp, shooting the bow, cutting snow blocks, and erecting the snowhouse. Bud came in at 3 P.M. with a seal which lies about thirty yards from our main camp. We will not get to the serious business of baiting a bear until this preliminary photography is finished.

Burr has asked Bud to charter a flight out of here next Wednesday, which means we have three days to complete all photography. It will take this long to complete everything except the kill.

After Wednesday, Bob and I will be alone. By that time we will have more seals we hope and will drag the skinned carcasses each day to lay fresh trails into camp to a bait anchored within bow range of our tent.

On it I will try my strategy that has worked so well on black bears—a wire from the bait that leads to a bundle of tin cans inside our tent. The tents have no windows but the rattle of the empty cans should alert us.

We will hunt with the snow sleds also and may do some scouting with the plane while hunting seals. I think we have a perfect location—a big bear track through here before camp was set up, a bear in here to tear the tents the day before we arrived, and one sighted a half mile from here two days later.

It is not possible to do our bear hunting job at the main camp with the ABC crew there. Too much activity. A generating plant running constantly to charge batteries and just too many people, generally speaking.

With all other scenes shot before the crew leaves, it will be up to Bob and me to come up with the key footage.

As an additional incentive to bring bears within bowshot, we will cook the seal blubber 'round the clock on a catalytic heater. With all of these things going for us, sooner or later a bear should wander our way.

Sunday, May 1, 9 a.m.—The temperature was twelve above at 7 A.M. A fog closed in and now it is snowing, reducing visibility to about 200 yards. We cannot shoot film. Bob, Burr, Simon, and I have had breakfast and are pondering what to do. Jerry, Steve, and Mike are still sleeping and there seems to be no need to wake them. Bob and I thought some of doing a little scouting for bear tracks with the sleds but decided against it as we might not find our way back to camp.

I don't believe I have mentioned Simon Ned in my notes. He is an Indian from Allakaket about 400 miles south of here. He does not know what tribe he belongs to but there are about twenty families in his village. He works for Wein Airlines which makes three flights a week into the village. The landing field is about a quarter of a mile away and Simon's occupation is taking the mail from the airstrip to the village. In his spare time he hunts, traps, and fishes. He owns one of the three snow sleds in the village. The rest of the families still have dog teams but all wish they had sleds which cost about $900 here. Simon also works for Bud about five weeks each fall in a commercial fishing venture.

Simon is forty-three years old and stands about five foot eight. He weighs 150 pounds and has six children, one of whom perished, along with his dog team, when they broke through the ice on their way to hunt caribou last fall.

Bud brought Simon in to help around camp. His chores include climbing the pile of ice to scan the area for bears the first thing every morning, bringing in ice for water, and washing dishes.

Bud got news by radio that Jim had reached Fairbanks with his damaged plane. He does not know how long it will take to repair it. It is doubtful if he will get back before the hunt is over.

In the meantime, Bob is doing a good job taking over the cooking. I tried to help with breakfast yesterday. The bacon turned out fine but trouble developed with the pancakes. They would not rise —only turn brown. I fought this for half a dozen unattractive samples, heavy as lead, with everybody offering suggestion. Burr said the batter needed lard which was added. No improvement. Bob said it needed eggs. No better. Finally after I had been replaced as cook, it was discovered that I was using Gold Medal cake flour instead of pancake flour. My replacement seems permanent.

Sunday, 8 p.m.—Bob and I made a snow sled survey today. We went east about two miles, then south for the same distance, and had intended to enlarge our circle but the fog cleared and we came back to camp to shoot film until 5:30 P.M.

We now have about everything needed for my film except the bear. All kinds of shots for almost any kind of eventuality. The light faded at five-thirty today. Usually we can film up to about eight-thirty in good light.

In the Arctic at this time of the year, we have daylight until about 10 P.M. and fair light through to about 2:30 A.M. when the sun comes up in the northeast. It slices down at an angle in the northwest and a sort of presunrise glow covers the north all night.

There are seven of us in the cook tent now. Five of them playing Black Jack and Bob is cooking. The battery-charging generator chugs outside and supplies current for the 150-watt bulb that hangs overhead.

Jerry has been sculpturing a polar bear from a large piece of ice that rises up about a third of a mile from camp. His tools are a machete and a pick. The bear is about life size and is beginning to look good.

Since it is Sunday, Bud does not come out to camp today.

Monday, May 2, 10 a.m.—Very thick fog this morning and not clearing. Twenty-two above at 8 A.M. Visibility was about two hundred yards. This is tantamount to a "whiteout" and one never knows where one's footing is. He could stumble into a drift and fall on his face. Or, equally perilous, a step could drop him six feet into a crevasse.

We ran into this condition in late afternoon the last day we flew. We had landed to gas up from cans carried with us and, while there was no fog, we could not determine exactly where the snow surface was. A rather sticky situation. We noticed this yesterday also, in later afternoon, when we finished filming. We stumbled back to camp like drunks.

Complacency is called for on this hunt but it is not always easy with no bear in sight and time rolling by. Card games help pass the time but there is only today and tomorrow for the ABC crew. It could actually be a week before they went out, however, if the fog holds out.

Tuesday, May 3, 8 a.m.—The fog cleared yesterday and we shot the last of needed film except a moonlight scene planned for midnight, but fog again prevented this. High yesterday was forty-seven.

Bob and I slept in the igloo last night just for the hell of it. Not much different from our tent except for the thought of impending disaster if it collapsed on us.

There is very thick fog now and not much to do. Bud has not been here since Saturday, although we expect him today if the fog lifts. Yesterday when it was clear, we could see the heavy fog bank to the south near shore.

I did some research yesterday on the bear-baiting business. We cut off the top of a five-gallon gas can and filled it half full of seal oil and set it to boiling over a heater outside the tents. Bob and I then went off downwind about one fourth of a mile to see if we could pick up the scent. We certainly could. It was almost as pungent as at stoveside. I am pleased with these results and am sure a bear could tune in on it from ten miles out. We will cook seal blubber, too. But this will come later when there are less people here. Too much activity now for a bear to come in.

Same Day, 8 p.m.—Absolutely nothing accomplished today except several walks in the fog. Bud and Jim flew in a half hour ago and brought some supplies. Jim's plane is repaired and he will be with us from now on, we hope. Bud expects the weather to clear tomorrow so that Wein can come in to take the ABC crew out. That will leave Bob and Jim and me from here on out with Bud flying in from shore occasionally.

I feel that we will get a break on the bears. We have to. This hard luck just can't hold. They were here and will come again.

We have two fine shows finished except for the kill. My snow sled sequence should be a good one. And Cliff has the ugrug to spice his up. Cliff said he would come back if conditions improved. In spite of the weather I am optimistic. Tomorrow the blubber pots will burn fiercely.

Wednesday, May 4, 7 a.m.—Weather not good. Visibility almost zero. Temperature is thirteen above and wind strong at fifteen to twenty knots an hour. Bob is cooking breakfast. The rest of the crew is not up yet. Just Jim, Simon, and I who are waiting patiently.

I have only praise for our Thermos tents. The Prairie Schooner, of which we have two, does everything that could be expected. It is shaped like a covered wagon, eight-by-twelve, with six and a half feet headroom. The tents are double, one inside the other. This cook tent takes a beating but stands up very well.

Jim and Simon sleep here. A three-burner propane stove stands inside the door and piled high, on both sides, are cartons of groceries.

The tents are pitched on eight to ten inches of snow over the ice. Some pieces of ⅜-inch plywood, brought out on the sled, make a floor, covering the rear two thirds of the tent. Between the back sleeping area and the kitchen, a moose hide, hair side up, serves as a rug and blotter to swallow up bits of food and small objects dropped by the dwellers. It has been estimated that the rug will yield a small fortune in poker money after this hunt.

Between the traffic and heat from the stove, a depression down to ice depth has developed just inside the door. Corrugated cartons, added as they become available, are used to build it up but tracked in snow melts on the cartons and we have instead a basin of paper pulp.

Another tent of this type, heated with an oil space heater, houses our sound man and assistant cameraman as well as the camera gear. Burr and Jerry live in a double-wall A tent heated with a space heater also. Bob and I sleep in a double Pop Tent. We have a catalytic heater to keep the chill off.

Thursday, May 5, 11 a.m.—Nothing whatever happened yesterday. A strong wind from the west held and the plane could not get in. I took a long hike looking for tracks but did not really expect to find any since they drifted over immediately in the wind.

About 10 P.M. last evening the wind went down but the snow continued. This morning when we woke up it was eighteen above, the wind was down and visibility was better. Spirits are higher now. It is possible that the crew might get out today.

I circled camp about two miles out after breakfast in beautiful tracking snow. The ride on the snow sled was exhilarating. No bears but white foxes have found a bag of fish left at our picture camp and had a feast.

I did some practice shooting. A great day to be hunting. An inch of tracking snow all over.

2 P.M.—Still a beautiful day. Forty above. Shot a seal two miles from camp. Weather is clear. We hear a plane. It seems likely that the crew will leave and I can get this off to mail.

May 6, Friday—The ABC crew got off at four-thirty yesterday. The Beaver plane was to come back today for their gear but it is still sitting on our airstrip as this was another foggy day.

The first thing we did after they left was to move camp—and none too soon. The hole Jim had dug to fish through was slowly flooding the area. Tent floors had melted through the snow down to ice. A bad situation. In Arctic camping tents should rest on snow, not ice.

We now have three tents instead of five. They are pitched on about three feet of snow (drifts that we leveled off), about 100 yards from the old campsite.

Bob and I have an eight-by-twelve, double-wall Prairie Schooner with an oil burner. To get this double canvas we simply erect one tent inside another.

Jim and Simon occupy a similar tent that is heated by a three-burner propane range. This is the cook and dining tent also. Between these two tents we have a Giant Thermos Pop Tent, not heated, that serves as storage for items that can stand freezing.

This morning we put the finishing touches on our new camp and shot a seal about a mile away. He was lying on the ice beside his hole. After skinning it, we dragged it behind the sled back to camp and then around an area three miles east, four miles north, and three miles south. Tomorrow we will extend the north trail to about ten miles. Open water is about fifteen miles in that direction.

Last chore today was to lash a seal down to an ice anchor about eighty yards from our tent and run a wire from it to a stake inside, on which we have hung some empty tin cans (our alarm system). Also the five-gallon gas can half full of seal oil and blubber was set on the heater atop an oil drum to give off scent continuously while we are here. Between the scent and the drags we hope to lure a bear into camp and to bow range. Temperature was twenty above today with an east wind.

Saturday, May 7—High today was twenty-eight and low eighteen. Bob and I dragged a seal behind the snow sled for ten or twelve miles today. About as far as we could go. Beyond this was very rough ice. We climbed on top of an ice pile but could not see open water, although a low cloud indicated water in that vicinity.

Eight or nine seals were lying by their holes but all had carefully selected their locations in flat areas where there was no cover to stalk up to them. Under the right conditions they can be approached to within seven or eight hundred yards with the snow sleds. If we had a child's sled with a frame covered with white material at the front, I believe we could get very close—lying on our bellies and propelling the sled with our hands and feet, watching through a peephole.

The Arctic seal must endure many interruptions during his sleep and sunning periods. At intervals of about one minute he raises his head to look quickly around. It is between these alert periods that one has an opportunity to squirm closer. The seals average about a hundred pounds each and have a layer of blubber two inches thick under their skins. The blubber is a beautiful, translucent pink that settles into clear oil after standing for about a month. This seal oil is used by the Eskimos for heat and when condensed makes a very succulent "dip" for almost any food they eat. Jim says it makes an excellent salad dressing. We shall see. . . . The liver is extracted from each seal for our own use and Jim has promised a fine feast of steak from the one we shot yesterday.

The frozen carcass of a Barren Ground caribou lies beside our tent and the skin provides a warm rug for inside. Our larder, besides roast and stewed caribou meat, consists of frozen steaks, chops, and fowl, canned goods, plus flour, macaroni, beans, etc. All water is melted from an abundant supply of salt-free ice stacked up in a pile fifty feet high beside camp.

We have two snow sleds in camp of the type that are replacing the dog team in Barrow. They will go almost any place except over the roughest ice and use about a half gallon of gas per hour. In addition we have a towing sled to haul supplies brought out from Bud Helmericks' headquarters at Colville River Delta. This sled is about thirty inches wide and twelve feet long. The runners are shod with 1/10" thick iron about three inches wide.

Sunday, May 8—Temperature is twenty. Very little to report. Heaviest fog yet. So thick it was difficult to travel with the snow sled although Jim and Simon managed to follow our drag north and found fresh bear tracks coming toward camp on our trail. If the bear had been nearby, they would not have been able to see him because of the fog and they hope they did not frighten him so he won't come back.

This has been a long, dull day. The wind changed to the southwest and late this evening snow began to fall. The heaviest snow I have seen in the Arctic.

Monday, May 9, Morning—Temperature twenty. A brisk wind all night, with snow. It is still blowing and snowing now but the sun is shining and visibility is boundless. This is the first sun and clear weather we have had in ten days.

Bud came out at noon but there will be no hunting today. Wein is expected here for the gear and Bud will have to meet the plane in Colville and lead him out to camp.

We have to stay in camp also, since there will be three barrels of gas to unload from the plane. Nothing can be planned definitely in this country. One is entirely dependent upon mechanical equipment and the weather. Bob flew back to Colville with Bud, to have a bath and spend the night. My turn next time.

At 9 P.M. Jim, Simon, and I dragged the seal north to the end of our trail. We got back at 11 P.M. through fog so thick we could barely make out our trail. It was ground fog, however, and we could look up through it and see blue sky.

Tomorrow is the beginning of the season when the sun does not dip below the horizon. I took a picture at 11:30 P.M.

Tuesday, May 10, 5 p.m.—Temperature thirty. No bears came in last night nor did the Wein flight come in today. Bud and Bob have not showed up either. There was a brilliant sun this morning but at noon a wind of about thirty knots sprang up. Much drifting of snow and again poor visibility.

Jim and Simon went seal hunting. We need a fresh one for our drag. They were caught in the blinding snowstorm that hit our tent

like pellets of ice. Jim had an unsuccessful shot at a seal.

First thing this morning I circled camp about two miles out to see if any bears had been near—no tracks. I then opened up our drifted-in path from the tent to my shooting stand overlooking the seal bait and the one leading to the photography position. Here a camera, prefocused, rests on a tripod protected from the elements by a white sheet.

Next I repositioned our heater and cleaned up the inside of the tent, adding more hanging arrangements for drying clothes. Took a Ski Doo and did some photos of ice formations and icicles. Tended the scent pot. Did some practice. Took a nap.

Wednesday, May 11—A beautiful day. Bud and Bob came out at 10 A.M. and we left immediately for hunting. I flew with Bud and Bob went with Jim.

Fifteen minutes out we saw a bear walking along beside a pressure ridge. This was the first bear we had seen for twenty-five days and it was quite a thrill. Bud asked did I want to try for him and the answer was "yes."

Fortunately we had sighted him at a distance and he did not see the plane, so we flew west on the ridge until we found a place to land several miles ahead. We then made our way back along the ridge on foot toward the bear to a spot that offered good possibilities for ambush, hoping the bear would continue on his course.

I found a place on a pile of ice where I would be out of sight if he came by on my side and high enough to shoot over if he came through on the other side. Bud and Bob found cover about twenty yards back of me to cover any action with the cameras.

We waited for an hour and a half, cramped and uncomfortable and cold, before we spotted him coming about a half mile away. He showed up dark against the bright snow, shuffling along in an aimless way with his mind on a good seal dinner, I suppose, as he investigated piles of ice and cracks in the snow.

At first he appeared to be coming straight by at close range on our side but at about 400 yards he swerved away from the ridge and seemed to choose a course through rough ice that would put him a 100 yards away as he passed me.

I had to make a decision. It seemed best to move out in front of him, which I did when he went out of sight behind the ice. The others moved with me and we again found cover with the cameras back of me as before.

The bear came into sight very quickly. Three hundred yards, two hundred, one hundred . . . coming on a course that would pass me at twenty yards or even closer.

But the wind was not good in our new position. At fifty yards his nose went into the air and he stopped to look toward us. Not sure, but suspicious, he turned sideways looking our way and sniffing. Having been charged twice before on other hunts and at closer range than this, I felt sure that he was trying to make up his mind whether he should come for us or run off, so I rose from behind my cover and released an arrow.

It looked good all the way. Immediately a red blotch appeared, close to the shoulder. He went down in the loose snow, recoiling from the hit and snapping at the arrow while lying on his side. Then he was back on his feet like a cat and took off on the double over the pressure ridge and beyond about a hundred yards where he went down again in some rough ice, this time for good.

A handsome trophy—a bear with ten gallons of seal oil in his belly. What a relief. After twenty-five days of bad weather and tough luck we get perfect conditions and went out to bag a polar bear just twelve miles from camp. We should have a good film.

May 12, Thursday—With good weather forecast I thought I should wire ABC to ask if Cliff would be interested in coming back as he had said he would.

Bud talked to Wein on the radio to inquire if we could go to Barrow on their Thursday mail flight. They advised that they had canceled the flight because of engine trouble, so Bud and Jim flew us in here at 11 P.M. I am sitting in my room in the Top of the World Hotel writing these notes.

Friday, May 13—In Barrow. Nothing of hunting news to report. Waiting for word from New York to see if Cliff is coming up.

This is a Barrow I have not seen before. Spring is here and black gravel is begininng to show on the streets in places but the snow sleds zip right through them just the same.

As we flew in yesterday we saw clouds of eider ducks over the town and the ice beyond. The natives are shooting them as they fly over the leads near where their whaling camps are set up.

A whale was taken here last Monday. It was about thirty feet long. We are trying to get some muktuk to take home.

I bought a kayak for the museum. I think it is the last one in town. We saw it on the roof of a shed and asked the owner if he would sell it. He said, "What were you thinking to pay for it?" I said that I was thinking of a hundred dollars. He said, "I was thinking of $125."

I paid him and made arrangements with Wein to crate and ship it. Simon is getting me an Indian-made sled and Jim has given me a pair of Indian-made snowshoes. Am dickering now for a mastodon tusk about nine feet long.

Saturday, May 14—George Thiele came in last evening from Fairbanks for the weekend. We had quite a reunion. We had hunted polar bears with him in 1960 and 1962.

We saw the sun at midnight tonight. There is good light here now, full twenty-four hours of the day. We can shoot pictures at any time.

Heard from ABC. They advise that Cliff is anxious to come back.

Sunday, May 15—Trying to get back out to camp but the weather is not good. Cliff wired that he will be in Friday. As soon as we can get out to camp we will do some seal hunting, fire up the blubber pot, and make a last-ditch stand to get a bear in to bait.

We have looked at enough Eskimos, have seen Barrow in all of its moods, and have escaped being run down by snow sleds. Arctic Research beat me to the draw on the mastodon tusk. They bought it for one thousand dollars.

Tuesday, May 17, 8 a.m.—We are still in Barrow and not too happy about it. If we have to be weathered in, we would rather be out in our camp on the ice. Bob, Jim, and I are the only ones in the hotel. Talked to Bud yesterday by radio. The weather was not good there nor here. It was snowing and visibility was poor.

Things look somewhat brighter this morning. There are still some snowflakes in the air, but we can dimly see the sun which means that the overcast is thin and might burn through.

10 a.m.—Bud is here. We're going back to camp.

Later—Had some trouble getting Jim's engine started. Temperature twelve. A pleasant flight to Colville. Saw many caribou, a snowy owl, and a flock of brant. In Barrow we saw snow buntings.

We made a stop at Bud's house and had tea and cookies. Then on to camp at 3 P.M. We saw quite a number of seals on the way back and since we need bear bait Bud took his plane and Jim the snow sled and went hunting. Both were back at 6 P.M. with five seals between them.

We had roast caribou for dinner, skinned the seals and went to bed. It is warmer here on the ice than on land.

Wednesday, May 18—Thirty below. Bob and I dragged a seal carcass about twelve miles northwest this morning. This is about two miles farther than we have been before. We crossed a fresh bear track about ten miles out. It was a small one. I made a stalk on a seal and missed him three times at 300 yards with a .244 rifle. . . .

Jim made a drag about eight miles northeast and shot two more seals, so we have plenty of bait.

We all got back to camp at 2 P.M. and finished up the roast. A misty rain has turned to fine snow and now another fog is setting in.

We have six seal carcasses piled in the bait area. Bob thinks a bear might gorge himself to the point of immobility and be an easy target.

We find seal hunting quite interesting. The seals lie in the sun on the ice with their heads close to their breathing holes. These holes are small at the top all winter, when the seals stay under the ice—just big enough, through six to eight feet of ice, for their noses to poke through for oxygen.

In the spring, about the first of May, they enlarge these holes until they can flip out on the ice for sunning. At the slightest sign of danger they disappear back down the hole and out of sight. Their sleep is never uninterrupted; we never saw one that did not raise his head about once a minute to have a look around. This takes about five seconds and since the head is down only about a minute, stalking a seal is tedious business.

One needs a good, accurate, flat-shooting gun, preferably scope mounted. The seals are usually some distance out on smooth ice where there is little cover for either man or bear to make a stalk. This is where the small sled I mentioned comes into the picture.

We fastened a piece of plywood about two by three feet, vertically, at the front of the sled. It is covered with white cloth and has a peephole for watching the seal as one propels the sled with his hands, lying flat on his belly as we did as kids. Propulsion is turned on during that minute the seal is sleeping and turned off immediately when his head comes up. With care a seal can be approached to within a hundred yards in this way.

Sometimes the seals are found within range (up to 300 yards) of a piece of ice that offers cover for a stalk. It is not practical to shoot beyond this range as they must be hit in the head or they will slip down their holes and disappear.

On smooth ice we can usually run the Ski Doo, carrying the small sled, to within a half mile before beginning the sled work.

We have been hunting the common hair seal. They weigh between 80 and 150 pounds. Their diet is almost entirely of shrimp and they must eat very well as the blubber under their skin is about two inches thick.

Thursday, May 19—We have been plagued with bad weather. Bob and I made the north drag this morning. We traveled first through a fine mist that iced our dark glasses and then turned to snow which made it difficult to see our trail on the return strip.

Unless one experiences them, it would be hard to imagine the problems an Arctic "whiteout" creates. Flyers must avoid them, if possible, since they cannot tell how far they are from the snow or ice during these storms. Landing, of course, is the greatest hazard of all and many planes have been lost during these times.

On the other hand, while walking, one cannot tell if a snowdrift is two feet up or is a depression two feet down. Patience is needed in the Arctic. What can't be done today is for tomorrow or even next week.

This afternoon we packed the foldboat and tents at the ice-cube camp and hauled them back to the airstrip. We also took some pictures.

At four o'clock the weather cleared and Bud flew out to camp saying he had a garbled telegram for me. None of us could make out the message, so Bud suggested that we fly over to a DEW line station about twenty-five miles or so away and call Barrow for confirmation on its contents. Bud said that over his transmitter there was so much static he could only make out something about Cliff Robertson.

The men at the radar station were extremely surprised to see us. "Who are you?" "Where did you come from?" "What do you want?" "How did you get here?"

I have not had a haircut in two months and my whiskers bristled over my face, so I kept my hat on knowing I did not look much like an upstanding citizen. When I told my inquirer that I had been camping in his front yard twenty-five miles out on the ice, hunting polar bears with a bow and arrow, it was almost too much, and there seemed to be a question in his mind whether to have us shot on the spot or quizzed considerably further.

He finally allowed me to call Wein at Barrow but nothing else. I explained to the girl in the Wein office that Helmericks could not understand the telegram they had sent out because of static on his radio and would she please read it to me from there. Yes, she would, just a minute. . . .

Ten minutes later she was back and said she couldn't find the telegram. I then told her to wire ABC in New York and ask them to send another telegram stating whether Robertson was coming back and when.

Our host at the DEW line station accompanied us out to the plane, wanting to make sure we had arrived in one, as we said, and to check the number Bud had given him. Nonetheless, we wondered how efficient our Distant Early Warning system is. We had flown straight in front of their screen coming in and had, for five weeks, been flying twenty-five miles north of their site.

We were back in camp at 7 P.M.

Friday, May 20, Noon—Twenty-six below. Wind twenty knots. Thick fog this morning but clearing now. We have done nothing so far today except have breakfast and visit in our cozy tent. If Helmericks comes out we will plane hunt on the way into Barrow to see if Cliff comes on the 6:30 P.M. plane from Fairbanks. We can hunt on the way back also. In fact we can hunt all night now, when the weather is good, since there is daylight around the clock.

Evening—No word from Bud. The weather is not good. Bob, Jim, and I made the seal drag north again. A bear had hit our trail about three miles from the far end but went the wrong way.

On the return trip we put the skinned seal carcass on the sled and Jim carved it all the way back to camp dropping off chunks of blubber at intervals close enough to keep a bear interested.

At 8 P.M. I made a new drag trail northeast for about twelve miles. Did not see a track and was back at ten-thirty. No word from Bud.

Saturday, May 21—A beautiful day. The sun was shining brightly when we got up. We expected Helmericks early. He came out at eleven-thirty.

To keep busy we strung the bear hide up on a vertical pole, using the foldboat double paddle to stretch out the legs. It looked fine hanging there between our tents and we took several pictures.

Bud reported a radio-phone talk with ABC who inquired first if Bob and I were all right and then said that Robertson could come back on Monday evening if this were agreeable with us. Bud told them to send him along.

Sunday, May 22, Evening—Today was a complete washout. Fog so thick it was not safe to venture out even in the Ski Doo. Bob and I tried it, starting on the northwest drag trail, but a snowstorm developed and we had to return. We took some pictures and had fried chicken for dinner at 9 P.M.

SUMMARY

Cliff Robertson came back Monday evening and stayed two days. We had no hunting weather during this time so there was nothing to do but wrap up the hunt. We did not have one hunting day in the last ten. Fog, fog, fog.

On several of these days we could have used the plane but we cannot see tracks without sunlight. I had hoped to get some bear to do but wrap up the hunt. We did not have one hunting day in pictures for the film.

Except for the bear sighted when we were setting up camp we saw only one bear in six weeks—the one I shot.

In reviewing the hunt certain conclusions seem obvious, although other factors, unknown to me, may have influenced the movements of polar bears during the six weeks we spent on the ice.

In the period between April 15 and the 20, eight bears passed within half a mile of camp. We saw one of these. The others were identified as seven different bears by their tracks.

No one disputes the fact that food and weather are the two chief elements that influence the movements of animals. Food is the most important and the food of polar bears is seal. Almost nothing else.

Ice covers the ocean in the Arctic at the time seals give birth to their young. Newborn seals cannot swim for several days, so the mother must make arrangements to overcome this problem. She locates her breathing hole underneath deep snow that has drifted against the side of an ice pile. At this hole, which she enlarges before the young are born, she digs a den in the snow, undetectable from topside, where she hopes her baby will be safe from the inquisitive nose of the polar bear until the family can go down into the water to safety.

Not every young seal survives these first critical days in spite of the mother's caution. The polar bear has a powerful nose and spends his days sniffing around the ice packs trying to locate a den and dig it out. We saw signs of his success in these efforts now and then.

I believe this seal birthing period ended a few days after we set up camp since the bears shifted their hunting activities to the leads that were opening up about fifteen miles north of us. I feel sure we could have had success in baiting bears if our camp had been nearer open water.

Camping on the ice pack is a unique experience. It can be done safely if the location is selected with care. It can also be more or less comfortable if one knows how to camp under these conditions. And while we were not successful, I am convinced that bears could be baited into camp by dragging seal carcasses behind snow sleds. One must be warned, however, that during the latter part of the season, when the ice is beginning to break up, it would be possible to be swallowed up by the sea through one misplaced step.

Another time, I would locate camp farther out on the ice nearer open water. The line between shore ice (which is ice that does not break up until the spring thaw) and the shifting ice floes farther out is quite clearly defined and does not change much from year to year, so with care a camp could be relatively safe farther out. The inexperienced would do well to hire an Eskimo who knows the ice. Otherwise one could be isolated on an ice floe and wind up as a guest of the Russians.

The entire hunt could be done with snow sleds but to avoid the almost endless fogs we encountered, one should be there in the early part of April, although temperatures as low as forty below zero could be experienced at this time. Also some method for preheating the sled engines would be necessary at this time of year.

Seals would be more difficult to find at this time also but if one purchased two or more in Barrow, before going out on the ice, it would be sufficient to lure bears into camp.

In addition to the seal drags, the blubber pot should burn continuously. This puts out a potent incense which, I am sure, can be picked up by a bear five to ten miles away in a proper wind. Our pot setup was trouble-free and operated twenty-four hours a day without attention. The flat-topped catalytic heater burned white gas and had a twenty-four-hour tank capacity. It sat on an empty oil drum and, to conserve heat and protect it from the wind, we covered it with a corrugated carton in which we cut a hole large enough to accommodate an open-end five-gallon gas can holding a small quantity of seal oil and blubber. These heaters burn at a uniform temperature—just hot enough to heat the seal oil or blubber to the right temperature. They require attention only once a day.

From such a location only snow sleds would be needed to hunt bears, either by tracking or by cruising around sweeping the area with binoculars from atop ice packs. This would be the ultimate in sportsmanship with either a bow or gun but, because of the hardships and the long time it takes with this method, I feel sure that most polar bears will continue to be located from planes. In 1967 polar bear hunting will be done under the permit system as a protective measure. Permits will be limited to the number of bears to be harvested.

Aside from man, the polar bear has only one enemy—the killer whale. In the water the bear is an agile and graceful swimmer but easy prey for these whales. Sometimes he comes out second best in an encounter with walrus, too, but in this case, he is the aggressor.

The Eskimo hunted the ice bear in two ways—with dogs or posing himself as a seal. In the former, while traveling along with his dog sled, a bear is sighted, and the dogs cut loose to bring the animal to bay. Then, amid a great bedlam of vicious dogs, snarling bear, and yelling humans, the Eskimo hunter advanced with his spear, bow and arrow, or later, his gun, and dispatched the bear.

Their even more daring and spectacular method was a sort of decoy game where the hunter spread himself prone upon the ice to simulate a seal when a bear was seen in the distance. He dressed in dark clothing and wiggled his feet like flippers and raised his head at frequent intervals to look around as a seal does. The bear would start stalking close like a cat after a bird, while the brave Eskimo carried on with his seal-like antics. Natives in the Arctic who have hunted this way told me that the bear could be counted upon to make his final rush from about fifty feet and just before this hazardous period the shot had to be made.

In the meantime, the resourceful polar bear will continue as master of the ice pack. He will prowl its white vastness and capture enough seals to grow big and strong and enjoy a happy existence where almost all other animals would starve. His keen nose and sharp eyesight, coupled with a fast left hook, serves him well and man, invading his realm, will never know whether he is the hunter or the hunted.

BROWN BEAR THE HARD WAY

The picture of this particular brown bear is hanging today in the offices of Field & Stream *in New York. Bob Brister is the shooting editor of the magazine, and he told me personally about this bear when he came back from the trip to Alaska and before he wrote the story. It was a close call as the bear had charged Bob's guide, Hap Mathis, without any warning in thick brush, and it was quite a scene there for a few moments.*

Brister is an excellent shot—having spent his life growing up in Texas and traveling all over the world to hunt and write about it. It is a good thing he is a fine shot. That encounter was too close for comfort.

Brown Bear the Hard Way

Bob Brister

Hap Mathis was breaking trail through a dense alder thicket when suddenly he dropped to one knee and flipped the sling of his .458 off his packboard in one swift, smooth motion.

A few yards ahead was something big and dark in the brush. Instantly I had the two-power scope on it, and when I started laughing Hap looked around incredulously.

"It's no bear," I told him, "just a pile of dirt."

From our position, the mound looked almost exactly the size of a big, dark Alaska brown bear. But Hap still wasn't laughing.

"Start backing up the way we came," he whispered. "Get to that clearing over there, and be ready to shoot in a hurry if you have to!"

Backtracking uphill through dense alder bushes is not easy, and when we finally made the clearing I pantingly demanded to know what all the excitement was about.

"If there had been a bear working on that new den in there, he just might have showed you," the oldtimer grumbled. "You live around those big devils forty years like I have and you just may change some of your Texas ideas about bears. Two guides got killed not far from here a couple of years ago because they stumbled up on a bear working on his den. Both had rifles, too, and got off a shot. But at the range we walked in on that den, one shot ain't likely to stop a big bear in time."

He handed me his binoculars, and I could make out the dark hole in the side of the steep, alder-thick ravine. The dirt around it was fresh, with some huge tracks not yet covered by the light mixture of snow and rain which had been falling all morning.

"Brownies are strange bears some ways," Hap mumbled around his ever-present pipe. "Let's just sit here a minute and see what happens. My judgment tells me there's a bear right here close someplace, and he's probably seen us close to his den. If so, he ain't gonna like it; a bear knows he's helpless when he goes into hibernation, and he just doesn't like the idea of any two-legged critters knowing where his hideout is. You see the size of those tracks in that fresh dirt?"

For half an hour we sat there, watching the alders and the slope below which led down to a gurgling, snow-fed creek called "Hot Springs." We were near the base of whitecapped Mount Peulik on the Alaskan Peninsula some eighty miles from the little fishing town and U.S. Air Force base at King Salmon. On the other side of the mountain, nearly twenty miles away and a hard day's walk up and down dozens of brushy ravines and hummocks in the tundra, was our base camp—outfitter Ray Loesche's snug, isolated cabins on the shore of Lake Ugashik.

As the falling rain began turning to snow, I wondered how wise we'd been to backpack into this remote valley. There was no place to land an airplane and we knew in advance we'd be confronted with a blizzard before we could walk back out again.

It had all started back in my home town, Houston, Texas, when one of my hunting partners, Houston architect Kenneth Campbell, invited Alaskan guide Ray Loesche and me to the same informal dinner at his home. Loesche was in Texas at the time booking hunts for the following year, and during the evening he mentioned a particularly big brown bear which he'd seen several times from the air in a little valley where no plane could land.

That sort of bear—and challenge—appealed to me. And in the comfort of Kenneth Campbell's living room I decided that backpacking in after an old monster that had been isolated for years would be a wonderful idea.

Now, shivering, wet to the skin, I pondered the radio reports we'd heard that morning of an incoming blizzard. In late October in that part of Alaska, we were asking for trouble.

Ray Loesche had not exactly liked the idea, but Hap Mathis, then his assistant guide, is an oldtimer in his 60's, a native of Alaska, and he helped me convince Loesche that it was a now-or-never situation; if the blizzard was very severe the bears would go into hibernation and the object of my hunt would be covered over in snow.

Since Campbell was after a giant moose he and Loesche had located, it was decided that Hap and I would go alone. We packed bedrolls, food, a small tent, and some emergency rations. Even if we got holed in for a few days, we could walk in around the base of the mountain. And when the weather let up we knew Loesche could fly over and drop in more supplies. With a little luck we could find that big boar of Hot Springs Valley and be on our way back before the bad weather ever hit. It all sounded so simple.

The walk in had taken almost all day because I'd persisted in stalking some caribou for pictures, and when we finally made Hot Springs Creek we were both tired and the weather was already starting to change. We'd stashed our heavy gear, including the food and bedrolls, in a little ravine near the creek and had gone on upstream looking for bear sign before making camp.

That was a bad mistake, and I made another when I killed more time by demanding to take pictures of the bear's den. Hap finally relented but first made me fire a couple of shots in the air to make sure the bear wasn't in there. The two shots reverberated up and down the valley—and nothing happened.

So we walked carefully down to the den and I realized just how large an Alaskan brown bear's winter residence can be. From the tracks, this was obviously a big boar, and Hap showed me how he'd selected the exact spot in the steep bank of the ravine where snow would pile up heaviest. Thus, the entrance would be protected through the winter by several feet of snow.

With gun shouldered, I eased into the gloomy interior, stopped to let my eyes adjust, and realized that the den enlarged to a circular "room" somewhat larger than the entrance. The bear had been working on it that day, judging from the loose dirt that fell on me every time I bumped the ceiling. It was still damp where his giant claws had scraped out earth and roots. Hap was outside clamoring for us to get started, and when I came out of the den I carefully flipped on the rubber scope cover to keep out the snow and rain.

We walked straight down to the creek, forced our way through the dense alders, and found we'd picked a spot too wide to jump. Hap went one way to look for a crossing, and I went the other.

I'd gone maybe 25 yards when there was a sudden, deep-throated "Wuuuff" and a huge, dark mountain of fur rose up above the alders. He was so close I could see his hair rippling in the wind, and in that split second he dropped down out of sight again and I could hear alders crashing.

Instinctively I'd flipped the rifle sling upwards and off the packboard, and took a precious second to clear the scope—all the time thinking I'd muffed my chance at the biggest bear I'd ever seen.

Then suddenly an alder swayed and the next instant a dark shape was crashing through like a freight train, heading straight for Hap.

I filled the scope with brown hair and brush and shot, and with a roaring, snarling, ground-jarring crash the bear rolled and broke brush, biting at the wound. When he came up, as if in slow motion, I saw him turn and come for me, and the gun seemed to fire itself head on into the bulk of brown hair and exploding brush. He rolled like a monstrous ball into the opening beside the creek, snarling and biting at his shoulder, and in the same instant was up and coming again. The bolt worked, slammed shut, and I knew it would be the last time; I'd have to save the shot until I could put it between his eyes at pointblank range. With only the creek and 10 yards between us I could see nothing in the scope, could only point the gun as a shotgun, holding for his head. And as the gun bellowed the bear jumped the creek and I knew I'd hit low. But then he hesitated, shuddered, and slowly collapsed like a huge brown tent into the edge of the creek.

Hap came ripping through the alders, pipe smoking like a chimney, yelling and slapping me on the back. "By God, I never saw a bolt-action fired like a machinegun before;" he whooped, "and thank God for it . . . I couldn't shoot with the back of that fat Texas head in my sights the whole time!"

It was then, for the first time, I realized what had happened in that time lapse of seconds. The bear had apparently been in the thicket beside the creek, stalking us or perhaps just hiding and believing at the last moment we'd found him. At any rate he had charged Hap, giving me that first crossing shot, which apparently had been a good one. When he'd rolled and turned for me, I'd stepped to the right from behind an alder to shoot . . . and Hap said at that instant I almost lost the back of my head—he'd been already starting to squeeze off his .458 when I popped out in front of him.

We both sat down, shivering suddenly from the combination of excitement and cold, and it occurred to me that we were being rather confident. There was a giant bear lying less than ten steps away which hadn't yet been proven dead or alive. "Don't worry about that," Hap chuckled. "I saw the fur fly that last shot; you made a perfect neck shot, best there is on a bear that close; who taught you to do that?"

I told him I'd held between the eyes and missed when the bear jumped, and he shook his head. "At that angle," he said, "you'd better be glad you missed; a bear's skull is thick and the slug might have glanced off with his head down and coming; lucky or not, you got him in the right place."

We eased up to the bear and Hap poked his eye with the .458. But it was all over. Judging from his position and the entrance holes of the bullets, my first shot had taken him in the shoulder, the second had gone through his leg and then into the chest as he rolled and roared coming up for me, and the third broke his neck. Neither of the first two would have stopped him in time, Hap decided.

"Look at those worn-down teeth," he whistled. "Now he's an old one for sure! See those porcupine quills in his lips and tongue? There's reason enough right there for him to be in a bad humor. He must have been having a tough time getting food to take on a porcupine." I pulled open the huge jaws and saw that the bear had indeed been in pain; his teeth were worn down and rotting with cavities, and two big porcupine quills were imbedded in his tongue while several more quills stuck in his lips.

"But look at this if you want enough reason for him to be mad at two-legged critters," Hap was saying. On the side of his head the bear had a long, ugly bullet scar. The shot had creased his jaw, then plowed into the top of his back—just missing the backbone.

With a sudden chill I wondered whether that hunter is still alive. From the angle of the shot, the bear had to be coming head on. Had the shot turned him, or had this been the same giant bear that killed those two guides two years before? One of them had gotten off a shot.

"You better quit speculating about that other hunter and worry about us," Hap grumbled. "It'll be dark before we're done skinning him, and it ain't gonna be easy as you think to find our gear down there."

I offered to walk down the creek, find the equipment, and get a fire started so we'd have no trouble finding it. The snow was beginning to stick to the ground, and the thought occurred to me that it could cover our little spike camp in a matter of minutes. But Hap shook his head. "Your friend here will weigh close to 1,400 pounds," he said. "I can't turn him over to skin him by myself, and unless we get this hide off him right now, we'll never get it off. It's gonna be freezing on him as soon as his body heat leaves him."

Hap seemed maddeningly slow with the skinning and fleshing tools, but he reminded me that the more fat he could get off the hide the easier we could carry it out. "If I do a real good job," he puffed, "the hide will still weigh over a hundred pounds, maybe a hundred and a half."

When he finally rolled up the dark rug and lashed it to his packboard, I argued that I should carry it; Hap is twenty years my senior. But he grumbled that Texans know very little about Alaskan packboards, and puffing his pipe like a bandy-legged steam engine, he made the last moments of daylight count. It was pitched dark when we reached the bend in the creek near our spike camp, and Hap wasn't sure if it was upstream or down from us.

Rather than take a chance on getting separated in the dark, he kept the flashlight and stayed put to signal me back to him while I took off upstream looking for our tiny pile of equipment. I began falling through the ice of little swamps and stumbling into hummocks and holes in the tundra called "tules" until my legs began to get rubbery. Still no sign of the equipment. The falling snow had covered everything—it was a futile search.

When I gave up and turned to go back to Hap, I expected the wind to be at my back. It was the only reference point I had in the dark to maintain direction. Instead, it was blowing straight into my face. Was I lost that easily? Then I realized the wind had a different, icy bite to it. The blizzard had arrived, and instantly I knew Hap and I could be in serious trouble. We were both wet, and the weather forecast had called for the temperature to drop down to zero.

Snow began blowing almost horizontally with the rising wind, and I had trouble making out even the outline of the brush. I was tiring fast from the repeated falls and trip-ups in the dark. I fired a signal shot and listened; if I could get the exact direction to him some precious steps could be saved. For nearly five minutes there was no answering shot, and a sort of numb panic gripped me. Why didn't he answer? Was the wind so strong he couldn't even hear the rifle? All I had was a metal match to start an emergency fire, a couple of candybars, and a soaked-through parka that was beginning to freeze stiff on my back.

Then I heard the heavy boom of the .458 straight ahead. I lunged through the brush, falling and getting up again, and finally saw the beam of Hap's flashlight probing up against the clouds like a miniature searchlight. The old trapper and woodsman had known I probably couldn't see the flashlight because of the brush and the ridges, but I could see that beam against the low clouds and sky.

When I reached him, utterly exhausted, Hap was shivering on his knees, trying to start a fire. The wood was wet, now frozen, but he had used a hatchet to cut some of the larger alder trunks and then split them open to get the wood in the very middle of each tree. He had his "fire insurance", a two-inch stub of a candle, lit and had made a pyramid of shavings and tiny sticks. But every time the fire would try to flame up the snow would put it out.

I took off my parka and made a windbreak of it, using my body to shield the wind and the parka to keep off the snow. The tiny blaze flickered and with numbed fingers we tried to whittle more dry sticks. For the first hour the fire was only a smoking, smouldering hope. But finally it was large enough to begin drying out the larger limbs. I looked at my watch and it was almost midnight. We had seven more hours until there would be daylight enough to find our sleeping bags and food.

The exertion of walking after and chopping wood began to take more and more effort; the temptation was just to lie down and go to sleep. Twice the hatchet slipped out of my numbed fingers and once it glanced off the knee of my hip boot. How stupid can fingers be just because they are cold? I found myself talking out loud to them.

Our clothes had begun freezing on our backs, and we dragged the bear hide to the fire, thawed the leather thongs binding it to the packboard, and rolled it out on the ground, hair side up. Then we wrapped ourselves up in it together to utilize our combined body heat and the thick hide's insulation to break the cold.

I had begun shivering uncontrollably, which Hap said was because of the exhaustion of nearly three hours of stumbling in the snow and tundra hunting for our gear. He told me to try and sleep, and finally in the protection of the hide some of the shivering began to subside. I woke up sometime later, checked to see if the fire was still alive, and tried to get up to put more wood on it. I couldn't move at all!

Hap awoke with my movements and helped me rock the hide back and forth; we were mummies in a frozen bearhide for a moment or so, but then the hide cracked loose and we pried it apart. The rest of the night we took turns chopping alder limbs, devoting half of them to the fire and the other half to building up a lean-to shelter for snow to bank against.

The wind kept howling higher, scattering our fire, so we began lying beside it on our sides to shield the fire and to warm one side while the other froze. Twice I got too close and the collar of my down jacket caught fire and burned my neck. I didn't realize it until I smelled it.

When daybreak finally came, 2 feet of snow covered the ground and the odds of finding our food and equipment had gone down with the temperature. Nothing looked the same, and we were so tired there could be no staggering around with a 150-pound bear hide.

"We've got to find some kind of shelter," Hap decided. "We can't travel until this blizzard quits."

Then I thought of the bear's den. It was close, and it would be warm and big enough for both of us. Also, the carcass of the bear was close and it would certainly be enough to feed us. We left the hide by the remains of the fire and marked it by hanging my blaze-orange hiking pack atop a close-by alder bush. Then we walked across the ridge and found the den.

We were so cold we just walked in—probably too fast—but there was no bear, and for the first time we were protected from the wind.

Instantly we started warming up and feeling better. Hap cut some wood and we made a fire at the entrance, then found there was enough of a chimney effect at the entrance that we could bring the fire inside. We moved several burning sticks in, and for the first time in hours got thoroughly, smokily warm.

Hay thawed the tough, red meat we'd hacked from the frozen carcass and we roasted it until it was burned on the outside. He said most bears have trichinosis, and the heat kills the germs. With or without germs, it was delicious; twenty-four hours had passed since we had eaten anything but a candybar each.

By midafternoon it was obvious the blizzard would be a two- or three-day affair and we'd have to spend another night. Shortly before dawn the wind changed, and we knew it immediately, because suddenly the den was full of smoke.

"We're rested and full of grub as we're ever gonna be," Hap decided. "Let's just go get that bear hide and start for base camp; longer we wait the deeper the snow's gonna be."

I asked about our sleeping bags.

"Hell with them," he grinned. "We'll mail yours to you next spring. We got all the load we can carry in this snow and the shape we're in now.

As soon as it was light we started out, and I was glad there were only a couple of feet of snow. Everything was covered over and it was like walking in the dark again; we couldn't see the holes in the tundra. I was also glad there were two of us; when one fell down the other could pull forward on his packboard to get him up again. Without help, I don't think either one of us could have made it.

Finally we cleared a ridge and could see the blue expanse of Lake Ugashik below. Our base camp cabins were tiny, dark dots against the snow. They looked close, but there were half a dozen creeks and ravines with steep, brushy sides to be crossed and we were getting very tired. Again I had that strange sensation of just wanting to lie down in the snow and go to sleep. We stopped to eat our last candybar and Hap developed leg cramps when he tried to get up with the bear hide. I switched packs with him and realized what a terrific load this man 60 years old had been carrying all along. He had to be tough!

The last few hours are not clear; just an interminable expanse of snow, stopping to breathe on the ridges, wanting to lie down and sleep. Hap was worrying we couldn't make the cabins by dark, but I was too tired and cold to worry. We just kept walking.

Kenneth Campbell had been outside in the yard of the cabin making some pictures of the trophy moose rack he'd killed and happened to see us coming across the willow flats. Thinking we'd had our sleeping bags and food along, he started yelling and joking at us from a distance . . . and then he saw the looks of us.

Only a few yards away were those wonderful warm cabins, hot coffee, whiskey, and food. It was all over . . . that long, cold, hard night of the bear.

MIKE CRAMMOND'S GRIZZLY BEARS

Of all the exciting stories of hunting grizzly bears, I can think of none more spine-tingling than these few encounters by hunter and photographer Mike Crammond. This particular story was written about a trip he made with a guide named Louis Capillo and wildlife illustrator Bob Kuhn—who ranks along with Carl Rungius as one of the finest animal painters in the world today.

What Crammond did in trying to photograph a grizzly sow with cubs may sound foolish to most hunters today, but one must remember that, to a photographer, the picture is worth anything.

Grizzly Bears

Mike Crammond

When a man begins to hunt, he has usually listened to many exaggerated legends about grizzly bears. Perhaps, then, in the back of every hunter's mind the conviction develops that he has not had all of hunting until he has faced a grizzly. I know it was thus with me. It was the set of large tracks which I found in the quarter inch of newly fallen snow in the Rocky Mountains slide, that incited me to do something about it.

By the following morning freshly fallen snow had reached two inches of powdered depth. It lay on the ground in such a fluffy manner that the leaves of small deciduous plants were able to support it above the brown-grey earth of the silted rockslides. Its icy texture allowed small crannies to form beneath the leaves. It was under these leaves that I began to search for the deliciously late fruit of the alpine strawberries. Bob Kuhn, the renowned wildlife illustrator, and Louis Capillo, our guide, had, on the night before, listened to my suggestion that we might be able to pick up the track of the grizzly again in the fresh snow, thence to follow it. Or, perhaps to find the bear feeding at the bottom of the slide over the edge of which we had dumped our mountain goat remains from two days previously. At any rate, Bob and Louis were following just a few yards behind me as I sought out the wild mountainside strawberries. They had been conversing in relatively subdued tones.

I had moved away from them, but before I did, a warning of the dramatic quality of the minutes to come was given me. With that indefinable sense of men of the wild, particularly Indians, Louis had stood momentarily very still. He had been looking in contemplation up the steep shale slide. He had to be sensing something because he was deaf as a post without his hearing aid. Added to this, the slide was obscured from view by the early morning fogs which intermittently blotted out everything from a distance varying from 25 feet to one hundred yards. He had shaken his head at his innermost thoughts and convictions, but I had noticed his reaction.

My own senses were alerted when nearby rocks rattled. The small pebbles drifted from under the skirt of white mist above, just where the slide blended into it. I saw the pebbles roll to a stop, wondering. There are often movements of earth on steep glacial slides. My gaze was drawn away from it. A scarlet strawberry beneath a browning leaf bent over with powdered snow had caught my attention. I stooped, picked it and another berry. They were chill and tart to the tongue, scented with their lovely fruity aroma. A rolling stone caught the corner of my eye. The fog thinned as in a moving picture scene. In an instant the big form of the grizzly showed clearly against the steep muddy shale. It was digging at a patch of small alpine plants, facing directly away from me.

I raised my gun. The hulking form became large and clear in the 'scope.

At barely fifty yards it filled the whole reticule. In fact, when it turned to face me I had the very unreal sensation that it was almost beside me. My eyes peered over the black gunmetal cover in order to be reassured. Without a moment more of centering the gun my grip tightened on the stock. My index finger felt for the dual spring pressure of the military trigger. As it went down to the harder pressure of the unleashed sear the 'scope crosshairs swung six inches low on the foreleg. This was in order to allow for a still rising bullet when shooting at that short distance.

Just as I squeezed off, the bear found me. It stepped quickly up-hill. At the instant of the detonation, it lunged to full height. Standing like a boxer on its hind legs, it swatted blindly at the air around it. Three times it danced in circles, lunging at nothing. Abruptly it turned its head down, biting at its foreleg.

A second later it raced for the cover of a shoulder height clump of weather bent juniper. Wraiths of fog had spilled across the mountain face again. The grizzly had disappeared into the bushes.

I ran up hill after it.

In the background I could vaguely hear Louis Capillo yelling for me to stop, to come back. Bob's excited hails affirmed his warning. Breathing very hard, at about fifty yards farther up the slope, I stared across a small ravine into the misted clump of forest green juniper. The powder-blue of fragrant berries showed clearly along the branches. Perhaps the distance was just over thirty-five feet from me.

At first I couldn't find a sign of the grizzly. As my eyes anxiously searched the twenty-foot long and fifteen-foot wide clump, the tawny hair of the bear's hump came directly into view. It was just above the higher juniper at the front side of the bushes. For a long moment I examined it. At no other point did any other portion of the animal show. The realization came abruptly that *it must be facing me*—not more than forty feet away.

Slowly, trying to control my breath with the thunderous beat of excitement-driven blood in my ears, I drew the 'scope sight down on the bushes. I was looking for a sign of the head. Nothing showed. At a spot that should be about ten inches below the top of what appeared to be the hump, I leveled the 'scope out, moved about three inches to the side. At that instant I squeezed the trigger.

The enormous form of the grizzly shot right out of the bushes into the air. Reaching a height of at least six feet in its jump it abruptly plummetted to the bottom of the ravine. It was about fifteen feet from me, eight feet below. As it struggled to get up, a billowing of hair, like the waving of wheat from a puff of wind, spread across its neck. The sharp, closeby detonation of a rifle sounded almost simultaneously, and I realized the animal had been hit by another's bullet. It raised its bloody, slavering jaws, attempted to regain its feet and move toward me. Almost instantly it fell back with whoosh of air from its lungs. I stood strangely stunned watching it. My gun was down.

Bob's figure hurrying ahead of Louis' caught my attention. He was yelling jubilantly.

"You got him, Mike! You got him!"

A sudden exhilaration filled me! Or, was it a deep seated release from the fear engendered by the animal when I found myself at close quarters—far too close. For a moment we all stood on the short ravine studying the unmoving figure. It was now pathetically just blood and limp muscle. I slid down the glacial silted gulley and lifted the very heavy head. The animal was dead. I turned to Bob.

"Thanks for your shot in the neck, Bob. I don't know what was the matter with me. I just stood there after he jumped out of the bushes!"

Bob laughed nervously. I stepped over and examined the bear more closely. Blood was flowing from four widely different portions of the carcass. I looked up, scratching my head at the same time.

"Did you shoot twice, Bob?"

"No. You shot him three times!"

"No!" I argued. "I hit him once," pointing, "from down there, where I first saw him, and once when he was in the juniper—"

Bob shook his head.

"You hit him twice from up here! Once while he was still *in the air!*"

I laughed. I was thinking that he was ashamed of shooting twice, and was making me feel better. He pointed adamantly to the top of the little gulley.

"Go look up there! Your shells should be there!"

Totally unconvinced by his suggestion, I nevertheless clambered up the bank. Sure enough! Beside where my shoe prints showed on the glacial mud, were two .303 British cartridge cases.

It was really time for me to scratch my head.

"By Gosh you're right!" I acknowledged.

"It was the fastest shooting I ever saw!" Bob grinned. "Don't you *really* remember?"

"No, honest to God, I don't! I know I saw him come out in that long jump, and I couldn't believe a grizzly could come twenty feet through the air. I vaguely remember having the gun on him, then seeing him try to struggle up again, when your bullet hit him in the neck."

Louis confirmed my shot in the air. In fact, he thereafter treated me with a "something special" air, as if I had proven myself in the Indian manner. It was very gratifying, but it would have been a hell of a lot more satisfying, if I could have remembered the act that achieved the recognition. Louis did say one thing at the time which has always stayed with me. "Mike, when you run after grizzly, you damn lucky you don't get kill!"

In fact, the words were still very clear in my ears when another Indian, a gutsy little short-legged assistant guide, stepped between me and a charging grizzly—less than fifteen feet from me. The bear's head was less than ten feet from him when he killed it.

That grizzly, taken in the Cassiar mountains, almost cured me of my inquisitiveness about bears.

My desires had long since switched from any wish to kill their kind to become a desire to photograph them for others to see. I was making an outdoors film in the Cassiar Mountain Range in Northern British Columbia. My guide was the well known big game guide and outfitter, Ches Delmonico of Dease Lake Lodge.

I had been in the field with him and his assistant guide Vincent Johnny for two days. We had seen a plethora of big game. The two of them were glassing a lush green alpine valley, searching for signs of caribou or Stone sheep, when Ches sighted the great yellowish hump down in the meadow. The animal was near the bottom end of the valley, at least a mile away. Ches became visibly excited.

"That's the biggest grizzly I ever saw!" he claimed emphatically. He trotted up to where I was changing the roll of color film in the movie camera. Closer at hand, Vince was nodding and agreeing with the same eager enthusiasm.

I felt my own belly begin to tingle with anticipation.

"Can we get closer to him?" I queried anxiously.

"He's right out in the open—" Ches hesitated with an awareness of my feelings about shooting bears. "But, you could *shoot* him. He looks like real trophy size!"

"I only want him on film!" was my stubborn answer.

Shrugging with wry nonchalance at my determination, Ches instructed Vince to tether out the horses right where they were. We would, he decided, stalk the grizzly the whole distance on foot. When I took the glasses to examine the slowly ambling yellowish hump in the meadow, the hugeness of its appearance made me take my loose cartridges from my side pocket. Wrapping them in my handkerchief, I placed them on top of my haversack. This was as a precaution against their clinking together accidentally when near the bear, and thus revealing our stealthy approach for filming. I meant to replace the bullets in my back pocket.

Ches called me over to take a look at the terrain and check the route of the stalk. Vince picked up my camera and rifle and brought them over while listening to the plan. He agreed the route was best. We began to work our way downward.

Due to the low nature of the bushes on that Alpine plateau, it took almost half an hour without being seen, to work our way down to the elevation of the bear. Finally, when we had struggled in a circle around the big yellow humped animal, right to the foot of a smooth glacially ground rock face, we could actually hear the nervous snorts coming from it. In a cold sweat of anticipation we inched up the back side of the six-foot rock elevation which was to be utilized to give the camera an unobstructed view of the bear and its actions.

Near the summit of the rock I unpacked the Bell and Howell 16mm machine, checked the lenses for position. Ches took that moment to peer over the top of the sparse shield of low bushes.

I heard him gasp.

"Damn! It's a sow with two cubs!"

Grizzly sows are notably and dependably belligerent toward nearby intruders of any kind. She wasn't able to see us, but she most apparently knew we were somewhere near. Her snorts were unmistakably angered.

Ches shook his head at me.

"Don't take any chances with her!" he admonished gravely.

Nodding, I quickly, and quietly, set the camera for light and distance. It seemed longer, but it required only a breathlessly finger-chilling moment. I had decided to lie flat on the rock top with the machine resting on my elbows braced on the stone. This was to form a tripod, instead of setting up the metal one. My hoarse whisper brought Vince up beside me. He agreed to take over the camera work if, and when, I took up my rifle to shoot. In my guts there was a cold and uneasy quiver. The old sow had given me the definite feeling that the whirr of the camera could trigger her into belligerent action.

Ches's harsh whisper jarred the rough edges of my nerves. "She's looking right at you!" he warned.

The button on the mechanism slid down. It triggered the noisy whirr of the film. Immediately the old sow whirled about to face the sound. She rose swiftly on her hind legs. Her neck was arched. Turning her beady eyes in my direction she acted with all the tensed venom of an angry cottonmouth snake. She dropped down on all fours to make one feinting lunge toward us. (Note. This is a commonly witnessed and preparatory grizzly movement, designed

225

to unnerve an opponent into turning aside, often used as a bluff, and always just before a headlong charge.) She again rose to her hind legs, head snaked forward. She eyed the camera for a short moment. Then, without further warning, she dropped onto all fours and began her charge. With my eyes glued to the camera viewfinder she appeared to be heading straight for me.

My nerve gave out, just as Ches gritted angrily. "You'd better shoot right now!"

Handing the camera to Vince at my elbow, I grabbed my rifle in time to see the sow once again rise up. It was just before she could enter an intervening hedge of bushes. She was ascertaining exactly where we were located, placing her target for when she came out. At that instant of her stillness, my finger squeezed a bullet off for her shoulder.

The missile splashed into a glacial pond, at an angle of error *at least eighteen inches above her and a foot to the left.*

She swung to standing position, facing the noise and splash made by the bullet. As she once more turned to face me, I fired for the heart region. The second slug smacked into the water behind her with the same apparent error in relation to my aim. I was unbelievably shocked. I simply wasn't that afraid of her. As the second white plume of spray settled on the glacial pond, she dropped quickly to all fours. She began her rush again, reared up to ascertain our location. I realized that these actions were in an effort to pick up the sound of the whirring camera.

Vincent Johnny was standing calmly on his feet beside me. He was holding the camera lens on her, with the button pushed down!

Shocked by what I thought were my misdirected shots, I drew the bead down on the grizzly's left haunch. This was in a desperate effort to compensate for the footage by which my bullets were missing her. Before she could once again drop down to charge us I squeezed an uncertain third shot. She crumpled into a heap.

Ches exhorted me to shoot her again.

Frankly my heart was not with the situation at all. I believed the last bullet had broken her spine. It was thus indicated by her sack-like slump to the ground. She was also the first animal in years I had missed with rifle—just too completely sure of myself.

I turned to argue with Ches. His yell and pointing finger jolted me. "Look out! Mike! She's up again!"

During the split second in which my eyes had been off her, the grizzly had regained her feet, seemingly unhurt. She was now coming toward me faster than ever. The ensuing hasty injection with the gun mechanism jammed the fourth shell diagonally in the receiver. Vince had the camera up again, whirring off film. Cold with sweat, my fingers fumbled the shell out and back in again. The ensuing hastily aimed slug threw black swamp mud up beside her.

She was now within twenty-five yards!

My wrist almost mechanically flicked home another injection of the mechanism. When I squeezed the trigger the hammer resounded dully on an empty chamber. The four shell clip was used up.

Ches was at my elbow.

"For Chris' sake, Mike—*shoot!*

A frantic search in my pockets for the shells which I had wrapped in my handkerchief brought the realization that those cartridges were still atop my haversack three quarters of a mile away. Vince had left the bag there as an unnecessary burden during the tough stalk down the valley. Chilled into clear thinking by the bear's nearing squeals, I reached into my back pocket. Over the years I have always maintained the habit of carrying one reserve shell there—at all times while hunting. Never was the length of time so greatly magnified for a shell to reach a rifle chamber.

The grizzly was now breaking out of the second juniper hedge. There was no question about her direction now. Her blunt head was directed at me. Drawing a bead on the lower joint of her left foreleg the aim took my last bullet into her right front shoulder. She went down, hind-over-snout.

Ches yelled fiercely. "Again, Mike!"

At his words the grizzly got up. Now carrying 400 grains of high velocity lead she again galloped toward me. Slavering blood and roaring at twenty yards she jellied my nerve. I was out of shells. Vince had in the meantime casually rewound the camera. He was recording the charge. Honestly he was—grinning!

I searched desperately for a tall tree, yelling to Vince to pick up his own haywire bound (actually) and typically Indian .30-30 Winchester, 1894, carbine. He held the camera on the bear, while I backed up scared as hell. On that whole valley floor there wasn't a tree more than two inches through, nor over sixteen feet in height. I know! I searched very hard for one. Ches, who could no more believe our predicament than could I, (that I was out of shells) began to back up with me.

As we retreated, Vincent Johnny, suddenly grasping the situation, carefully set down the camera. With one swift movement he picked

227

up his carbine, and in the same swing moved forward with the barrel up. He walked straight toward the charging grizzly!

At fifteen feet from him the bear broke through the remaining low hedge of bushes. His gun cracked. His first bullet struck her on the skull. It spun off the slanted bone with a whining ricochet that sounded like a dropping bomb. The next two shots were so fast that they sounded like one. One of them screamed off in a similar ricochet to the first. The other one dropped her big body right in front of him. A quick jump took him over her to place another bullet into the base of her skull.

I was ashamed of myself. But, examination of the bear and the situation showed some reasons. Not only did the sow have cubs, but she had a front leg with a foot severed almost completely, presumably by some accident while she had been growing. It had left her with a stump terminating with a black half pad. This, alone would have made her contentious or pugnacious of disposition.

As to my own poor shooting, my rifle had been damaged during transit on the plane flight to Watson Lake. One of the heavy air bumps which we had hit over the mountains had apparently shorn off the gold bead front sight and twisted the blade, as well as the rear sight. This had remained unnoticed during the hunt because I had no desire to use the rifle due to my preoccupation with taking color film. (When we tested the rifle the following day it actually shot eighteen inches high plus the same distance to the left at fifty yards. Two days later, when it had been corrected, a single shot brought me a Stone ram at 150 yards—right in the heart).

That evening of the grizzly charge as we sat beside the campfire, Vince shook his head. "Grizzly bear, good bear, Mike. You shoot him, he come toward you! Not like black bear, go run in the bushes, where you gotta go after him! Grizzly bear he always come toward you!"

It was one piece of wisdom with which I had no contention. It had twice been all too truly proven to my satisfaction.

PLENTY OF BEAR

No collection of hunting stories—let alone a bear book—would be complete without a story by Russell Annabel. His hunting and fishing stories appeared in all the major outdoor magazines for decades and he wrote a number of excellent books on both subjects.

This story first appeared in Field & Stream *in 1937 and was later incorporated into a collection of stories in a book entitled* The Field & Stream Reader, *published by Doubleday & Company, Inc. (New York, 1946). Other famous outdoor writers appeared in this same book, among them Nash Buckingham, Archibald Rutledge and Zane Grey. It was put together by the editors of the magazine during the tenure of Editor-In-Chief Dave Newell—who also wrote several stories for the book.*

Alaska still has a lot of bears in it, but nothing like the days when Annabel and pals hunted it—as you will see by this fine story.

Plenty of Bear

Russell Annabel

Maybe it will help if I tell you about the experience Gunn Buckingham and I had at Chinitna Bay. It was one of those rowdy blue-and-gold June mornings, with a whiplash wind roaring in from the open Pacific. We had climbed to the rim of a shallow, brush-grown basin in which we hoped there might be a stray Kodiak. As we came out on the crest and looked down I spotted one—a fair-sized bear standing on the bank of a frozen streamlet at the base of the hill.

Buckingham slammed a cartridge into the chamber of his rifle, and then startled me by asking, "Which one of 'em shall I take?"

"What do you mean 'which one'? There's only one bear down there."

"There's two."

"There's one."

This might have continued indefinitely if I had not happened to glance up the ridge on our left. A biscuit-toss up the slope was a circular patch of tall dead redtop grass, surrounded by deep snow drifts. Leading into the grass was a line of deep-wallowed bear tracks, but there were none to show where the animal had come out. Looking closely, I made out a brownish object partially screened by the weaving grass. It looked like a moss-covered boulder, but it wasn't, because suddenly it turned over, and four immense brown paws showed above the wind-brushed redtop.

Buckingham said: "Holy smoke! We must have got into a convention of bear," and started shooting.

The basin erupted Kodiaks. There had been at least five in the brush below, and they tore out in all directions, smashing through the alders like elephants. The one in the grass island reared straight up at Buckingham's first shot. He looked like a woolly hangover from the ice age. I could have sworn he was as tall as the spruce trees behind him.

Buckingham squinted along his rifle sights, and fired again. The heavy soft-nose struck with a wicked "whoomp," and the bear crumpled without a kick left in him.

The point is not that you may be caught in a bear stampede during your hunting trip, but that, square mile for square mile, the bear population of Alaska exceeds that of any other country on earth. There are so many species and sub-species in the territory that even the scientists who have studied them cannot agree on the precise number. And they come in an amazing variety of colors: white, blue, black, brown and yellow. If your wife insists that you bring back a bear pelt to match her new bridge set, you can safely undertake the job.

A couple of years ago an Indian hunter named Charlie Toughluck, up in the Nelchina country, killed a blue glacier bear with snow-white ears. Nellie Neal, who runs a roadhouse at the head of Kenai Lake, is the proud possessor of a red grizzly pelt. This extraordinary trophy came from the Sinjack Mountains, two hundred miles above the arctic circle. One look at it will convince you that there are in this world stranger things than we have dreamt of in our philosophy.

Early spring—between May 20 and June 20—is the best time to hunt Kodiaks. Not only are the pelts better then, but the bears are easier to locate. The alders are not in foliage, and the bears stand out so plainly against the naked drifts that often you can spot one from two to three miles distant, without using binoculars.

Outfit at Seward, and cruise around the Kenai coast to Kodiak Island, or to the low-lying tundra hills of the Alaska Peninsula. Or charter a gasboat at Anchorage and hunt the west coast of Cook Inlet. Put into Chinitna, Iniskin, or Illiamna Bays—all good spring bear ranges. At Chinitna you will have the thrilling experience of hunting on the slopes of Mount Redoubt, a live volcano with a plume of smoke and steam rising from an icy cleft at its summit.

Hunting Kodiaks in the autumn is a pretty unsatisfactory sport. The bears are all down in the flats, and the flats are knee-deep with mud and slush. The alders are thicker than hair on a dog's back, and the weather is rotten.

It rains on the Alaskan coast in September. Boy, how it rains! They tell a story about a schoolma'am who related the Biblical account of the flood to a class of young Alaskans. It didn't go over so well. One small sourdough stood up and allowed that it had been raining for nigh on a month and a half, and the creek out front hadn't come up a foot.

Of course, if you are tough and don't mind sloshing around in mud-holes with a wild north wind whistling around your ears and rain sluicing down your back, go to it. You may be lucky enough to knock over a bear or two, but the pelts won't compare with spring pelts, and nobody will envy you the trip. You'll spend a good share of your time drying socks, wiping mildew off your boots and gun cases, and trying to keep the sugar from turning to syrup.

If you have a few rounds of ammunition left after taking your limit of bear, spend a day or two shooting leopard-seal. Cruise along the river mouths, with a phonograph playing in the boat's stern. The seal, believe it or not, will follow the music.

Maybe you have shot at some difficult targets in your time, but wait until you have tried to hit the sleek brown head of a seal bobbing in a gasboat's wake. It requires a technique which makes trap-shooting a child's pastime by comparison. And the really swell thing about it is that the Territorial Government will pay a substantial bounty for the nose and whiskers of each seal you succeed in killing.

In case seal shooting doesn't square with your marksmanship, try hunting whales. Anybody should be able to hit a whale. In the spring, herds of little belugas, the sacred white whales of the Aleuts, swarm in these waters. And occasionally a big 50-footer comes in from the ocean. Better leave these alone, however, for you may have trouble on your hands if you happen to annoy an old bull whale when he is engaged in the springtime business of courting a lady whale.

Buckingham and I made this mistake once, and I still believe the ensuing mix-up caused the gray streak in my once auburn locks. The barnacle-backed bull we fired at was so enraged by one little .30 slug that he lobtailed all over the place, and came within five feet of smashing our boat to kindling and sending us all to Davy Jones' locker. Cheechakos can get themselves into more trouble!

By all means supplement your store grub with local seafoods. They make a tall-water chowder on this coast which cannot be equaled in the round world. The ingredients, it seems, are a jealously guarded secret.

I just happened to be standing at the galley skylight one day when the cook was preparing the noble dish; so I can report that it contains, among other things, sea celery, fillet of silver hake, halibut cheeks, cockle clams, bacon, diced onions and—this appears to be its crowning glory—fried cubes of king salmon milt. The dangerous thing about ordering a bait of this superlative chowder is that it may cause you to forget bear hunting altogether. However, I advise you to pull yourself together and take a chance. You'll never regret it.

Will Kodiaks charge? Sure they will. I have never seen a wild animal that wouldn't charge under the proper set of circumstances. Fool around long enough with a porcupine, and he'll do his fighting best to fill your boots with quills. A week-old seal pup, cornered on the beach, will come at you with the worst intentions in the world.

As to the percentage of Kodiaks that will charge through sheer bad temper and hatred of man, you'll have to consult somebody else. I know four or five men who have been badly mauled by Kodiaks which, so they say, came busting unexpectedly out of the brush, all ready for war. I knew two men who were killed by Kodiaks after they had shot at the animals and failed to stop them. And I know others who have committed every indiscretion from falling over Kodiaks to popping them with .22 rifles to see them jump, without getting even a dirty look in return.

My advice is: don't take any chances. Know your rifle thoroughly, don't stop shooting until you are positive your bear is dead, and never, never under any circumstances, follow a wounded bear into the alders. Failure to follow this last cardinal tenet of bear hunting has caused most of the hair-raising tight scrapes you read about. An alder jungle is no place to meet an angry bear of any species. A ragged old female Kodiak with a pair of gangling cubs growled at me in a hillside thicket one day, and I nearly broke my neck trying to locate her so that I would know which way to light out of there.

A tragedy that took place down near the Canadian boundary has haunted me for years. Big Axel Johnson, a trapper, came home to his cabin in the early autumn twilight and found a Kodiak breaking into his meat cache. Johnson had no rifle with him, but was carrying a heavy double-bitted ax.

The bear charged, and as it came bounding at him Johnson split its skull with the ax. But the vitality of the animal was such that it mauled him terribly before it died. Johnson dragged himself to his bunk and scrawled a last note to his partner. It read: "Dear Jim—The bear killed me, but, by Heaven, I killed him too."

Don't get excited if you happen on a Kodiak whose fur gleams like polished silver. Take your guide's advice and let the beggar go his way in peace—the color is an illusion. These silvery-looking bears

are really the color of a new burlap sack, and are not considered good trophies. Some quality of the sunlight reflecting from the snow makes them look like platinum blondes.

The darker the pelt, the better the Kodiak trophy. Just set your heart on an 11-foot bear with fur the color of rare old hand-rubbed mahogany, and keep saying over and over to yourself: "I'm going to get him. I'm going to get him, by golly, if it takes until June 20." And maybe you will. Stranger things have happened.

Your crew will subject you to the usual sourdough horse-play, if they think you are the right sort of guy and can take it. Here's one they will try to put over.

Back in town, after the hunt is over, they'll tell you about an extraordinary pink bear pelt owned by a member of the local fire department. Naturally, you are eager to see it. So, taken in tow by the skipper, guide, packer, cook and engineer, you go up to the fire hall. Here, the chief conniver opens a shower door, and within you see one of the fire laddies soaping and scrubbing himself. After a dazed moment or two you get it—then, of course, it's up to you to buy drinks for the whole framing lot of them, plus a box of cigars for the fire department.

Maybe I shouldn't reveal this, but it's the only revenge open to me after the whole-souled way I fell for the lousy joke. Anyway, they'll get you with the ice-worm stunt, or the old one about the barrel of pickled bear tongues, or any one of a dozen others designed to put cheechakos in their proper place.

You won't find many black bears in either Kodiak or grizzly country; but go up to the Glacier Lake, ten miles southeast of the headwaters of Knik River, or over among the grassy Kenai hills near the forks of Chicaloon River, and you'll find them thicker than fiddlers in hades. It is best to pack in; but if you are pressed for time, charter an airplane at Anchorage.

Pitch your camp high on a hillside where you can look out over a wide scope of country, and get busy with your binoculars. The bears will be up in the timber-line blueberry patches, putting on fat for hibernation. It's easy to locate them, for their black coats stand out against the autumn hillsides like headlights on a raft. There are some big ones, too—6- and 7-footers. The first of September is the time to start hunting.

A good thing to remember is that all blacks are pirates and have a mighty yearning for the white man's grub. A camp left unguarded in black-bear country is a sure invitation for trouble. For some unfathomable reason, blacks have never learned to recognize a tent entrance. Or maybe they prefer to make their own entrances and exits. At any rate, whichever the case, they always tear a large hole in one side of your tent going in, and another large hole in the opposite side going out.

This custom of theirs has reduced legions of strong men to tears. It is beyond the power of language to describe the havoc and confusion a black bear can create inside a cook tent. Tin cans are a cinch for him—he crushes 'em in his mouth like gumdrops. And chances are, having discovered that good things come in tin, he'll hammer your camp stove flat as a pancake, trying to get something edible out of it.

Some time back, the Game Commission discovered that black bears are predators, and made outlaws of the species by lifting all protection. They were, it appears, killing moose calves, which was only natural of them, considering their fondness for fresh meat and the lack of watchfulness which characterizes moose mothers. While a cow will fight to the death for her calf if she happens to be present when danger threatens, she has the bad habit of leaving her infant cached in a thicket for a considerable period of time each day. A black bear comes along, finds the calf curled up in the alders—and the result is a square meal for the bear and another pain in the neck for the Game Commission.

Up in the tall Knik peaks, however, where there are no moose, the situation is different. Here, if a bear wants fresh meat in any quantity, he is faced with the prospect of going up against the rapier horns and iron courage of an eternally watchful old nanny goat. This has had the effect of making vegetarians of the Knik black bear.

When I was up on the Glacier Lake trapping goats for the Biological Survey, I once saw a black bear make an elaborate stalk for an old nanny and a pair of kids. He scrooched up a ravine on his belly, bounded like a flash across an open shale pitch, and floated softly as a midnight shadow down a daisy-starred swale to within fifteen feet of where the little family of goats was peacefully enjoying the noonday sun. Just as he was getting set for the final rush at one of the kids, the nanny stood up and faced him.

Having looked an irate nanny in the eye at close range myself, I know exactly how the bear felt. She looked as big as a buffalo, her horns were yards long, and suddenly there didn't seem to be any percentage in carrying the thing any further. That must have been the way the bear felt, for after a moment's hesitation he turned and shuffled off down the mountain.

A scrawny little 300-pound bear gave me a scare one day. I was sitting under a trap-line cache on Metal Creek, a tributary to Knik River, making a cup of tea. Suddenly I heard a commotion in a near-by high-bush cranberry thicket. In a moment, out came the black bear, whoofing and popping his jaws in no uncertain manner.

As my rifle was down in the canoe, I swarmed up one of the cache legs to the roof, and sat there, slapping mosquitoes, for two solid hours while the bear did sentry duty below. Finally he wandered off, looking back over his shoulder at every few paces to growl at me. Don't ask me what had put him on the war trail. Maybe he had been disappointed in love, or maybe he just didn't like the idea of my being around there. At any rate, I am convinced he would have given me a bad time of it if he had caught me out in the open without my rifle.

Indian hunters will tell you that a fighting black is more to be feared than either the grizzly or the Kodiak, for the reason that the latter two species seem always to be in a frantic hurry about mauling a man, while the black will rip and tear at a victim as long as there is a spark of life remaining. This explanation of the Kodiak's tactics may account for the number of men who have lived to tell the tale after being mauled by the big brownies.

The grizzly, of course, is the trophy of trophies, the goal of every sportsman's desire. He has glamour and a reputation for ferocity which has made him the undisputed emperor of the bruin tribe. His fame has been told in story and song since the days when men hunted him with slate-headed lances and made clothing from his hide.

No camp-fire gathering is a success without at least one grizzly yarn to make the chills run up your spine, and no sportman's den is properly fitted out unless there is a grizzly trophy or two in it for the owner to brag about. Ask any hunter to name the world's ranking big-game animal, and he'll tell you it's a toss-up between the grizzly and the Siberian tiger, with the sladang crowding them close for honors.

Your best bet for grizzlies in Alaska is the range of shale hills lying between the headwaters of Wood River and Yanert River. Go in by pack-train in the early fall from the Alaska railroad station at Healy. It's an easy three-day trip, with only one pass to climb.

Camp at the mouth of Little Grizzly Creek, on Wood River, and hunt the hanging basins and creek heads. This is grand country—high, wild and open, with only a sparse fringe of spruce along the stream banks. On all sides the mighty snow peaks of the Alaska Range loom mile-high into the blue.

There are innumerable small creeks plunging down from the high glaciers, secret valleys tucked away between the shoulders of the hills, windy ridges where bands of white bighorn sheep and woodland caribou gather. And it is the finest grizzly country between Seward and the Endicotts. Count Tolstoy and I once saw eighteen grizzlies here in two weeks.

It is a good idea to do your hunting on horseback—you cover more ground in a day and have opportunity to watch the hillsides instead of your footing. When you have located a bear, anchor your horse to a boulder and crawl as close as you can before going into action. Try to put your shots into the chest cavity—a soft-nose through a grizzly's barrel won't keep him down. He'll roll over a few times, and claw up a lot of moss and earth; but the first thing you know, he'll snap out of it and start for distant places.

And when you have one down, put in an extra couple of shots for luck—the taxidermist can fix up the holes so that you would never know they were there—and then sit down for a cigarette. Time enough to go over the kill to have your photograph taken when you are absolutely sure that the bear is dead. An action photograph of you, trying to beat an Alaskan grizzly to a tree, will be small consolation to your wife and children if your guide has to ship you home in a box.

SPECIAL OFFER FOR BOOK CLUB MEMBERS

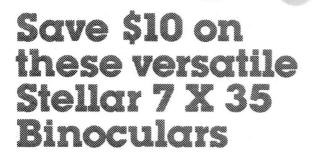

Save $10 on these versatile Stellar 7 X 35 Binoculars

They're ideal all-purpose binoculars — good for a wide range of outdoor activities from football games to bird watching.

Look at these features:

- ☐ **Fully coated optics.** Both lenses and prisms are coated to give them maximum light-gathering power and to insure bright, clear, sharp images.
- ☐ **Quick, accurate focusing.** A right-eye adjustment compensates for differences in vision of the two eyes. A center focusing wheel permits fast adjustment.
- ☐ **Magnification.** "7 X" refers to the magnifying power of the binoculars. It means an object 700 feet away will appear to be only 100 feet away. "35" refers to the diameter in millimeters of the objective lenses, which determines the amount of light admitted. The larger the lenses, the greater the amount of light and the later in the evening you can use the binoculars.
- ☐ **Field of View.** The Stellar Binoculars provide a 393-foot field of view at 1000 yards.
- ☐ **Weight.** 21½ ounces.

The binoculars come in a soft vinyl case with carrying strap. You also get a shoulder strap and four lens covers.

Suggested Retail Price $49.95. Your Club Price only

$39^{95}

plus delivery and handling

Stellar 7 X 35 Binoculars are fully guaranteed against any defects in workmanship.
